ROUTLEDGE LIBRARY EDITIONS:
MARRIAGE

Volume 12

CONCILIATION IN SEPARATION AND DIVORCE

CONCILIATION IN SEPARATION AND DIVORCE

Finding Common Ground

LISA PARKINSON

Routledge
Taylor & Francis Group
LONDON AND NEW YORK

First published in 1986 by Croom Helm Ltd.

This edition first published in 2023
by Routledge
4 Park Square, Milton Park, Abingdon, Oxon OX14 4RN

and by Routledge
605 Third Avenue, New York, NY 10158

Routledge is an imprint of the Taylor & Francis Group, an informa business

British Library Cataloguing in Publication Data
A catalogue record for this book is available from the British Library

ISBN: 978-1-032-46071-0 (Set)
ISBN: 978-1-032-46599-9 (Volume 12) (hbk)
ISBN: 978-1-032-46607-1 (Volume 12) (pbk)
ISBN: 978-1-003-38253-9 (Volume 12) (ebk)

DOI: 10.4324/9781003382539

Publisher's Note
The publisher has gone to great lengths to ensure the quality of this reprint but points out that some imperfections in the original copies may be apparent.

Disclaimer
The publisher has made every effort to trace copyright holders and would welcome correspondence from those they have been unable to trace.

New Preface to 2023 Reissue *Conciliation in Separation and Divorce*

Family mediation's development since the 1980s has been a switchback of ups and downs, rather than a steady progression. *Conciliation in Separation and Divorce,* published in 1986, described the first steps towards setting up independent, community-based family mediation services to assist separating and divorcing couples to reach agreed settlements, instead of taking disputes to court. Action was needed at grass roots level, since there was little prospect of prompt government action to implement the Finer Committee's recommendations (Report 1974) on unified family courts and 'conciliation' (this term was soon replaced by 'mediation'). Small groups of family law professionals, mainly lawyers, court welfare officers and social workers seeking reform of the 'adversarial' system, formed local committees to set up family mediation services in their area.

Out of court family mediation services were set up in many regions during the 1980s and 90s and soon widened their scope from child-related issues to any or all issues in separation and divorce, including finance and property. An interdisciplinary pilot project involving family lawyers and other professionals working together as co-mediators led to a joint working party with the Law Society to draw up professional practice rules for lawyer mediators. A national association of family mediators was formed and a Code of Practice issued, together with standards and requirements for family mediators' training and practice. Forty years after the Finer Report, a unified Family Court was finally created under the Children and Families Act 2014. This Act also introduced a requirement for applicants to the family court (subject to certain exemptions) to attend a Mediation Information and Assessment Meeting (MIAM) with an authorised family mediator, prior to filing an application for a child arrangements or financial order. The MIAM has two main purposes: first, to help potential litigants consider mediation and options for out-of-court settlement, and secondly, for the mediator to explore and assess the suitability of mediation in the circumstances. Individuals attend separately, because safety and suitability cannot be assessed with both parties together. The Family Mediation Council (FMC) has published Standards and Guidance for MIAMs which list the tasks involved and indicate the range of knowledge and skills needed by mediators. These include assessing indications of domestic abuse and/or circumstances where a child may be in need of safeguarding, providing relevant legal information to participants, having a good understanding of child development and children's attachments, and using negotiation and conflict management skills. National standards for mediators' training and practice are regularly reviewed and updated by the FMC and the Family Mediation Standards Board. Five national associations of family mediators and the Law Society's Family Mediation Panel are represented on the FMC's management board. An FMC survey in 2019 indicated that around 37,000 mediations were undertaken in that year and that when each party attended a MIAM, 73% accepted mediation and went on to reach full or partial settlement. 46% of mediations concerned child-related matters, 25% finance and property and 29% all issues in separation or divorce. Individuals on low incomes can qualify for mediation free of charge and in 44% of the above cases, one or both participants qualified for public funding.

Despite steps to encourage the use of mediation, statistics suggest that around one third of separating couples in England and Wales take disputes to court and that 49–62% involve allegations or findings of domestic abuse. Domestic abuse cases surged in periods of lockdown during the Covid pandemic. The Family Solutions Group, a sub-group of the Private Law Working Group, reported that '*the numbers of parents making applications are unmanageable and family courts are stretched beyond limits.*' Mr Justice Cobb, Chairman of the Private Law Working Group, observed in his Foreword to the Report that '*many parental disputes are not **legal** disputes and a **legal** response may indeed be unhelpful for many families.*' The Family

Solutions Group recommended closer collaboration between family law professionals and statutory and voluntary agencies. Government Ministers, rather than focusing on cost savings in their own department, need to develop interdepartmental policies to reduce the social and financial costs of prolonged parental conflict and mitigate its harmful impact on children and young people.

During mediation's developmental phase, the voice of the child remained largely unheard, although, even in the early days, some mediators with a background in family therapy talked with older children on their own, when this was considered appropriate and with the consent of both parents. Child-inclusive mediation is now widely available, provided by qualified family mediators with additional training in its principles and pre-requisites and in specified knowledge and skills. At the child's request, the mediator shares children's messages and suggestions with their parents so that these can be taken into account in arrangements for the children. Research studies report significant benefits. Young people say that talking about their situation and concerns with a family mediator reduces their anxieties and helps them to feel better. Children's participation in mediation also increases parental co-operation and improves communication in the family.

I hope this reissued account of family mediation's early history will spur fresh determination to promote mediation for parents, children and family members undergoing separation, divorce and other situations of family change, who need skilled, impartial assistance to understand their options, plan for the future and maintain the vital attachments and relationships that sustain them through life.

Lisa Parkinson, Bristol, November 2022

Notes

1. Finer Committee *Report of the Committee on One-Parent Families* (1974) HMSO Cm. 5629
2. Parkinson L. *Family Mediation* 1st edition Sweet & Maxwell 1997, 4th edition LexisNexis 2020
3. Family Mediation Council www.familymediationcouncil.org.uk
4. https://www.familymediationcouncil.org.uk/2022/08/02/standards-guidance-and-assurance-for-miams/
5. https://www.familymediationcouncil.org.uk/wp-content/uploads/2022/05/FMC-Manual-of-Professonal-Standards-Regulatory-Framework-v1.4.1-Updated-1-March-2022pdf

6. Family Mediation Council (FMC) Survey January 2020
7. https://www.judiciary.uk/publications/what-about-me-reframing-support-for-families-following-parental-separation Family Solutions Group Report, 'What About Me?' 12 November 2020, par 34
8. ibid, Executive Summary, para. 12
9. ibid, Foreword
10. University of Exeter Wellcome Centre Healthy Relationships Project, Report and Key Findings March 2022 The_Healthy_Relationships_Project_Report_and_Key_Findings.pdf
11. ibid

CONCILIATION IN SEPARATION AND DIVORCE

FINDING COMMON GROUND

LISA PARKINSON

CROOM HELM
London • Sydney • Dover, New Hampshire

Croom Helm Ltd, Provident House, Burrell Row,
Beckenham, Kent BR3 1AT
Croom Helm Australia Pty Ltd, Suite 4, 6th Floor,
64-76 Kippax Street, Surry Hills, NSW 2010 Australia

British Library Cataloguing in Publication Data

Parkinson, Lisa
Conciliation in separation and divorce: finding common ground.
1. Divorce mediation
I. Title
362.8′286 HQ814

ISBN 0-7099-4053-X Pbk

Croom Helm, 51 Washington Street, Dover,
New Hampshire 03820, USA

Library of Congress Cataloging in Publication Data

Parkinson, Lisa, 1940–.
Conciliation in separation and divorce

Bibliography: p.
Includes index.
1. Divorce mediation—Great Britain. 2. Divorce—law and legislation—Great Britain. I. Title.
KD764.P28 1986 346.4101′66 86-2662
ISBN 0-7099-4053-X (pbk.)

Printed and bound in Great Britain by
Biddles Ltd, Guildford and King's Lynn

CONTENTS

To Tim, Diana and Jonathan

FOREWORD

In 1946, Lord Denning presided over a committee to look into procedure in divorce and other matrimonial cases. The committee's report emphasised the importance of doing everything possible to reconcile couples whose marriage was on the rocks. This recommendation led almost immediately to substantial public funding for marriage guidance work.

Two decades later the Finer Committee on One-Parent Families shifted the focus to conciliation. The court should of course be alive to any sign that reconciliation was possible, but equally it should give effect to the policy of the law that dead marriages should be decently buried.

Since the Finer Report, conciliation has become almost an industry – but still very much a cottage industry, with only sparse and spasmodic public funding. Over the years a lot of questions have come to be asked about it. What exactly is conciliation trying to achieve? What should the conciliators be trying to do? What should their professional skills and training be? What is the best relationship between conciliation and the legal system? How far is there a risk that conciliation will be used to promote the interests of the stronger against the weaker? Does conciliation save money? What is the success rate of conciliation schemes? What in any case is the test of "success"?

The aim of this book is to contribute to the continuing debate about these and other issues. It would be impossible to find anyone better equipped to write it than Lisa Parkinson. After a distinguished academic career at Oxford University she became a trained social worker and saw at first hand many of the adverse consequences of the divorce process. She played an active part in setting up the Bristol Courts Family Conciliation Service, and as its first co-ordinator worked tirelessly to promote the idea of conciliation and to secure the future of that service. Since 1983 she has been the Training Officer of the National Family Conciliation Council.

This book is therefore based on unrivalled personal knowledge and experience of conciliation as it has developed in this country over the years. But it is far more than that. A glance at the bibliography will show the width of the author's reading, and a glance at almost any page of the text will show how deeply Mrs Parkinson has thought about the issues involved. This book is thus quite indispensable to anyone seriously interested in the legal and social work aspects of divorce and other family litigation. It also raises issues of very great importance for those concerned with legal and social work theory.

S. M. Cretney

ACKNOWLEDGEMENTS

Unfortunately it is quite impossible to thank individually all the conciliators, legal practitioners and researchers in Britain and other countries who have taught me a great deal and helped to shape my ideas about conciliation in the course of countless informal discussions and formal debates over almost ten years. One of the most positive aspects of conciliation is the network of people who share a common interest in the subject and who respond to the challenge to explore its potential value and possible or actual disadvantages. Conciliation is essentially an interdisciplinary bridge-building process and I am extremely grateful to many practitioners in different disciplines who have helped to make connections both in ideas and in their practical application. In particular, I should like to thank those who have read and commented so willingly and helpfully on draft chapters of this book, notably Professor Stephen Cretney, Robert Dingwall, His Honour Judge Forrester-Paton, Olivia Hardie, Yvonne Korn, Mavis Maclean, Diana Parker, Janet Walker and Tony Wells. Their views may differ from my own and although they have given me a great deal of help I should like to emphasise that any errors or deficiencies in the book are my sole responsibility.

I am also aware of the debt I owe to those whose personal experience of marriage breakdown, divorce, remarriage and step-families has helped me to recognise not only how well people cope against the odds but also how the odds need to be made more even. The experience of some of these families has been used to illustrate some common problems, but the names I have given them are fictitious and identifying details have been changed. I have felt justified in quoting their difficulties because many people have said to me that they would like their own painful experiences to serve some useful purpose in changing traditional approaches to divorce and family break-up, both in the legal process and in the attitudes of society as a whole.

Although many of us share the wish to make divorce a less damaging and destructive process for the adults and children concerned, I doubt very much if the book could have been written without the constant encouragement and practical help of my husband, Tim, who has not only given me tremendous support but has also instructed me in the use of a word processor and has sorted out the technical tangles I got into from time to time. I am now firmly converted to using a word processor – but it does help to have a resident expert.

Lisa Parkinson

INTRODUCTION

Ten years ago, the word "conciliation" was scarcely used, whereas hardly a week goes by today without some mention of it in the press in connection with an industrial dispute or in relation to marriage breakdown and divorce. As with many words that have gained sudden popularity, "conciliation" means different things to different people and it is still occasionally confused with "reconciliation" although the distinction between the two terms is now more widely understood. The current enthusiasm for conciliation as a method of settling disputes can result in it being seen as a magic remedy for all kinds of interpersonal conflict, without basic assumptions being examined. More searching questions about its objectives, methods and results are now being pursued and this study of conciliation in separation and divorce recognises that there are inherent difficulties and contradictions in the practice of conciliation, as well as strong arguments in its favour. Conciliation has been hailed as a humane and effective method of settling disputes which should be used as far as possible as an alternative to litigation, but it may not be immediately clear why new services are needed to provide it, since many problems are sorted out by solicitors without court proceedings and the concept of the welfare state has propagated a rapid growth of counselling and social services dealing with all kinds of personal and family problems.

One of the reasons for the recent focus on conciliation is increasing public concern about the social and economic consequences of large-scale divorce. It is well known that divorce increased sharply during the 1970s. The number of couples who divorced in England and Wales in that decade (1.2 million between 1971 and 1980) was three times the number who divorced in the 1960s (0.4 million between 1961 and 1970)[1]. The divorce rate increased sixfold in England and Wales between 1960 and 1980[2] and although it has levelled out since 1979, the level remains very high, since on current trends it is predicted that one in three marriages will end in divorce within 35 years of marriage[3]. Figures from the 1982 *General Household Survey* show a marked increase in cohabitation but although the marriage rate fell in the 1970s, especially for couples marrying at younger ages, there is no evidence so far that the increase in cohabitation is affecting the divorce rate, since cohabitation in this country seems to be mainly a prelude to marriage rather than an alternative to marriage[4].

Marriage remains very popular, and the experience of a failed marriage does not necessarily lead to disillusion with marriage itself. A study by Leete and Anthony (1979) showed that 55.5 per cent of men and 48 per cent of women who divorced in 1973 remarried within four and a half years of their divorce and about 60 per cent of those who remarried did so within a year of the divorce. Over a third (36%) of all new marriages in 1983 involved a remarriage for one or both partners and in almost half of these cases both partners had had at least one previous marriage[5]. Marriages involving a previous divorce for one or both partners seem more likely to end in divorce than first marriages at similar ages[6]. Teenage marriages are also at particular risk of divorce and girls who marry in their teens are more likely to have husbands in semi-skilled or unskilled jobs[7]. Haskey (1984) showed that certain social and occupational groups are much more prone to divorce than others: for example, the divorce rate in the armed forces is over two and a half times the national average. In 1979 the divorce rate for husbands in social class 1 (professional) was less than half the national rate, whereas the rate in social class 5 (unskilled) was more than twice the national rate and particularly high among the unemployed, who are disproportionately drawn from the unskilled. Haskey found that the divorce rate of unemployed husbands in their fifties was even double that for social class 5[8]. Unemployment is also closely associated with chronic ill-health, depression, criminal offences including child abuse, and the reception of children into care[9].

This clustering of social ills can lead to erroneous assumptions about their cause and effect and may increase the tendency to see divorce as a modern disease which needs to be prevented or treated. It is relatively easy to count divorces which are formally recorded and to overlook the many unrecorded disruptions of marriage and family life which occurred in the past. In the nineteenth century, many marriages were ended by the death of one partner but historical evidence suggests that there were also many informal separations. John Stuart Mill wrote in 1832 that "marriage is really . . . a lottery, and whoever is in a state of mind to calculate chances calmly and value them correctly is not at all likely to purchase a ticket"[10]. Nowadays, divorce has become a major social trend affecting thousands of men, women and children but we should be careful not to assume that unhappy marriages end in divorce and that marriages which last are invariably happy and harmonious. However, the divorce rate almost certainly reflects the actual rate of marriage breakdown much more closely than it used to do, since divorce in the nineteenth century and the early part of this century was the prerogative of the very wealthy and divorce law was then designed to support the existing patriarchal system[11]. Public policy and legislation in Victorian times took little account of the marital and family relations of the poor, unless they threatened to become a charge on public funds: in the middle of the last century it was considered that "the only legal reason why a husband should support his wife is that she may not become a burden on the parish"[12]. In the course of this century, changes in public opinion and legislation have gradually dismantled the social, legal, financial and religious barriers to divorce and there is now a universal access to divorce which is both welcomed and feared. Divorce now tends to be seen as the remedy for severe marital problems, but if it is embarked on hastily, without the petitioner weighing up or even knowing the probable consequences, another equally acute set of problems may replace the problems of the marriage.

Another reason for the growing interest in conciliation is recognition that it "might encourage the parties to come to terms with their often deep-seated feelings of resentment and anger, rather than to seek an unattainable catharsis in a judicial forum"[13]. As a legal process, divorce dissolves the legal ties of marriage between husband and wife but it also frequently splits parents and children and whole families, especially where relatives and friends take sides with one partner against the other. Public opinion about the rights and wrongs of divorce is also sharply polarised, with pressure groups fighting for the husbands, wives and children whom they variously perceive as the main victims of divorce. Each proposed change in divorce law generates more argument about the hardships it is expected to cause for particular sections of the population or about its overall effect in weakening the institution of marriage and the stability of society as a whole. One of the few areas of agreement between conflicting social and political ideologies in relation to divorce is that the adversarial traditions of the English legal system contribute in no small degree to the emotional, social and financial costs of divorce. Dissatisfaction with this system and with the delays caused by congestion in the divorce courts has prompted a search for more positive and effective ways of settling legal problems connected with separation and divorce. As an alternative to adversarially conducted court proceedings, conciliation seems to offer a number of advantages, particularly in its emphasis on the value of mutually agreed decisions and co-operation between couples who remain parents of their children, despite their divorce.

A third reason for what might be called "the conciliation movement" is the evidence from research that although counselling and welfare services have proliferated since the middle of the century, relatively few people turn to them for help in solving the difficulties they encounter during the process of separation and divorce. A survey conducted in 1981 by Millward Brown Market and Social Research[14] found that two-thirds of the divorced men and women interviewed had not sought any help from a statutory or voluntary agency in relation to their divorce. Almost all of them thought, however, that there should be more pre-divorce counselling and that the present legal system was out of date. Nearly 80 per cent said that divorce would be better handled by a special family court and one in three – more men than women – wished they had tried harder to save their marriage. One in three also said they had had problems over custody and access arrangements for their children, and "children" who were interviewed (adults whose parents had divorced) felt that their parents had tried to make them side with one parent against the other. One in three felt they had emotional problems as a result. Most of the divorced parents felt they had no difficulty getting on with their step-children: the step-children disagreed almost 100 per cent. Another study conducted by Murch at Bristol University in 1973-74[15] found that although many of the recently divorced people in the sample had consulted their family doctor – whose treatment was likely to take the form of psychotropic drugs[16] – only 1 per cent had sought help from a marriage guidance counsellor. It seems that the marriage guidance councils are still widely perceived as mending, not ending, marriages in trouble[17] and this widespread belief is confirmed by the National Association of Citizens' Advice Bureaux who reported that "the counselling service of the Marriage Guidance Council is often not acceptable to couples who have decided that their relationship is irretrievable"[18]. Citizens'Advice Bureaux receive well over 600,000 inquiries per year about family and personal matters, of which a large proportion concern separation and divorce and they consider that there is a substantial need for information and help which is not met either by the legal system or by existing services. The Probation Service has a statutory responsibility to provide a welfare service in the divorce courts but the low priority given to this work by the Home Office[19] means that no additional resources have been made available and welfare officers are under considerable pressure. Separating and divorcing people may be reluctant to approach a statutory agency which is associated with the treatment of criminal offenders and although this stigma has been reduced in many areas by setting up separate teams of welfare officers specialising in civil work, they are officers of the court and their work is backed by the court's authority. Similarly, local authority social service departments are associated with receiving children into care, and parents whose home life is in turmoil may fear being found inadequate by a social worker with statutory responsibilities for the welfare of children. When couples disagree about the ending of their marriage and about arrangements for the future, both partners are likely to turn to solicitors for advice and often for partisan support. If disagreements are then handled in a combative way by solicitors and barristers, they may escalate into a prolonged and bitter legal battle at considerable cost to public funds. Expenditure on matrimonial legal aid totalled £61 million in 1983-84 out of a gross civil legal aid bill of £105 million[20]. It can be argued that large sums of public money are being spent on helping families to split up in destructive ways and that relatively little is spent on helping couples to consider the options available to them and to separate, if necessary, without severe conflict and distress.

Another argument for the introduction of conciliation services is that under the present system, insufficient attention is given to children's needs and feelings, partly because solicitors who advise and act for husbands and wives do not represent their children. If parents fight each other in court over custody or access arrangements, one parent generally emerges as the winner and the other as the loser, but in reality they both lose and so do their children, because any possibility of co-operation may have been permanently lost. The number of children affected by divorce has risen dramatically in the last twenty years. On current divorce trends it is estimated that one in five children in England and Wales will experience parental divorce before reaching the age of 16[21] and possibly multiple separations as well. Of the 160,000 children per year whose parents divorce, two-thirds are under eleven years old and a quarter are under five. Recent empirical studies in Britain[22] suggest that a crucial factor for children is the way in which decisions are taken and explained to them by their parents. If children are deprived of information and reassurance concerning this major upheaval in their lives, they may become deeply distressed and anxious, and in the longer term their development may be impaired by the loss of adequate support[23]. Children whose parents managed to co-operate, despite the ending of their marriage, were found in one study[24] to show a lower than average rate of emotional disorder compared with their age-group as a whole, whereas children whose parents continued to fight after the divorce, or who felt rejected by the parent who left home, were liable to develop stress-related physical illnesses, behaviour problems, depression, or failed to progress at school. Longitudinal studies[25] have found a disturbingly strong association between a child's experience of family break-up before the age of five and later negative developmental outcomes, including higher risks of stress-related physical illness, psychiatric disorder and serious crimes committed against the person. These negative consequences do not result automatically from separation and divorce: many children cope adequately with stress and succeed in adjusting to changed circumstances. The priority, therefore, is to identify measures which reinforce parents' resources and reduce children's vulnerability to the effects of a crisis in the family. Wallerstein and Kelly's five-year study in the United States[26] showed that parents' capacity to respond to their children's needs may be seriously diminished if they themselves are overwhelmed by the experience of marriage breakdown and divorce, suggesting that the most effective way of helping children may be to provide more help to their parents, particularly during the crisis of separation.

The kind of help adults may need or find acceptable cannot be provided in isolation from the legal process, since the process of obtaining a divorce requires compliance with compulsory legal procedures. A system of helping couples to reach mutually agreed decisions instead of getting embroiled in litigation needs therefore to be integrated with the legal process of divorce. The practice of conciliation in separation and divorce must fit in with this legal framework or at least avoid conflicting with the requirements of the law. Much can be learnt from other countries' experience of family law reform and conciliation, since the problems of large-scale divorce are not confined to Britain and many countries have developed non-adversarial methods of settling disputes. Most industrialised countries have experienced a simultaneous increase in divorce and these common trends in Europe, North America and Australia show that national factors of causation cannot fully explain an international pattern[27]. Some of the problems associated with divorce may be insoluble without fundamental economic and social change[28] and new initiatives, such as the introduction of conciliation services, should not simply act as palliatives which remove the pressure for reform.

Conflict tends to generate anxiety at both a personal and public level and this anxiety may generate a naive faith in conciliation as though it were a magic wand which can be waved over antagonistic couples, replacing their hostility with reasonableness and harmony.

It is disconcerting to find that the philosophy of conciliation can be harnessed to serve different ends and that its practice, ironically, can lead to disputes among professionals. In this ideological battle, the initial "c" of conciliation stands in many people's minds for communication, collaborative effort, co-operation and compromise, but research findings suggest that it can also stand for coercion and control. Arguments about conciliation, like the conflicts of divorce itself, should not be seen as inevitably negative and destructive because they may stimulate development and growth instead of passive acceptance and stagnation.

This study of conciliation is intended to contribute to an open debate about its potential advantages and disadvantages. Practice manuals for conciliators are needed and will undoubtedly follow, but first we need to consider the context in which conciliation is developing in this country and the problems we are seeking to solve. Before we try to refine the performance of the conciliation "motor", we need to consider the terrain it is meant to cover, the lay-out of the roads, who is meant to be driving, and the appropriate speed for the traffic. This study is intended therefore to encourage further exploration of the complex and difficult common ground which lies not only between many disputants but also between the professionals who become involved in their difficulties.

The following summary offers some sign-posts to the topics addressed in each chapter. Chapter 1 provides a short historical survey of divorce law and procedure in England and Wales, since the practice of conciliation in separation and divorce needs to be set in its legal context. Support for conciliation is often bracketed with the campaign for a family court, and chapter 2 considers the lack of co-ordination between overlapping jurisdictions which can result in matrimonial proceedings being taken in the same case in more than one jurisdiction in England and Wales or in different parts of the United Kingdom. Chapter 3 looks briefly at the nature of conflict and at different methods of settling disputes, drawing some parallels between conciliation in industrial disputes and conciliation in divorce. Chapter 4 traces the early history of divorce conciliation in Britain, from its beginnings in Bristol from 1975 onwards to the formal inauguration of the National Family Conciliation Council in 1983. The word "conciliation" is used to describe a variety of different schemes and procedures and chapter 5 discusses four different approaches, both in and out of court. Chapter 6 examines the role of the conciliator in more detail, in relation to questions of selection and training, the problems of confidentiality, the use of practical skills and the relevance of theoretical knowledge. Chapter 7 identifies some aspects of unequal bargaining power and the ways in which conciliators can help to balance power between couples or family members without taking sides with one of them. In chapter 8 it is recognised that conciliation involves a number of assumptions and some inherent contradictions, especially where children are concerned. The controversial questions of whether, and if so, how, children should be included in conciliation are discussed, with brief illustrations from two case examples. Chapter 9 reviews research findings from England, Australia, New Zealand, Canada and the United States which point to the complexity of monitoring and evaluating conciliation services and the many questions which remain unanswered. Finally, in chapter 10, wider applications of conciliation are considered and the recent recommendations of the Committee on Matrimonial Causes Procedure (the Booth Committee) are related to current developments and possible directions for the future.

Notes

1. K. Kiernan, *The Structure of Families Today*, OPCS Occasional Paper 31 (London, 1983).
2. Central Statistical Office, *Social Trends 15* (HMSO, London, 1985).
3. J. Haskey, "The Proportion of Marriages Ending in Divorce", *Population Trends 27* (OPCS/HMSO, London, 1982).
4. Office of Population Censuses and Surveys, *General Household Survey* (HMSO, London, 1984); J. Eekelaar, *Family Law and Social Policy*, 2nd edn (Weidenfeld and Nicolson, London, 1984).
5. OPCS Monitor, *Marriages 1983* (OPCS, London, 1984).
6. Central Statistical Office, *Social Trends 14* (HMSO, London, 1984).
7. J. Haskey, "Social Class and Socio-economic Differentials in Divorce in England and Wales", *Population Studies*, vol. 38 (1984), pp. 419-38.
8. Ibid.
9. M. Harris, "How Unemployment Affects People", *New Society*, 19 January 1984.
10. John Stuart Mill, letter to Harriet Taylor, quoted by F.A. von Hayek in *John Stuart Mill and Harriet Taylor* (Routledge and Kegan Paul, London, 1951), p. 69.
11. J. Eekelaar, "The Democratisation of Family Law", paper given at the British Society for Population Studies Conference on the Family, University of Bath, 14-16 September 1983.
12. J.F. MacQueen, *The Rights and Liabilities of Husband and Wife* (1849), p. 213.
13. Law Commission No. 112, *The Financial Consequences of Divorce* (HMSO, London, 1981), par. 37.
14. *Woman* magazine, 27 February 1982, pp. 23-6.
15. M. Borkowski, M. Murch, V. Walker, *Marital Violence* (Tavistock Publications, London, 1983), p. 158.
16. R. Chester, "Health and Marriage Breakdown: Experience of a Sample of Divorced

Women", *British Journal of Preventive Medicine*, vol. 25 (1971), p. 231.
17. J. Brannen and J. Collard, *Marriages in Trouble* (Tavistock, London, 1982) and P. Hunt, *Clients' Responses to Marriage Counselling* (National Marriage Guidance Council Report No. 3, Rugby, 1985).
18. National Association of Citizens' Advice Bureaux, *Evidence Paper E/6/82* (London, 1982). The total number of inquiries concerning personal and family matters received by Citizens' Advice Bureaux in 1984 was 664,000, an increase of 17,000 over the previous year's figures (*NACAB Annual Report 1984*).
19. *Home Office Statement of National Objectives and Priorities for the Probation Service in England and Wales* (London, April 1984).
20. *Law Society's 34th Annual Report on Legal Aid 1983-84*, Appendix 4B.
21. As 2 above.
22. Y. Walczak with S. Burns, *Divorce – the Child's Point of View* (Harper and Row, London, 1984); A. Mitchell, *Children in the Middle* (Tavistock Publications, London, 1985).
23. M.J. Wadsworth and M. Maclean, "Parents' Divorce and Children's Life Chances", *Children and Youth Services Review* (in press).
24. M. Lund, "Research on Divorce and Children", *Family Law*, vol. 14 (1984), pp. 198-201.
25. M. Wadsworth, *Roots of Delinquency* (Martin Robertson, Oxford, 1979).
26. J. Wallerstein and J.M. Kelly, *Surviving the Break-Up* (Grant McIntyre, London, 1980).
27. R. Chester, "Mass Divorce and its Implications", in C. Guy (ed.), *Relating to Marriage* (National Marriage Guidance Council, Rugby, 1985).
28. C. Smart, "Marriage, Divorce and Women's Economic Dependency", in M.D.A. Freeman (ed.) *The State, the Law and the Family* (Tavistock Publications and Sweet and Maxwell, London, 1984).

1 THE LEGAL PROCESS OF DIVORCE IN ENGLAND AND WALES

It is still taken largely for granted in this country that the dissolution of marriage should be a judicial process administered by courts of law, and although there is an increasingly strong view that the decisions associated with divorce should be taken by divorcing couples themselves rather than by the courts, there is little question of divorce becoming merely an administrative process regulated by a Registrar of Births, Marriages, Divorces and Deaths[1]. In Denmark, where the divorce rate parallels that of England and Wales, far ahead of other EEC countries, nearly nine out of ten divorces are granted by County Governors (public administrators) and in Norway, too, divorce is mainly an administrative process rather than a judicial one (Schmidt 1984). As long as divorce remains a legal process controlled by the courts, as in all parts of the United Kingdom, legal concepts and rules are bound to exercise a powerful influence over the way marriages are dissolved. This influence can be applied to helping divorcing couples reach well-informed and mutually agreed decisions for the future or, by focusing attention on the past, it can increase hostility, bitterness and guilt. A legal process which facilitates agreement can help couples to re-organise their lives and relationships in a humane and civilised way, whereas a process which concentrates on establishing which spouse is the guilty party increases antagonism and discourages constructive solutions. Research studies (Chester 1971, Hart 1976, Wallerstein and Kelly 1980, Ambrose, Harper and Pemberton 1983) show that divorce is a very painful process for most people and it is unrealistic to expect a legal process to eliminate personal pain and grief. However, legal proceedings have the capacity to alleviate or exacerbate pain, depending on their structure and atmosphere, the moral judgements they convey and the extent to which they help to solve the complex and sometimes intractable problems of marriage breakdown.

The law of divorce in England and Wales was based historically on the concept that divorce should be granted to an innocent partner who seeks relief from the other partner's intolerable misconduct. The doctrine of the matrimonial offence assumes the innocence of one party and the guilt of the other, thus forcing them into the positions of accuser and accused without acknowledging that both partners are often jointly responsible for the breakdown of their marriage, in various ways or degrees. The need to reform an outdated divorce law has been a matter of considerable public concern throughout most of this century. Under the Matrimonial Causes Act 1937 the offences of cruelty and desertion were added to adultery as grounds for divorce and for the first time a no-fault ground was included: that of the spouse's incurable insanity. There was however no means of obtaining a divorce with the consent of both partners because "it was widely thought that to allow divorce with consent would destroy the institution of marriage and the sanctity of family life" (Cretney 1984, p. 101). The petitioner was not allowed to be equally at fault for the failure of the marriage (Eekelaar 1971) and any evidence that a divorcing couple had colluded with each other in the presentation of the petition was an absolute bar to divorce being granted.

The disruption caused by the war resulted in a sharp increase in the number of divorces (from 6,915 in 1940 to 47,041 in 1947) and in 1951 Mrs Eirene White presented a private member's bill in the House of Commons which would permit divorce to spouses who had lived apart for seven years, without requiring one of them to accuse the other of a matrimonial offence. This bill caused alarm that the institution of marriage was being threatened and the government responded by setting up a Royal Commission on Marriage and Divorce (the Morton Commission 1951-56) to consider the reformers' arguments that the concept of the matrimonial offence was archaic, punitive and inconsistent with people's actual behaviour and expectations in marriage. The contrary arguments were marshalled by the Church of England, whose representatives explained to the Commission that the doctrine of the matrimonial offence was "entirely in accord with the New Testament" and that divorce was "a very dangerous threat to the family and to the conception of marriage as a lifelong obligation" (evidence to the Morton Commission 1952 pp. 160 and 142).

The Morton Commission was persuaded by the force of these arguments to oppose reform, and when the Commission reported in 1956 all except one member favoured the retention of the matrimonial offence as the ground for divorce (Cretney 1984). The Commission's conclusion was that divorce law should provide relief where a wrong had been done and that the irretrievable breakdown of marriage should not be allowed as an alternative ground for divorce (1956 par. 69 xiii). These recommendations drew fierce attack from some quarters (McGregor 1957) and in 1963, despite the Church of England's previous opposition to reform, a group of churchmen, lawyers and laity was convened by the Archbishop of Canterbury to consider whether the concept of the irretrievable breakdown of marriage could provide an acceptable legal ground for divorce. In the same year, the Matrimonial Causes Act 1963 allowed collusion between divorcing couples to become a discretionary bar to divorce instead of an absolute bar, a change described by a former President of the Divorce Division (now the Family Division) of the High Court as "revolutionary" (Simon 1970), because it enabled the court "to allow the implementation of agreements or arrangements which can dispose without acrimony of such matters as maintenance, damages, custody of and access to children, and property disputes, and to obviate long and damaging contests" (p. 3231). This revolutionary development failed, however, to make any significant impact on the way divorce proceedings were conducted, because long-established legal traditions assumed divorcing couples to be antagonists whose conflicting interests should be dealt with through formal confrontations in court. Legal rituals designed to achieve justice in criminal trials may not be appropriate in matrimonial and family law, where couples frequently have common interests and responsibilities as parents. If clashes between them are treated by solicitors and the courts as a battle for moral and material victory, the legal process encourages prolonged warfare and incites them to seek vindication or revenge. The system of providing separate legal advice to each party and where necessary separate representation in court is intended to ensure as far as possible that individual interests and claims are adequately protected, so that the court's decisions in contested cases are based on full consideration of the available evidence. However, this system is also criticised for increasing rivalry and antagonistic attitudes and these connotations have given rise to the label "adversarial system" – a label which is often used pejoratively to imply that separate legal representation promotes litigation, even where both parties wish to settle their affairs with as little acrimony and expense as possible. The image of the gladiatorial divorce lawyer was borne out by some historical accounts of legal practice in the divorce courts. John Mortimer recounted in his autobiography (1982) that in the 1950s the matrimonial offence of "cruelty" was used by lawyers to describe almost any activity in which even the best-intentioned respondent might have engaged. Mortimer concluded from his own experience at the Bar that a barrister could easily build a career in "undefendeds" (undefended divorces) provided that he could learn "to fit each and every marriage into the three immutable categories of adultery, cruelty and desertion" (p. 99).

Once the powerful machinery of divorce was set in motion, husband and wife became insignificant figures crushed under a weighty legal process which ground along under its own momentum, with apparently little concern for those whose lives it was reshaping so drastically.

The Morton Commission's opposition to divorce reform proved however to be "little more than a ripple on the surface of a tide that was moving strongly in the other direction" (Finer Report 1974 par. 4.32). In 1966 the Archbishop of Canterbury's group published their report *Putting Asunder*, expressing their view that "as a piece of social mechanism the present system has not only cut loose from its moral and juridical foundations: it is, quite simply, inept" (p. 32). The group advised that

> we should learn to think in terms not of "innocent" and "guilty" partners, but of the condition of the matrimonial relationship . . . If, after hearing the evidence, the court decided that the relationship was "dead", . . . it would not be giving a decree in favour of the petitioner or endorsing his or her conduct, but simply giving effect to a finding of fact (p. 50).

The newly established Law Commission endorsed this view in *Reform of the Grounds of Divorce: The Field of Choice* (1966), stating that a good divorce law should buttress, rather than undermine, the stability of marriage, but when, regrettably, a marriage had irretrievably broken down, the law should "enable the empty legal shell to be destroyed with the maximum fairness, and the minimum bitterness, distress and humiliation . . . in a way which will encourage harmonious relationships between the parties and their children in the future" (pp. 10-11).

The Law Commission's recommendations paved the way for the Divorce Reform Act 1969 which introduced the irretrievable breakdown of marriage as the sole ground for divorce. However, this reform was not as progressive as it appeared, because the irretrievable breakdown of marriage had to be established by one or more of five "facts", three of which corresponded to the old matrimonial offences of adultery, cruelty and desertion. These facts were incorporated in the Matrimonial Causes Act 1973, the current divorce law in England and Wales, as follows:

1. that the respondent has committed adultery and the petitioner finds

it intolerable to live with the respondent;
2. that the respondent has behaved in such a way that the petitioner cannot reasonably be expected to live with the respondent;
3. that the respondent has deserted the petitioner for a continuous period of at least two years immediately preceding the presentation of the petition;
4. that the parties have lived apart for a continuous period of at least two years immediately preceding the presentation of the petition and the respondent consents to a decree being granted;
5. that the parties have lived apart for a continuous period of at least five years immediately preceding the presentation of the petition.

Even in 1984, over 70 per cent of the petitions filed in England and Wales were based on fault, the largest category (41%) being based on allegations of "unreasonable behaviour" by the respondent and the second largest (28%) on adultery[2]. Eekelaar and Clive (1977) found that the respondent (who is the husband, in seven out of ten divorces) was far less likely to accept a petition based on "unreasonable behaviour" than one based on other evidence but very few respondents ultimately defend the divorce because of the enormously high cost and difficulty of doing so. According to the Lord Chancellor's Advisory Committee on Legal Aid[3], legal aid is not normally granted to defend a divorce petition if it is clear that the marriage has broken down irretrievably and that the defence will be unsuccessful. The Judicial Statistics for 1982 showed that only 0.57 per cent of petitions filed in that year were set down for trial as defended cases in the High Court and very few of these are ultimately heard because the respondent generally decides for one reason or another not to proceed (Cretney 1984). However, research evidence (Eekelaar and Clive 1977, Gibson 1980, Davis 1981) has shown that petitions based on allegations of "unreasonable behaviour" arouse strong reactions in respondents. If they are prevented from putting their side of the case, the unresolved conflict may be transferred to issues relating to money, children and property, for which legal aid is more readily available. These issues provide warring couples with a new arena in which the marital battle can be fought. Eekelaar and Clive (1977) found that parents in "unreasonable behaviour" divorces were far less likely to have agreed the arrangements for their children than those involved in adultery or two-year separation cases. Petitioners who cited "unreasonable behaviour" were more likely to oppose the other parent's access to the children and disputes over custody and access arrangements were much more common than in other cases. In the United States, Weiss (1975) likewise found that disputes over children provide a battleground in which parents fight out the unresolved conflicts of their broken marriage. It is therefore particularly worrying that "unreasonable behaviour" is a much more common basis for divorce where there are children of the marriage than where the couple is childless (Eekelaar and Maclean 1983).

The Divorce Reform Act 1969 has not established no-fault divorce as the norm: fewer than a quarter of all petitions filed in 1984 were based on two years' separation with consent and 6 per cent on five years' separation without consent[4]. A petitioner who does not want to wait two or more years for a divorce may be driven to use one of the fault-based facts which permit a "quickie divorce". Hurtful and inflammatory accusations are thus encouraged rather than curbed by a divorce law which has not yet abolished the matrimonial offence as the basis for divorce. The attempt to superimpose the concept of irretrievable breakdown of marriage on top of the concept of the matrimonial offence has produced a kind of historical and moral layer-cake, in which a thin layer of twentieth century liberalism has been spread over a thick slab of Victorian moral values. A law which is ill-attuned to people's needs is likely to be abused. In a survey of over 300 divorced people commissioned by *Woman* magazine in 1981, 27 per cent stated that their petition had been based on false allegations in order to speed up the divorce[5]. If there is no evidence of fault nor of two or more years' separation, the court cannot grant a divorce, even if the marriage has broken down irretrievably and both partners accept the need for divorce. In March 1985, the Court of Appeal refused to grant a divorce to a wife who failed to prove unreasonable behaviour by her husband to support her claim that the marriage had broken down irretrievably[6]. The husband agreed that there was no chance of making the marriage work again but the Court's ruling obliged the couple to preserve a marriage that was probably deeply unhappy for both of them and for their children. In another case referred to the Court of Appeal in 1984[7], the wife was granted an injunction to exclude her husband from the matrimonial home for an indefinite period, on the grounds of his violence towards her and his general ill-treatment of her and of their elder daughter. Yet the wife's petition for divorce had been dismissed in the divorce court because the judge had not found sufficient proof in the petition of "unreasonable behaviour". It is disturbing that divorce courts dissolve so many marriages so quickly, on the basis of allegations which are often fiercely denied by the respondent, and yet some couples are left in an intolerable stalemate without the relief of divorce. This unsatisfactory situation falls a long way short of achieving the objectives of a good divorce law, as defined by the Law Commission (1966).

Until 1984, special leave had to be obtained to present a petition for divorce within the first three years of marriage and there had to be evidence of exceptional hardship on the part of the petitioner or "exceptional depravity" on the part of the respondent. Apart from the difficulty of distinguishing exceptional depravity from ordinary depravity, research findings (Law Commission 1982 No. 116) indicated that the three-year ban delayed but did not prevent divorce and that the recent substantial increase in petitions for judicial separation was very largely due to their use as a short-term measure, pending divorce. These findings suggested that couples whose marriage broke down very quickly were likely to go through two sets of legal proceedings to end their marriage – judicial separation followed by divorce within two years or so. The Matrimonial and Family Proceedings Act 1984 abolished the discretionary three-year rule and substituted an absolute bar on divorce proceedings being commenced within the first year of marriage. The immediate effect of this change was a 6 per cent increase in petitions filed in 1984, compared with the previous year, to a record total of 178,940 (*The Times* 16 August 1985). This increase was expected to continue during 1985 and then to taper off gradually, while the number of petitions for judicial separation has dropped, as predicted.

The 1984 Act also laid down guidelines[8] on the extent to which the courts should take account of either party's conduct when assessing claims for financial provision and property transfer in connection with divorce proceedings. The Matrimonial Proceedings and Property Act 1970, which was re-enacted in the Matrimonial Causes Act 1973, allowed the courts considerable discretion in assessing the weight to be given to either party's misconduct when determining their financial obligations. Lord Denning argued forcefully in the Court of Appeal decision of Wachtel v. Wachtel that detailed examination of allegations of misconduct would be contrary to the principles of the Divorce Reform Act 1969 and that conduct should be taken into account in relation to financial orders only if it were seen to be "both obvious and gross"[9]. Lord Justice Ormrod, in his judgement in the same case, observed that the part played by each party in a marriage is not easily assessed in a court of law and that fault rarely lies only in one direction:

> The forensic process is reasonably well adapted to determining in broad terms the share of responsibility of each party for an accident on the road or at work because the issues are relatively confined in scope, but it is much too clumsy a tool for dissecting the complex inter-actions which go on all the time in a family. Shares in responsibility for breakdown cannot be properly assessed without a meticulous examination and understanding of the characters and personalities of the spouses concerned, and the more thorough the investigation the more the shares will, in most cases, approach equality[10].

The Law Commission (1981 No. 112) accepted that it would place an impossible burden on the courts to assess each party's share of responsibility for the breakdown of their marriage and the Matrimonial and Family Proceedings Act 1984 provided a statutory reformulation of the Wachtel decision by directing that the court must have regard to the conduct of each of the parties "if that conduct is such that it would in the opinion of the court be inequitable to disregard it" (s. 3 g). The 1984 Act thus re-stated the policy that conduct should normally be disregarded by the courts when making financial and property orders. Although there was sharp controversy at the time over the instruction to take account of exceptional misconduct, preliminary reports on the effects of the Act suggest that a year later the courts were paying no more attention to conduct than they had done previously and that solicitors were generally discouraging their clients from embarking on recriminations in the hope of obtaining a more favourable financial settlement. It is possible however that in some cases both parties might be advised to cross-petition each other to protect themselves in subsequent proceedings over finance and property.

The humiliation and distress which many petitioners used to suffer in recounting details of their marriage breakdown at an open court hearing (Elston, Fuller and Murch 1975) was alleviated not by a reform of the law itself but by a procedural change which attracted little public attention. The surge in the number of divorces particularly from 1971 onwards and the high cost of holding a judicial hearing in each case put increasing pressure on the courts and on the legal aid fund, which met the main cost of these hearings. Concern to reduce the soaring costs of legal aid, rather than humanitarian concern to make divorce proceedings less punitive (Gibson 1980) was apparently the main reason for the introduction in 1973 of the "special procedure", by which undefended divorces based on two years' separation in which no children were involved could be obtained by post without any court attendance in connection with the decree. This procedure was extended in 1975 and again in 1977 to cover all undefended divorces, whether or not children were involved. The "special procedure" has thus become the normal procedure (92.5 per cent of all decrees granted in 1982 were granted under this procedure) but its name remains unchanged. Petitioners are now spared the public ordeal of giving evidence about the breakdown of their marriage in open court but the "special procedure" does not lessen the private ordeal experienced by many couples and may even deprive them of a necessary opportunity to vent their feelings. Further changes of procedure are under consideration to encourage direct discussion and negotiation between them about matters connected with their divorce, but no formal provision for this has yet been made (1985) within divorce procedure.

The decree of divorce is pronounced in two stages, the decree nisi and the decree absolute. The task of checking divorce petitions and their supporting documents is undertaken by divorce court registrars but registrars cannot (at the time of writing) pronounce a decree nisi. This has to be pronounced by a judge in open court (a batch of decrees is usually pronounced collectively) but as the documents have already been checked and the parties are not present, the use of the judge as a rubber stamp seems pointless. As the decree nisi is not the final decree, divorcing couples may not be certain whether and when they are actually divorced. Six weeks after the pronouncement of the decree nisi, the petitioner may apply for the decree to be made absolute but if this is not done the respondent has to wait a further three months before he or she may apply for the decree absolute. The historical and legal reasons for this two-stage process may not be understood by divorcing couples, who may find two separate applications to the court, on the decree alone, both confusing and cumbersome. In about 3,000 divorces per year, neither party applies for the decree to be made absolute and these marriages remain in a legal limbo and possibly in emotional limbo as well.

The Divorce Reform Act 1969 was described in its long title as an Act which should among other things "facilitate reconciliation". If anything, it may be said to have done the reverse. Researchers in Bristol (Davis 1981) found that 25 per cent of the respondents interviewed did not accept that their marriage had broken down irretrievably or were uncertain whether it had done so. Although this does not necessarily mean that these divorces could have been avoided, the legal process gives the respondent neither time nor encouragement to discuss the possibility of reconciliation with their spouse, whose decision to end the marriage may have stemmed from profound misunderstandings and lack of communication. The requirement under section 6 (1) of the 1973 Act that the solicitor advising the petitioner must file a certificate stating whether the possibility of reconciliation has been discussed is an absurdity on several counts: the law's requirement is technically satisfied if the solicitor states that the prospect of reconciliation has not been discussed and the requirement does not apply at all where the solicitor is advising a petitioner under the Green Form scheme. As the majority of petitioners are advised under this scheme, the law's apparent concern to facilitate reconciliation has been reserved for the minority whose financial means are above the prescribed limits of the Green Form scheme and, even then, the procedure is seen by many solicitors as no more than a dead letter which should be repealed[11]. About a third of the petitioners in the Bristol study who had consulted a solicitor said that their solicitor had not checked specifically that they really wanted a divorce (Davis 1981). Although it may have been obvious in many cases that a reconciliation was out of the question, there is cause for concern that some petitioners, at least, find themselves on a conveyor-belt to divorce without other alternatives being fully explored.

Children and Divorce

The Matrimonial Causes Act 1857 empowered the divorce court to make such order "as it may deem just and proper for the custody, maintenance and education of the children" and the Guardianship of Minors Act 1971 (re-enacting the Guardianship of Infants Act 1925) directed that courts must regard the welfare of the child as the first and paramount consideration. The Denning Committee (1947) had expressed concern that the welfare of children in divorce proceedings was wrongly subordinated to the interests of their parents and the Morton Commission (1956) recommended that steps should be taken to ensure that divorcing parents considered their children's future welfare and to give the courts more effective control over questions relating to the children. The Morton Commission proposed that there should be a rule that the decree nisi should not normally be made absolute unless and until the court was satisfied that the proposed arrangements for the children were satisfactory, or the best that could be devised in the circumstances. Legislation to enact this rule was introduced in 1958 and re-enacted in section 41 of the Matrimonial Causes Act 1973.

What the law intends and what happens in practice may be two very different things. Although the welfare of the child is paramount in law, applications for custody of or access to children are treated as ancillary to the decree proceedings and consideration of them may be delayed by preliminary correspondence between solicitors and by administrative delays in the court system. Moreover, if a child's parents disagree, it may not be at all easy for a judge to determine what arrangements may be in "the best interests of the child"(Mnookin 1975, Freeman 1983, Cretney 1984). In the absence of clearly defined and reliable criteria, a great deal depends on the relative weight given by judges to particular factors or circumstances. One of the many difficulties in making these assessments is that the subjective accounts given by parents under stress may be inaccurate, incomplete or distorted by their own needs and feelings. An adversarial approach to disputes encourages couples to denigrate each other as parents and to appeal to a higher authority to settle the argument for them. In dealing with these contested cases and with other cases in which there is particular concern about the children's welfare, the courts need assistance in assessing family circumstances and the interests of the children concerned. Under the Matrimonial Causes Rules 1957, probation committees were required to assign a probation officer to the High Court "with a view to assisting the court in making an order or provision with respect to the custody, maintenance or education of a child" and the Matrimonial Proceedings (Children) Act 1958 used the term "welfare officer" for the first time and specified that the welfare officer should be a probation officer. When divorce jurisdiction was extended to divorce county courts under the Matrimonial Causes Act 1967, probation committees were asked to appoint welfare officers in these courts and the Matrimonial Causes Rules 1977 re-enacted earlier legislation by providing for a judge or registrar to refer any matter concerning the welfare of a child to a court welfare officer for investigation and report. The divorce courts have complete discretion in determining when to call for a welfare inquiry and initially very few were ordered. During the 1960s and 1970s, the number increased dramatically from 880 in 1960 to 10,717 in 1970 and then almost doubled to 20,475 in 1980 (James and Wilson 1983). In 1981, probation officers prepared 21,870 reports concerning access and custody[12], representing a welfare inquiry in about one in five divorces involving children. In spite of this heavy reliance on welfare officers, their role has never been clearly defined and there is disagreement as to whether their primary task is to make investigations and assessments on the court's behalf or to assist divorcing and divorced parents to reach agreement over arrangements for their children.

Eekelaar and Clive (1977) found in their examination of court records from ten divorce courts in England and Wales that the intervention of welfare officers rarely resulted in existing arrangements being altered and that the court changed a child's residence without parental agreement in only about 5 per cent of contested custody cases. However, almost a third of these cases took over a year to reach a final court hearing and the researchers concluded that "there is room for adapting our procedures to the urgency of these situations, in recognition of the importance of their resolution in the interests of the children concerned" (par. 13.30). They also pointed out "the limited effect that legal proceedings can have in these complex emotional and social conditions" and recommended that welfare officers should not simply collect information for the court but concentrate on helping divorcing parents to resolve questions concerning their children (par. 13.30).

When the "special procedure" was extended in 1977 to all undefended divorces including those involving children, a new system of judicial appointments was introduced, known as the children's appointment or section 41 appointment[13]. The petitioner, even if the children are in the care of the other parent, is required to attend an appointment in the judge's chambers so that the arrangements for the children can be considered: the decree of divorce cannot be made absolute unless the judge declares that the arrangements for the children are satisfactory or the best that can be devised in the circumstances. When the Lord Chancellor announced this new system in the House of Lords, he admitted that "inevitably, it is very difficult for the Judge to do more than approve whatever arrangements the petitioner proposes" (*Hansard* HL 15 June 1976). Researchers at Bristol University (Davis, MacLeod and Murch 1983a) found that judges took an average time of four and a half minutes per appointment and that judicial satisfaction was pronounced in 90 per cent of cases. Maidment (1976) found that only 1 of 95 cases failed to obtain judicial satisfaction. In an observation of 402 appointments at four county courts, Dodds (1983) reported that judges rarely ordered a welfare report and that the criteria for doing so varied considerably between different judges. Some of the judges said they regarded the appointments as a cosmetic exercise intended to allay public concern about the effects of divorce on children. A parent who sets out to deceive the judge may succeed in doing so and the arrangements that are proposed for the children may be changed immediately after the appointment or never implemented. Parents who were interviewed in the Bristol study said that they found the procedure ambiguous and confusing. The respondent parent (usually the father) attended the appointment in only 32 per cent of cases and as problems concerning the children may be covered up by a petitioner parent anxious to obtain a divorce, neither parent may make these problems known to the court. By 1985, some county courts were actively encouraging both parents to attend the appointment and take part, with the help of a welfare officer if needed, in discussion about arrangements for their children but this constructive use of the appointment is by no means established practice throughout the country and there is great variation between different courts and different judges.

The court is asked in a divorce petition to dissolve the bonds of marriage, not the bonds of parenthood, but there is a common assumption that after divorce only one parent should have sole custody, care and control of the children. The law does not provide precise definitions of these terms and personal experience suggests that many divorcing parents do not know that they can apply for joint custody, with day-to-day care and control in the hands of one parent (Parkinson 1981). We seem to have a self-perpetuating situation in which parents apply for sole custody, believing this to be normal practice and the court rubber-stamps the arrangement, thus reinforcing sole custody as the norm. Figures provided by the Lord Chancellor's Department show that only 12.7 per cent of custody orders made in England and Wales from January to September 1985 were for joint custody, whereas just over 86 per cent were sole custody orders (77 per cent to the mother and 9.2 per cent to the father). There is great disparity between different regions and different courts in relation to joint custody orders: 18.6 per cent of custody orders made by courts in the South-Eastern Circuit in this nine-month period were for joint custody, compared with only 5.5 per cent made by courts in the Northern Circuit. Considering the large number of custody orders made in matrimonial proceedings (62,134 from January to September 1985), there is a remarkable dearth of empirical evidence as to whether joint custody orders increase parental conflict, encourage co-operation or simply make no difference to the existing situation. Pearson (1982) found that many custody disputes in the United States were not about practical arrangements for the children but about the notion that one parent, usually the father, is disposable after divorce. There seem to be many unproven beliefs about joint custody, but significantly, Patrician (1984) found that legal labels such as "sole custody" and "non-custodial parent" influence parents' attitudes and expectations and that these labels contribute to conflict and dissatisfaction. Maidment (1984) argued that the fact that sole custody orders grant sole rights to one parent and remove them from the other encourages parents to treat their children as possessions to be won or lost, although in a contested custody case everyone experiences loss to a greater or lesser extent. It is questionable whether the divorce courts should so willingly deprive one parent of parental rights and responsibilities, especially if the concept of joint custody has value in helping to reassure children that neither parent has abandoned them. Maidment (1984) proposed that the divorce court should make only a "children's residence order" which would specify which parent has day-to-day responsibility for the children while recognising that both parents have a continuing parental role. However, it would be irresponsible to overlook those cases in which one parent's involvement in the children's lives appears to be actually harmful to them, perhaps because the parent is mentally ill or violent. In such cases, an application for sole custody would enable the court to consider whether custody should be granted to one parent only or to neither parent, and whether the other parent should have any access to the children.

The Role of Solicitors in Divorce Proceedings

Individuals on the brink of separation or divorce need specialist information and advice on the many questions and problems that face them, and many of them turn to solicitors without being aware of other possible sources of information and help in relation to marital difficulties, separation and divorce (Ambrose, Harper and Pemberton 1983). These difficulties commonly involve emotional, psychological and housing problems as well as legal and financial ones, but the Bristol study showed that most divorcing people consulted solicitors and that very few consulted social workers, counsellors or priests (Borkowski, Murch and Walker 1983). The "special procedure" opened the way to do-it-yourself divorce but research findings (Davis, MacLeod and Murch 1982a) showed that only a small proportion of childless couples were likely to conduct their own divorce without the help of a solicitor, whereas 99 per cent of petitioners who had children sought legal advice, usually on the divorce itself. Solicitors have considerable influence in directing people towards legal action or away from it and a great deal depends on how they balance the role of adviser, counsellor and negotiator with that of advocate and champion. People approach solicitors with very different expectations and often in a state of great anxiety and confusion. Ambrose, Harper and Pemberton (1983) found that some of the men in their study particularly valued their solicitor's partisan support in helping them to press their claims instead of accepting an unfair settlement or beating a full-scale retreat. One man commented that his solicitor helped him to "dig my heels in over access and joint ownership of the marital home" (p. 73), whereas others referred to the difficulties of understanding legal language and several complained that their solicitors were provocative and combative. Comments included: "He tried to stir up complications" and "He tended to state things in a way which I knew would provoke adverse reactions" (p. 78). The Bristol researchers (Davis, MacLeod and Murch 1982b) found that many divorcing individuals wanted their solicitor to give them a calm and objective appraisal of their position and of the likely outcome if they took their case to court. Forty-two per cent of those interviewed reported that maintenance had been disputed at some stage and 29 per cent said that they had disagreed about arrangements for their children. Disputes over maintenance were frequently linked with access problems. The parents in this study were not particularly dispute-prone as all the divorces had been undefended and they were not currently involved in court proceedings over custody or access: 29 per cent of those who stated that there had been conflict in their case said that their solicitor had encouraged them to reach agreement and only 15 per cent said that their solicitor had urged them to fight their case through the courts. But those who avoided litigation had not necessarily resolved their difficulties and 18 per cent said that they were dissatisfied with their existing access arrangements.

These research studies show that solicitors do not necessarily take a sharply adversarial stance in matrimonial proceedings and that they often restrain their clients from litigation. In December 1982 a group of solicitors formed the Solicitors' Family Law Association with the aim of promoting a more sensitive, constructive and non-litigious approach in matrimonial proceedings. Sixty solicitors based mainly in the London area were founder members of the Association, which grew rapidly to a membership of about 700 by November 1985. The Association's Code of Practice (Appendix C) emphasises the need for constructive negotiations to help couples settle their affairs and avoid litigation. If all solicitors undertaking matrimonial work followed this Code of Practice, congestion in the divorce courts would be considerably lessened and expenditure on legal aid might fall dramatically. The Chairman of the Association (Cornwell 1983) reported that out of approximately 110 matrimonial clients who consulted him during 1983, only two became involved in a contested court hearing and only two of the divorce petitions which he issued were based on "unreasonable behaviour". He also stated that none of his clients rejected his approach to go in search of a more "adversarial" solicitor. It is not known however to what extent his clients were representative of the divorcing population as a whole.

Although the litigious divorce solicitor may be out of fashion, members of the species still exist and the absence of litigation does not prove that divorcing couples actually agree with each other. The Bristol study (Davis, MacLeod and Murch 1982b) indicated that fully fought court proceedings over custody or access may be the tip of an iceberg of partially submerged disputes which may affect families for many years after the divorce. Research in Sheffield suggests that these unresolved disputes put great strain on second marriages (Burgoyne and Clark 1984). The Bristol researchers found that almost one-third (31%) of divorcing parents who were not involved in contested proceedings over custody or access at the time of their research had no communication with the other parent or only hostile communication. A breakdown in communication or continuing conflict may result in access stopping altogether or taking place infrequently. Failure to exercise access may indicate lack of interest on the part of the non-custodial parent but it often seems to be linked with unresolved conflict. Maidment (1976) found no access at the time of the divorce petition in one-third of divorces and irregular access in a further 14 per cent. Eekelaar and Clive (1977) found similarly in their national study of divorce court records that one-third of the families reported no access one year after separation and this proportion increased to nearly one half at the time of the divorce. A court order for reasonable or defined access seems to bear little relation to whether access takes place or not (Maidment 1976) and "a law which, in practice, allows sole custody rights to one parent in the majority of cases and which allows access decisions and practice to go largely unchecked is, by implication, encouraging parental irresponsibility on divorce" (Maidment 1984 p. 166). A number of studies of the impact of divorce on children (Hetherington, Cox and Cox 1979, Wallerstein and Kelly 1980, Lund 1984, Walczak 1984, Mitchell 1985) point to the importance from the child's point of view of maintaining regular contact with the parent who leaves home.

Wallerstein and Kelly (1980) found that children who felt abandoned by a loved parent were liable to show overt or underlying depression of varying intensity and that this was often accompanied by "disabling symptomatic behaviors" (p. 248).

Some access disputes are not referred to the court because the parent seeking access fears making matters worse or doubts the effectiveness of a defined access order, in the face of determined opposition from the custodial parent. The court has power to make a matrimonial supervision order where there are entrenched difficulties, or other cause for concern about the welfare of a child[14], and these orders may remain in force until the child reaches the age of 18. Figures kept by the Department of Health and Social Security show that, of the 36,000 supervision orders which were operative in 1982, more were made in matrimonial and other family proceedings than under the Children and Young Persons Act 1969. However, the social worker or probation officer to whom the supervision order is allocated does not always know the court's reasons for making it, and the existence of a supervision order by no means guarantees that access will take place. It is ultimately very difficult for the court to enforce an access order, because sanctions such as imprisonment for deliberate breach of the order or a warning that custody of the children might be transferred to the other parent may be impracticable because of the hardship that might be caused to the children (Samuels 1981).

Another major factor determining whether disputes are referred to the court is the availability of legal aid. Legal aid was withdrawn from undefended divorce proceedings in 1977, although it continues to be available for the "ancillary issues" of children, maintenance and property. Initially, there was a sharp drop in the number of applications for legal aid in matrimonial proceedings but from 1978 onwards the number increased rapidly. The Lord Chancellor's Advisory Committee on Legal Aid noted in their *32nd Annual Report (1981-82)* that the proportion of divorces involving contested ancillary matters was rising at a much faster rate than the divorce rate[15]. The number of legal aid bills paid for matrimonial proceedings in the divorce county courts more than doubled in the four-year period from 1979-80 to 1983-84[16] and the Advisory Committee reported (*Annual Report 1983-84*) that gross expenditure on matrimonial legal aid totalled £61 million in 1983-84 out of a total civil legal aid bill of £105 million[17]. The median cost of legal aid for each party in matrimonial proceedings in 1983-84 was £590 in the county courts and £1,219 in the High Court, representing increases of almost 20 per cent and 16 per cent respectively over the previous year's median costs. The Advisory Committee commented (1983-84) that litigation is a particularly inappropriate method of settling disputes in matrimonial cases because the bitterness engendered by prolonged litigation is likely to undermine the effectiveness of any arrangements eventually agreed or imposed by the courts, while the cost of prolonged litigation puts additional pressure on already strained family finances (par. 129).

The limited costs which solicitors can claim for providing legal advice and assistance under the Green Form scheme[18] and the lower rate at which this work is paid, compared with the almost unrestricted costs that can be claimed for legally aided cases, may encourage some solicitors to contest ancillary issues concerning financial matters, property and children, instead of persevering with patient and often frustrating negotiations. Davis (1983a) suggested that "we have at present a "top-heavy system of financing which gives us the worst of both worlds, not allowing solicitors to give adequate time to divorcing clients, and yet encouraging an adversarial approach" (p. 12). A person who is not eligible for legal aid and who cannot afford the costs of private litigation may be forced to give up, whereas a legally aided person can contemplate a prolonged legal battle. The Law Society does however impose a statutory charge which gives the legal aid fund a first charge on any property recovered or preserved by a legally aided person in proceedings in which property is in issue. It is essential that legally aided individuals understand the implications of this charge before they risk incurring high legal costs. The Legal Aid Advisory Committee (*Annual Report 1982-83*) commented that many of the difficulties that arise in connection with the statutory charge are caused by ignorance and the Committee urged solicitors to explain the implications of the charge to their clients "clearly, fully, early and frequently" (par. 83). Legally aided proceedings also delay settlement since the administrative process of assessing a legal aid application and granting a certificate takes considerable time. The Law Society reported in 1985 that the average time taken to issue a certificate in 1983-84 was 55 days and that 19 per cent of applications took more than twelve weeks to be processed (*Legal Aid Annual Report 1983-84*, Appendix 2G). The granting of a certificate is only the beginning of court proceedings which may be prolonged. If there is no contact between the children and the absent parent during this time, or very stressful contact, the children may react by refusing to go on access visits and the rift between them and their father (or less frequently their mother) becomes increasingly hard to repair. A complex and overburdened legal machine does not provide the swift and sensitive response which families need, and the principle of the paramount welfare of the child may achieve little practical result if parents have lost the will or ability to co-operate by the time their case comes to court.

Justice and Welfare: the Conflict of Opposing Principles

The Matrimonial and Family Proceedings Act 1984 put into effect the Law Commission's recommendation (1981 No. 112) that the court should give first consideration to children's interests when exercising its powers to make financial provision and property adjustment orders. Under the new legislation, the courts are therefore directed to give priority to the needs of the children of the family, rather than apportioning a couple's income with the aim of achieving equality between them as adults. The courts are also now empowered to order a final settlement (the "clean break") and to dismiss a former spouse's application for periodical payments (maintenance), with or without her consent. It is recognised, however, that such an order is unlikely to be made where there are young children (Law Commission No. 112) and that the court must take account of a dependent wife's ability to obtain employment.

The balance between justice and welfare is more uncertain in preliminary proceedings to determine the right of occupation of the matrimonial home, pending a final decision in divorce proceedings. The courts traditionally followed the policy that the parent with de facto custody or a court order for custody would normally be granted the exclusive right of occupation of the home at least in the short term, because this arrangement was likely to be in the best interests of the children. However, in the case of Richards v. Richards[19], the House of Lords ruled that in determining a dispute over the occupation of the matrimonial home prior to divorce, the question was whether the order was "just and reasonable", having regard to factors specified in the Matrimonial Homes Act 1983, which include the conduct of both spouses. The welfare of the children, although a relevant factor, was not to be regarded as paramount. The courts have thus been given inconsistent guide-lines on the priorities they should follow in all matrimonial proceedings, because the inherent conflict between justice for spouses and the welfare of children has not been fully and satisfactorily resolved. In practice, children's emotional as well as material needs may still be pushed aside by parents intent on fighting their own battles and the House of Lords' decision in the Richards case was seen by some as "a striking example of the hollowness of much rhetoric supporting the cause of children in divorce" (Eekelaar 1984 p. 137). The upheaval experienced by children when their parents separate is usually profound, since it frequently involves a change of home and school as well as the emotional disruption caused by one parent leaving home. Southwell (1985) found in a study in a large northern city that nearly half of the children were moved out of the family home, either because it was sold or because it was occupied by the non-custodial parent. Murch (1980) found only one-third of children still living in the family home shortly after divorce and Mitchell (1985) found that nearly a quarter of the children in her Scottish sample had moved home three or four times, one of them five times and one girl more times than she could remember. This girl was sad that she never stayed long enough in one place to make friends. The provision in the 1984 Act that children's interests should be the first consideration may influence court orders concerning the sale of the matrimonial home, but hasty decisions may still be taken by one or both parents in the crisis of separation. At this stage many couples need help in working out plans for the future and their anger, distress and lack of information frequently make it impossible for them to solve their problems on their own.

Reforming Divorce Law and Procedure

This brief survey has drawn attention to some of the ways in which current divorce law and procedures aggravate disputes between divorcing couples or force conflict underground. There is therefore considerable concern about the need to reform both the substantive law of divorce and divorce procedure. Following the Law Commission's recommendation (1981) that legal procedures in matrimonial cases should be systematically reviewed, the Lord Chancellor appointed a Committee on Matrimonial Causes Procedure (known as the Booth Committee, after its chairman) to recommend procedural reforms which might mitigate the intensity of disputes, encourage settlements and provide further for the welfare of the children concerned, "having regard to the desirability of achieving greater simplification and the saving of costs"[20]. The Booth Committee's terms of reference excluded consideration of the substantive law and the structure of the courts administering matrimonial and family law. These matters were under separate review in 1985[21] but this piecemeal approach is unsatisfactory, because it is almost impossible to plan effective reforms in one area without knowing what is likely to be happening in the system as a whole. Divorce law in this country continues to fall between the two stools of justice and welfare and these different principles create a clash of values and expectations, intensifying the conflicts of divorcing and divorced couples instead of alleviating them. Consideration of the Booth Committee's final recommendations in relation to procedural reform (Report 1985) will be deferred to chapter 10 in order to trace the development of conciliation in separation and divorce, since the integration of conciliation with divorce procedure forms a major plank of the Committee's proposals. But even if conciliation becomes an integral part of procedure in the divorce courts, there are other courts to consider as well. Matrimonial and family law in England and Wales is administered in a fragmented and uncoordinated fashion which compounds problems that are already far from simple. This uncoordinated system forms the subject of the next chapter, since there would seem to be limited value in reforming one court system while maintaining outdated traditions in other courts which also deal with the problems of marital breakdown and separation.

Notes

1. The idea of a Registrar of Births, Marriages, Divorces and Deaths was mooted by Dr Bob McCreadie, Lecturer in Law, Edinburgh University, in a paper given at the 1984 Scottish Conference on Divorce Conciliation. A report on the conference was published by the Scottish Council for Single Parents and the Scottish Family Conciliation Service (Lothian), Edinburgh, 1985.
2. Statistics provided at the Law Commission-Bristol University Seminar on "Reform of the Ground for Divorce?", 6 December 1985.
3. Lord Chancellor's Advisory Committee on Legal Aid, *34th Annual Report 1983-84*, par. 141.
4. As 2 above.
5. *Woman* magazine, 27 February 1982, pp. 23-6.
6. *The Times*, 23 March 1985.
7. Galen v. Galen reported at *Family Law*, vol. 15 (1985), pp. 256-7.
8. Matrimonial and Family Proceedings Act 1984, section 3 (2) (g).
9. Wachtel v. Wachtel (1973) Fam. 72 [1973] 1 All ER 829.
10. Ibid.
11. *A Better Way Out* (Law Society, London, 1979).
12. Matrimonial Causes Procedure Committee, Consultation Paper (Lord Chancellor's Department, London, 1983), par. 1.9 (d).
13. *Matrimonial Causes Act 1973, Section 41.*
14. Under section 44 (1) of the Matrimonial Causes Act 1973, the court may make a

supervision order if there are "exceptional circumstances making it desirable that the child should be under the supervision of an independent person". In 1983, 37,000 supervision orders made in matrimonial and other family proceedings were operative, of which 22,000 were assigned to local authority social services departments (*DHSS Review of Child Care Law 1985*).

15. Lord Chancellor's Advisory Committee on Legal Aid, *32nd Annual Report 1981-82*, par. 89.
16. Law Society's *34th Legal Aid Annual Report 1983-84*, Appendix 2A (ii).
17. Lord Chancellor's Advisory Committee on Legal Aid, *34th Annual Report 1983-84*, par. 134, note 71. Net public expenditure on matrimonial legal aid totalled £43 million in 1983-84.
18. The cost of the advice and assistance which a solicitor may provide to a petitioner in an undefended divorce case before asking for an extension under the Green Form scheme was raised to £90 in 1985. The initial financial limit for advice to a respondent is £50.
19. Richards v. Richards [1984] 1 A C 174.
20. See 12 above, par. 1.1.
21. See chapter 10.

2 SEPARATE COURTS AND SEPARATE REMEDIES

The problems of helping separating and divorcing couples to sort out their difficulties with the minimum bitterness, distress and financial cost to themselves and to the state are compounded by the problems of fragmented and overlapping legal systems. For over a century, two different systems of matrimonial law have existed side by side in England and Wales, applying different rules and remedies to similar human predicaments. These divisions and anomalies were examined by the Committee on One-Parent Families (Finer Committee) set up in November 1969 by Richard Crossman MP, then Secretary of State for Social Services, to "consider the problems of one-parent families in our society, ... the extent to which they can obtain financial support when they need it; and the ways in which other provisions and facilities are of help to them"(Finer Report 1974, par. 1.1). The Finer Report provided a detailed history and analysis of the two systems of matrimonial law administered in England and Wales, one by the High Court and the divorce county courts, the other by the magistrates' domestic courts. Although the members of the Finer Committee remarked that "long acquaintance with this duality may blunt the power to recognise its peculiarities" (par. 4.15), their own scrutiny was sharp and critical. They noted with irony that when divorce legislation was first enacted in England and Wales under the Matrimonial Causes Act 1857, the reformers "regarded legal intervention into matrimony, maintenance and the custody of children as so delicate and important that the jurisdiction had to be entrusted to professional judges of the highest rank"[1]. The proceedings could be heard only in London and at least three judges had to sit in each divorce or nullity case (Cretney 1984). This legislation was of course inaccessible to the majority of the population as no legal aid was available.

The Domestic Jurisdiction of Magistrates

In 1878, further legislation was introduced to provide a simpler system of justice "designed for what were considered to be the special and cruder requirements of the poor"[2]. Under the Matrimonial Causes Act 1878, magistrates were empowered to grant a separation order with maintenance to a wife whose husband was convicted of aggravated assault upon her ("ordinary" assault was apparently not considered sufficiently serious to justify a court order). This provision was an extension of the criminal law administered by lay magistrates in courts that were known as "police courts" because of their close association with the police. When the second Royal Commission on Divorce and Matrimonial Causes (the Gorell Commission) was set up in 1909, the magistrates' courts were dealing with about 15,000 applications per year for separation orders, whereas petitions for divorce or judicial separation in the High Court numbered only about 800 annually. Until 1949, when the Legal Aid and Advice Act enabled wives on a low income to take divorce proceedings in the High Court, the limited domestic jurisdiction of the magistrates' courts provided the only access to legal protection and financial support available to working-class wives.

Despite increasing pressure in the last ten years for a single, unified family jurisdiction in England and Wales[3], we still have two uncoordinated and overlapping systems. There is no hierarchical connection between the two:appeals from the magistrates' domestic court are not heard in the county court and magistrates do not sit with judges in the county court as they sometimes do in the crown court. Not only do the two jurisdictions administer two different systems of matrimonial law which may be based on different principles: they use different terms to describe the same concept. The term "joint custody" does not exist in the magistrates' jurisdiction, where the term "actual custody" is the equivalent of "care and control" in the divorce court[4]. Lawyers familiar with legal terminology may not realise how confusing these terms are to the lay person, especially if he or she is in a state of shock. There is evidence (Dodds 1983) that some unrepresented fathers have difficulty in completing legal documents and may misunderstand some of the questions. Personal experience also suggests that many people need explanations of legal terms in language they can understand and at a pace they can cope with. Even highly educated people can be bewildered by the existence of different courts using different terminology for similar orders relating to children. The introduction of yet another term, "custodianship", under the Children Act 1975[5], which enables foster-parents or relatives other than natural parents to be granted custody of a child, is bound to increase the already considerable public confusion about the legal alternatives open to parents and parent-substitutes in situations of family break-up.

Davidoff, a Home Office statistician, estimated (1984) that there were about 260,000 domestic proceedings in England and Wales in 1983, of which about 10,000 involved applications for custody or access orders under sections 8, 10 or 14 of the Domestic Proceedings and Magistrates Courts' Act 1978. In almost all these cases, a maintenance or interim payments order was made at the same time. There were also about 12,000 applications under guardianship proceedings and in just over half the successful applications a maintenance order was made as well. These figures provide evidence that a forum other than the divorce court is needed. With the increase in cohabitation, there are many unmarried couples who have children from current or previous relationships and there are also many married couples who need legal remedies that are not as final as divorce. Guymer and Bywaters (1984) found that a large proportion of applications to the domestic court were withdrawn, often because a reconciliation was said to have occurred. Some of the applicants who were interviewed acknowledged that they had initiated proceedings as a form of "shock tactics", hoping that reconciliation would be the outcome. Although this did seem to happen sometimes, even in some cases after an order was made, very few referrals were made to the probation service in connection with possible reconciliation and Guymer and Bywaters doubted whether a referral to the probation service would have been acceptable to many applicants. They saw the court clerk as a key figure who could maximise the possibilities of reconciliation in a number of ways, particularly by introducing an early hearing system at which couples could be encouraged to enter into informal discussion and negotiate direct agreements with each other.

Reconciliation may be a central issue in the domestic court, whereas in the divorce court it receives scant attention. The Justices' Clerks' Society (1982) has also argued that magistrates' courts are more widely distributed geographically than the county courts and that lay magistrates are closer to the community than professional judges. The consumer view, however, is that proceedings in the domestic court may be "uncomfortable and sometimes traumatic"(Guymer and Bywaters 1984 p. 28). Some magistrates' courts have new, purpose-built domestic courts but others use old buildings in which civil and criminal cases are heard side by side. In some courts, magistrates sit on a high dais and applicants have to give evidence from a prominent dock, as though they were on trial. Since 1979, magistrates' courts are required to form special panels of magistrates to sit in the domestic court, in recognition that special knowledge and skills are needed to deal with matrimonial and family cases. Observation of the domestic court in operation suggests, however, that apart from the variable calibre of individual magistrates, there is often a substantial gulf both of communication and understanding between magistrates and applicants. This gulf is more noticeable in the south than in the north, where there is still a strong tradition of seeking matrimonial relief from the magistrates' court. Regional variations are very marked: the Justices' Clerks'Society (1982) reported that the decline in the use of the magistrates' domestic courts from 1971 (when the new divorce legislation came into force in the county court) to 1980, varied from 16 per cent in Birmingham to a massive 88 per cent decline in Bristol.

The Finer Committee recommended unequivocally that "the whole of the matrimonial jurisdiction of the magistrates should be abolished" (par. 4.379), but instead of moving towards a unified family court, as the Finer Committee recommended, the Domestic Proceedings and Magistrates' Courts' Act 1978 retained the matrimonial jurisdiction of magistrates and brought it more in line with the divorce jurisdiction of the county courts. The 1978 Act enabled magistrates for the first time to make maintenance orders based on agreement between the applicant and the respondent (section 6), but section 12 preserved the concept of the matrimonial offence under more anodyne names. "Wilful neglect" became "failure to maintain" and "cruelty" became "unreasonable behaviour", as in divorce law. Guymer and Bywaters (1984) found that almost three-quarters of the applications to the domestic court were uncontested and only ten per cent involved a contested hearing. This may give a misleading impression of agreement and acquiescence. A more realistic picture can probably be obtained from the number of applications for enforcement orders to deal with accumulated arrears of unpaid maintenance.

The High Court and the divorce county courts do not have any special machinery for administering and enforcing maintenance orders. Orders made in these courts are in practice usually registered in the magistrates' court before they can be assigned to the Department of Health and Social Security which will then pay supplementary benefit to the applicant, according to entitlement and irrespective of whether maintenance is being paid regularly or not. Husbands who did not want the divorce in the first place may become even more resistant if their former wives make an application to the magistrates' court, having already taken proceedings in the divorce court. The administrative reasons which oblige wives to register their order in the magistrates' court may not be at all clear to their former husbands, especially if they have not consulted a solicitor through fear of incurring legal costs. The resulting combination of misunderstanding and resentment, which is linked very often with problems over access, is scarcely conducive to the payment of maintenance. The problems of enforcing maintenance payments are paralleled by the problems of enforcing access orders. Men who have been granted reasonable or defined access to their children may find that access is nonetheless refused by the mother, for one reason or another, and that the court is unable or reluctant to apply sanctions to enforce the access order. The courts regard access and maintenance as separate issues but they are closely linked in the minds of many parents, who may use them as instruments of retaliation against each other.

Davidoff (1984) estimated that about two-thirds (177,000) of applications to the domestic courts in 1983 were for enforcement or variation of maintenance orders or for attachment of earnings. An enormous amount of time is spent by magistrates in assessing men's ability to pay maintenance and ordering them to do so, but Gibson (1982) showed that only a small minority of wives with orders enforceable in the magistrates' court actually receive realistic maintenance on a regular basis. One-third of the women with care of their children who were interviewed by researchers in Bristol (Davis, MacLeod and Murch 1983b) said that they were dependent on supplementary benefit at that time, and although over 70 per cent received some maintenance occasionally or regularly, in only 12 per cent of cases was this their sole source of income. Graham Hall and Martin (1984) found in their examination of 205 maintenance orders that 41 per cent were paid satisfactorily and that 42 per cent were in arrears because of unemployment or poverty. They suggested that collecting officers should have more powers to enforce the payment of orders in the minority of cases (about 4 per cent of their sample) in which the order was apparently flouted deliberately.

The Matrimonial and Family Proceedings Act 1984 provoked fierce controversy about husbands' financial obligations following divorce and the right of wives to life-long maintenance. But as Eekelaar (1984) pointed out, it is unfortunate that the question of post-divorce maintenance is almost invariably expressed in terms of a former wife's right to continuing support, thus encouraging the view that the issue is solely between two adults, or between the wife and her former husband's new family. "The reality is that, unless there have been children, few wives seem to make a claim for maintenance at all, or, if they do, they are seldom successful" (Eekelaar 1984, p. 111). While the battle is waged over reform of the private law of maintenance, insufficient attention is paid to the impact of social security and taxation policies. Divorced wives in middle and upper income groups may benefit from tax concessions and increased financial independence, whereas wives in lower income groups are particularly liable to fall below the state poverty-line. "Thus, existing divisions within the divorcing population are being exacerbated by discriminatory social policies"(Davis, MacLeod and Murch 1983b p. 224). The Law Commission (1981) complained that the courts are operating the rules of maintenance in a factual vacuum, without adequate information about the interaction between the private law of family maintenance and the public law of national insurance, taxation and social security. "We do not know how much maintenance is in fact ordered to be paid by the courts. Still less do we know in what proportion of cases such payments are actually made, and for what period of time they continue" (Law Commission 1981, par. 8).

The problems relating to the financial support of children after their parents separate are not merely legal and financial. Essentially, they involve psychological, moral and social values about parents' continuing responsibility for their children following separation or divorce and about the rights of children to know and continue to see both their parents, whether they are married, unmarried, separated or divorced. Magistrates in the domestic court are empowered under the Affiliation Proceedings Act 1957 to order a natural father to pay maintenance for the support of his illegitimate child. These proceedings are concerned with financial support and magistrates cannot make additional orders at the same time concerning the father's access to his child, although this may be an extremely important issue from the child's point of view. The child may be the offspring of a longstanding relationship and as attached to his or her father as any legitimate child is likely to be. Some magistrates make a point of informing the father that he can apply for access under the Guardianship of Minors Act 1971 but they are not required to give this advice. In any case, the need to embark on fresh court proceedings may deter fathers from pressing their claim to access, especially if they fear that this will only cause further antagonism, making access impossible or fraught with conflict.

Domestic Violence

When either spouse seeks a divorce or judicial separation or when a mother is seeking support for an illegitimate child, there is in each case only one jurisdiction to which application can be made. In cases of domestic violence, on the other hand, there are no less than four jurisdictions offering some measure of legal protection. Potential applicants are faced not only with the problem of the violence itself but also with the problem of understanding the different forms of protection available. Since 1977, the four jurisdictions under which protection can be sought are: 1) divorce or other matrimonial proceedings under the Matrimonial Causes Act 1973; 2) High Court proceedings; 3) the Domestic Violence and Matrimonial Proceedings Act 1976, which is the only jurisdiction available to a cohabiting person seeking protection from violence; 4) the Domestic Proceedings and Magistrates' Courts Act 1978. In principle, criminal law can also be invoked, but criminal law is more concerned with punishing offenders than with protecting battered wives, to whom civil law offers better but still inadequate protection. Both the county courts and the magistrates' courts can make personal protection and exclusion orders but the county courts have wider powers to make non-molestation orders as well, on grounds that can include mental as well as physical violence. Moreover, county court exclusion orders can apply to a wider area surrounding the matrimonial home.

The number of applications for injunctions has increased enormously in recent years, almost doubling in the three-year period from 1978-79 to 1981-82. The average cost per legally aided applicant increased in the same period from £194 to £424[6]. The Booth Committee (1983) expressed concern about injunction proceedings on three particular grounds: first, because they often exacerbate conflict and bitterness between couples who might have been able to work out an agreed solution to their problems; secondly, because the urgency with which these applications must be treated allows the respondent very little time in which to obtain advice and prepare his case; and thirdly, because there is no effective sanction against an applicant who seeks this form of relief without proper cause. Both the Booth Committee (1983) and the Lord Chancellor's Legal Aid Advisory Committee (*Annual Report 1983-84*) expressed concern about the extent to which ouster orders are sought, believing that some applications are merely a strategy to obtain sole occupation of the matrimonial home. Neither of these committees commented on the inadequacy of court orders in protecting women (and also men) from physical and emotional violence in the home. A recent study (ed. Pahl 1985) emphasised how little public attention is actually focused on the very severe problem of domestic violence. These problems will be discussed further in chapter 6.

Wardship

Parents in dispute over their children have the possibility of recourse not only to the magistrates' domestic court and the divorce court but also to a third jurisdiction, the wardship jurisdiction of the High Court. This jurisdiction is the oldest one dealing with the welfare of children and also the widest in the range of remedies and powers at its disposal. In wardship proceedings, the child becomes subject to the High Court's protection as soon as application is made and custody is vested in the High Court, which may grant care and control to the applicant, subject to the court's directions. The Matrimonial and Family Proceedings Act 1984 enabled the High Court to transfer wardship proceedings to a county court, where High Court jurisdiction may in any case be exercised by a circuit judge sitting as a High Court judge or by a barrister sitting as a deputy High Court judge. A fundamental feature of the wardship jurisdiction is that "unlike most litigation in this country, which is determined according to the so-called adversary principle, the court is not limited to resolving a particular dispute which the parties have chosen to bring before it" (Cretney 1984 p. 350). The wide powers of the court under wardship may account for its increasing popularity. In 1951, there were only 74 wardship proceedings. By 1977, the number had risen to 1,500 and by 1982 to 2,300 applications[7]. Once wardship has been invoked, no important change in arrangements for the child can be made without the court's consent and the child cannot be taken out of England and Wales even for a holiday without the court's permission. A parent may seek the extensive powers available to the court under wardship, for example to prevent a child being taken out of the country by the other parent, or in an attempt to regain children who have been snatched by the other parent. A parent may apply to have the child made a ward of court because rapid action is needed, but he or she needs to be aware that the court then becomes the legal parent of the child and the court may not accept the views of the parent making the application.

The local authority or any other interested party may also initiate wardship proceedings as a means of receiving children into care or keeping them there when other proceedings might fail, as for example where parents have requested the return of a child in voluntary care and where there are no grounds for a section 3 resolution under the Children and Young Persons' Act 1969. There are possible areas of conflict if the wardship jurisdiction overrules the powers of a local authority in whose care the child already is, or where the High Court has to assess conflicting recommendations from social workers in two different local authorities. Hayes (1984) pointed out that wardship has a vital protective and monitoring function within the framework of child care law and that it can be used to fill a serious gap in the law where a parent is unable to challenge the decisions of the local authority. In the case of "D. v. Barset County Council"[8], the High Court had to decide between two proposals, either accepting the local authority's proposal that a two-year-old girl should be placed with long-term foster-parents with a view to adoption, or that she should be returned to the care of her maternal grandmother. Her grandmother, then aged 38, had looked after her grandchild for several months, after the 18-year-old mother left the family home and went to live in "Barset", about a hundred miles away. The local authority rejected the grandmother's proposal, which was supported by the mother despite previous difficulties between them, that the little girl should live with her grandparents and have regular contact with her mother. The High Court took a different view, however, and the senior social worker in charge of the case was criticised for serious errors of professional judgement and practice. The court decided that the child should live with her grandparents and 16-year-old uncle, with whom she grew into a "bright, settled, happy and secure child" (Hayes 1984 p. 239).

This case illustrates the ways in which disputes over child custody arise not only between parents but also between parents and grandparents and between the family and the local authority. If the dispute is handled in an adversarial manner, the parties (the local authority may be one of the parties, in this sense) tend to take up polarised and antagonistic positions and contradictory views of the child's best interests may be argued from opposite sides of the court. Wardship jurisdiction is the only jurisdiction capable of giving adequate consideration to the interests of the child, the parents and the local authority, but Eekelaar (1984) warned that the vague criterion of the "best interests of the child" contrasts unfavourably with the more defined grounds available for care proceedings and that extension of wardship jurisdiction could "seriously threaten the delicate balance between family autonomy and children's rights" (pp. 184-5). In wardship cases, the court can call on the services of the Official Solicitor to represent the child as a guardian ad litem and to act as an adviser, investigator and supervisor on the child's behalf. However, partly in response to the pressures on the Official Solicitor's department, a Practice Direction (1982)[9] from the Court of Appeal stated that in general a welfare officer's report is sufficient in wardship cases.

The provision of legal aid for parents in wardship cases differs from the provisions applicable in matrimonial proceedings and the Lord Chancellor's Advisory Committee on Legal Aid has described the present uncoordinated system of granting legal aid in civil cases as "chaotic" (*Annual Report 1983-84*, par. 57). The Committee recommended that "once the jurisdiction and procedures have been rationalised, legal aid for parents and children . . . should be subject to a single test, including perhaps a new criterion based on the interests of the child" (par. 157).

A Family Court in England and Wales

The unified family court recommended by the Finer Committee (1974) could remove the divisions and duplication in our present system of matrimonial and child care law, in which different aspects of family problems are artificially divided and dealt with in separate courts or in separate hearings in the same court. The demand for the family court is now very strong, though a few sceptical voices can be heard in the general chorus of support. The Lord Chancellor, in the course of a lengthy debate in the House of Lords on the Matrimonial and Family Proceedings Bill (*Hansard* HL 21 November 1983) observed that although he was attracted by the concept of a family court, he did not believe it would "usher in the millennium in the way that some of its supporters seem to suppose" (p. 36). However, he announced that "given the strength of support for the idea of a comprehensive court with exclusive jurisdiction in all family matters", he had agreed with the Home Secretary that "we should now re-examine the idea of a unified family court, starting with a detailed study of the resource implications in terms of finance, manpower and accommodation". Judge Jean Graham Hall, an outstanding champion of the family court (Graham Hall 1970, 1978), has argued in a further paper written jointly with a county court registrar (Graham Hall and Martin 1983) that cost need not be an obstacle or a cause for delay in setting up a unified family court. Support for the family court has also come from the British Association of Social Workers, who issued a discussion paper on the family court in August 1984 (BASW 1984) and from the Law Society's Family Law Committee, who issued a consultation paper and held a conference for interested organisations and professions in May 1985. The detailed structure of the family court and the extent of its jurisdiction remain matters for debate. Many of its supporters envisage a family court dealing with divorce and other matrimonial proceedings and all civil proceedings relating to children, including wardship, guardianship, custodianship, adoption, and care proceedings in the juvenile court, but there is disagreement as to whether it should also deal with juvenile offenders, on the lines of the Children's Panels in Scotland. In November 1985 the Association of County Councils launched a fresh campaign for the introduction of the family court, backed by many statutory and voluntary organisations, Members of both Houses of Parliament, and other individuals. As Baroness Faithfull observed in launching this campaign, "children and families simply cannot afford to wait another 20 years, when legal issues involving children and families have multiplied rapidly, but are still being dealt with in an out of date and confusing variety of court situations" (Family Courts Campaign 1985).

Scotland

A unified system of matrimonial and family law in England and Wales would not however provide a comprehensive system operating throughout the British Isles. The law and the legal system in Scotland differ from those of England and Wales in ways that can only be touched on here. There is no summary jurisdiction in Scotland corresponding to the domestic jurisdiction of English magistrates. Jurisdiction is shared between the Court of Session in Edinburgh and the sheriff courts and these courts administer the same laws jointly, unlike the dual system in England and Wales. Scottish divorce law was reformed by the Divorce (Scotland) Act 1976 which brought divorce law in Scotland broadly in line with that of England and Wales. The sole ground for divorce is the irretrievable breakdown of marriage, which has to be established by one or more of the same "facts" as in English law. Until 1984, all Scottish divorce cases had to be heard in Edinburgh at the Court of Session and a "pursuer" (as a divorce petitioner is known in Scotland) living outside Edinburgh usually consulted a local solicitor who then instructed an Edinburgh solicitor, who in turn engaged an advocate (barrister) to draft the summons. This system was of course extremely costly and slow and poor communications could result in a defender (respondent) not knowing whether s/he was divorced or not (Mitchell 1981).

Since May 1984, divorce proceedings can be heard in local sheriff courts as well as in the Court of Session and this change may help divorcing couples to feel a little more in control or at least aware of what is happening. However, divorcing parents rarely attend court in person. Evidence about the arrangements for the children is provided in writing by means of sworn affidavits and the courts rarely request further information about the children (Eekelaar and Clive 1977, Mitchell 1981, Seale 1984). Seale (1984), in a study undertaken by the Central Research Unit of the Scottish Office, found that nearly half the affidavits about children did not mention whether the child had any contact with the non-custodial parent and access was not granted by the court in 86 per cent of cases because it was not requested. In some of these cases, access may have been agreed informally between the parents but Mitchell (1981) found some divorced fathers very distressed at having been deprived of access to their children because they had not understood that it was necessary to apply for it. A further study by Mitchell (1985) found that 25 per cent of children lost contact at the time of separation and a further 15 per cent saw the absent parent at rare intervals. Approximately 7,000 divorces were granted in Scotland in 1980 and a welfare report was called for in 347 cases but these included cases which were later abandoned or which became labelled "asleep" because no further action was taken within a year (Seale 1984). Seale found that there was no consensus on the information which should be contained in a welfare report (which may be prepared by an advocate or a social worker in Scotland, as there are no probation officers or specialist court welfare officers in Scotland). She found that the quality of reports varied greatly and that information about the children was generally very sparse, often being limited to a statement that they were "happy and well cared for".

Custody orders made in Scotland may not be recognised in England, where a contradictory order may be made in the same case. A report published jointly by the English and Scottish Law Commissions on the Custody of Children (1985) showed that a father who starts divorce proceedings in Scotland may be awarded custody of the children by the Scottish courts, even though an English court had awarded custody to the mother. Attempts are being made to prevent parents taking custody proceedings simultaneously in different parts of the United Kingdom. Under new rules proposed by the English and Scottish Law Commissions, only one court would be able to make a custody order at a particular time and an order made in one part of the United Kingdom would be enforceable in another.

International Child Custody Disputes

There is a growing problem of child kidnapping in "tug of love" cases, which may lead to simultaneous custody proceedings in the United Kingdom and overseas, over the same child. In the case of Re G. (a minor)[10], three different courts and the Official Solicitor acting as guardian ad litem became involved in deciding with which parent a five-year-old child should live. The Court of Appeal allowed the father's appeal that the mother's application to the High Court for wardship should be dismissed and that the child should be returned to the jurisdiction of the Canadian court. The parents in this case had previously managed to reach a series of agreed decisions about the care of their two children, during a very unsettled four-year period following the break-up of their marriage, during which time the mother moved from Canada to South America, back to Canada and then to New York and the West Indies before coming to England. When communication broke down between them, no effort seems to have been made to help them reach a joint decision. Instead, armies of professionals were mustered to take a decision which the parents might have reached themselves, had they received adequate help.

The Child Abduction and Custody Bill 1985, which is due to be implemented in 1986, is aimed at helping parents and others with custody rights to obtain the return of a child unlawfully taken abroad or to enforce a custody order made in their favour. It would enable Britain to ratify and implement two international conventions on child abduction (the Hague Convention and the European Convention) which seek in different ways to provide an internationally agreed approach to child kidnapping. But the Hague Convention is in force only in France, Portugal, Switzerland and Canada and many countries have shown no interest in signing it. If the whereabouts of the child are unknown, conventions are of no help and time is usually on the side of the abducting parent. The longer the child is with that parent in another country, the harder it becomes to insist on his or her return without causing more disturbance and distress to the child. The practice of snatching children and taking them to another country has increased with the growth of international marriages and the high incidence of divorce. Some parents hope to retain custody of their child by making an application in their country of origin with the child in their possession, and in most cases it is the old story of possession being nine-tenths of the law. These desperate actions by parents who snatch their children take no account of the effects on a child of being suddenly uprooted from a loved parent and a familiar environment: this may result in serious emotional disturbance in the child and a loss of trust in both parents.

Conclusion

Judge Abella, a Canadian judge, reviewed the functions and results of different legal systems in relation to disputes over children and concluded that existing structures, procedures and laws are inadequate to the gargantuan task of adjudicating children's rights when their parents divorce (Abella 1982). She questioned whether it is realistic to expect a legal process to alleviate the emotional distress of the families involved and whether the adversarial system attracts a disproportionate amount of blame for failing to solve problems which may lie well beyond any legal remedies. No system can guarantee justice, however elaborate and sophisticated its rules. The more we construct formal institutions to resolve marital and family disputes, the greater the risk that each institution will be used to defeat another institution, so that yet another institution is needed to resolve the institutional conflicts of competing systems. The assumption is readily made that the disputants themselves are incapable of settling their disagreements and until recently they have been given little opportunity and encouragement to do so.

Modern systems of matrimonial and family law consist of many different elements, including substantive law, legal procedure, the structure and administration of the courts, the availability of legal aid and the values and practice of the legal profession. Each of these elements and all of them in conjunction play a significant part in the course a particular dispute takes and in its eventual outcome from each party's and the children's points of view. There are various crossroads at which those caught up in disputes may have a choice of route, if they are aware that the choice exists, between aggrieved surrender, prolonged warfare or negotiated settlement. We need to consider how disputants can be helped to make a rational and well-informed choice of route, before pursuing one particular path which may lead in the opposite direction from the path chosen by the other party. In many cases, there may be a third path which disputants could explore together at least for a limited time, which might enable them to work out decisions acceptable to them both. This third path towards dispute settlement forms the main subject of the next chapter.

Notes

1. *Finer Report 1974*, Appendix 5, par. 36.
2. Ibid.
3. See for example Graham Hall 1970, 1973, 1978.
4. Domestic Proceedings and Magistrates Courts Act 1978, Part 2, sections 36-7.
5. Part II of the Children Act 1975 introducing the legal concept of custodianship was implemented on 1 December 1985.
6. Lord Chancellor's Legal Aid Advisory Committee, 32nd Annual Report, 1981-82, Table C.V.
7. *Judicial Statistics 1951, 1977* and *Judicial Statistics Annual Report 1982*, Table 4.6.
8. Hayes (1984) identified the local authority in this case by the fictitious name of *Barset*, as she was quoting judicial criticisms of the authority which would not have received publicity, as the case was unreported.
9. Practice Direction (Children: Joinder as Parties) [1982] 1 WLR 118.
10. Re G. (a minor), case reported in *Family Law*, vol. 14 (1984), pp. 244-5.

3 DISPUTE SETTLEMENT AND CONCILIATION

A Family Court counsellor in the Family Court of Australia[1] has drawn a useful distinction between "settling disputes, that is, putting a stop to overt conflict, and on the other hand, achieving a resolution, which may be defined as genuine agreement or harmony. Settlement may include various forms of disengagement, including withdrawal or surrender. Resolution, on the other hand, implies that both parties are truly satisfied with the outcome" (Madison 1982 p. 8). This distinction between settlement and resolution of conflict distinguishes a settlement which one or both parties feel forced to accept from a genuine agreement which is mutually acceptable. It also draws attention to the fact that other people may be concerned only to end a dispute quickly, whereas the disputants themselves may be looking for a solution which meets their own personal needs as fully as possible. Some methods of settling disputes may be designed primarily to serve public interests, in which case little notice may be taken of the quality of the settlement from the point of view of the two main protagonists. Other methods may concentrate on achieving a satisfactory solution for the two parties concerned, without counting the social and financial costs to society in general of a prolonged and painstaking process of settlement.

An evaluation of different methods of settling disputes involves some understanding of the nature and function of conflict. Conflict has positive functions in strengthening the cohesion of groups and reinforcing identity and it can also generate creative energy, whereas consensus may foster inertia and indifference. The polarity between conflicting forces can create tensions which are not invariably destructive: they may promote the growth of new relationships or adaptations of existing ones. The German sociologist Georg Simmel (1908, trans. 1955) pointed out early this century that "there probably exists no social unit in which convergent and divergent currents are not inseparably interwoven". Even if one could conceive of a completely harmonious group, it "could show no real life process" (p. 15). The awareness that conflict is both necessary and inevitable can reduce anxiety about its divisive and destructive effects and may enable people to keep this anxiety at manageable levels while they consider possible solutions. Positive and negative feelings are often closely intertwined in intimate human relationships and their co-existence can cause a great deal of confusion, conflict and pain.

Deutsch (1973) distinguished manifest (direct) conflict from underlying (indirect) conflict which may be channelled into other areas or issues. If an attempt is made to settle a particular dispute, the focus of effort may be confined to the manifest conflict, whereas if resolution is the aim, much greater effort may be needed to locate the roots of the conflict and resolve it fully so that it does not surface again somewhere else. There is also a difference between intrapersonal conflict, or conflict within the individual, and interpersonal conflicts which arise between individuals or groups (Folberg and Taylor 1984). Internal conflict may result from unacceptable perceptions of the self, unresolved personal experience and relationships, or from personal needs which cannot be reconciled with obligations and commitments to others. Interpersonal conflict between couples or groups of people may express a clash of interests or values, or both, and is commonly accompanied by problems of communication. We tend to use the words "conflict" and "dispute" interchangeably but they are not necessarily synonymous. A conflict may not become a dispute if it is suppressed or denied or if it is not communicated to the other party or parties involved (Abel 1973). Felstiner and colleagues (1980-81) identified three stages in the evolution of a dispute: 1) the "naming" stage when a grievance is perceived and identified; 2) the "blaming" stage when responsibility for the grievance is attributed to another person or group; and 3) the "claiming"stage in which a remedy is sought to rectify or compensate for the grievance. A dispute is likely to refer to one or more specific claims but it may also be a channel for deep-rooted personal conflict. Those of us who attempt to settle disputes need to consider whether we are trying to settle the overt dispute or the underlying conflict, as the two objectives are very different and require different methods. We also need to consider who is in control of the dispute and its outcome: the parties or the dispute-settler. Roberts (1979, 1983) provided a valuable analysis of the structural characteristics of four different dispute-settling processes. These four processes are:

1. Simple bilateral negotiation between the two parties.
2. Negotiations conducted by proxy through representatives, relatives or friends.
3. Adjudication and arbitration.
4. Conciliation.

1 Simple Bilateral Negotiation

Couples who negotiate directly with each other may do so from the strength of a fundamentally good relationship and/or because of their mutual concern to avoid a damaging dispute, either for themselves or their children. If they disagree, they will probably try to sit down together to work out what to do. The essential feature of bilateral negotiation is that control over decisions is retained by the parties themselves, without being surrendered partly or completely to other people or the state. Decisions are based on the parties' own values and priorities, not on those of another person or authority. If both parties are equally motivated to find an acceptable solution and evenly balanced in terms of their emotional, psychological and material resources, the settlements they reach may seem fair and reasonable by objective criteria. However, many couples are not evenly balanced and the weaker or less knowledgeable partner may be coerced or exploited by the more powerful one. Negotiations conducted without advice and safeguards do not guarantee well-balanced outcomes and relatively few couples in dispute may even attempt them, because the tensions between them may be too stressful and overwhelming. As the level of stress increases, one party may capitulate or both of them may appeal to other people to manage and direct their conflict for them.

2 Negotiations by Proxy

Couples who cannot cope with direct negotiation and who doubt their own judgement or resources usually seek advice and support from their family and friends, and often from professionals as well. If each consults a professional separately, the two professionals may diagnose the problems differently and give conflicting advice on the action which should be taken. Separate legal advice to each party may focus on their individual rights and grievances without exploring mutual concerns and this tends to discourage direct communication. Solicitors sometimes advise estranged couples not to have any contact with each other, even where there are children of the marriage and no risk of violence. As Roberts (1983) explained:

> the nature of the help will depend on the kind of partisan involved: a relative or friend may give "moral" support, encouraging a

> disputant or calming him down if he gets too upset; a professional adviser may give specialist advice about the implications of particular courses of action, about the consequences of failure to reach an agreement and about avenues which might be explored in negotiation further along the line (pp. 544-5).

An adversarial legal system assumes that the two parties have conflicting interests and in the absence of settlement or withdrawal, the dispute may be referred (subject to factors such as the parties' wishes, and the availability of legal aid) to an arbitrator or judge.

3 Adjudication and Arbitration

The essential characteristic of adjudication and arbitration is that the judge or arbitrator has the power to impose a decision on the disputants. In arbitration, the parties may agree beforehand to abide by the arbitrator's decision, whereas in adjudication they can be compelled by law to accept the judgement whether they wish to do so or not, with sanctions such as imprisonment if they flout a court order. The adversarial system, which provides formal rules for the presentation and evaluation of conflicting claims, is a necessary means of settling some disputes which cannot be settled in any other way and the provision of "an impartial decision-maker before whom competing litigants can submit their claims in the expectation of a just determination" (Abella 1982 pp. 4-5) is a source of symbolic as well as pragmatic authority in containing violent and intractable disputes. Arguably, adjudication should be used as a final resort, after other methods have failed to settle the dispute.

Adjudication may take many forms, from friendly, inquisitorial procedures to highly controlled and ritualised testing of evidence (Roberts 1983). In an unrestrained adversarial system, lawyers may champion their clients in a legal duel in which the lawyers dominate the action, relegating the disputants to the subservient role of "seconds". The disputants may then feel that they have lost all control of the conduct of their dispute and the eventual outcome may leave them bruised and disillusioned. In other cases, the opportunity to press their claim may provide a form of emotional catharsis which enables them to accept the court's decision.

4 Conciliation

Conciliation may be defined as a structured process in which both parties to a dispute meet voluntarily with one or more impartial third parties (conciliators) who help them to explore possibilities of reaching agreement, without having the power to impose a settlement on them or the responsibility to advise either party individually. However, the term is often used much more loosely, as though it were a benign label which can be applied to conciliatory advice and help to either or both parties, from any source. For example, the Home Office Working Party on Marriage Guidance defined "conciliation" as "the moderation of bitterness and reduction of areas of disagreement" (Marriage Matters 1979, par. 4.84), without specifying whether the process must involve both parties and an impartially placed conciliator.

The practice of conciliation as a method of settling disputes has increased so rapidly in many countries and has received so much publicity that it is easy to gain the impression that it is a new idea. The *Shorter Oxford English Dictionary* gives five different definitions of the verb "to conciliate", of which the earliest, in use from 1545, is "to gain (goodwill etc.) by acts which induce friendly feeling". A second definition, in use from 1573, is "to reconcile, make accordant", and a third, "to soothe, placate", dates from the later part of the eighteenth century. This last definition fits the onomatopoeic quality of the word. It sounds like spreading oil on troubled waters or pouring water on flames, with the implication that conflict is being extinguished or suppressed. Yet the earliest definition did not convey the idea of extinction and suppression: on the contrary, it called for constructive action to harness the energy of conflict in a search for positive solutions. These distinctions are significant, because they indicate that conciliation, like adjudication, can take different forms and produce different results.

The English words "conciliate" and "conciliation" have Latin roots, but the philosophy and practice of conciliation can be traced well before Roman times. Conciliation was the principal method of resolving disputes in ancient China (Brown 1982). Confucian teaching held that constructive, rational discussion helps disputants to reach lasting agreements, whereas a formal process of confrontation, followed by an imposed decision, may leave them embittered and uncooperative. The Chinese legal system in the fifth and sixth centuries BC was notorious for its injustices and corruption and Confucius may have had pragmatic reasons for preferring conciliation, but the practice of conciliation embodies values which are fundamental to his philosophy – the values of mutual understanding and respect, rational discussion and harmonious co-existence. These values are upheld in modern China by People's Conciliation Committees who offer an alternative forum to the courts for the settlement of personal and family disputes. Conciliators meet with both parties, usually on neutral ground, to help them explore possibilities of reaching agreement. As a Chinese conciliator observed graphically in a televised conciliation discussion with a young married couple who were initially very hostile to each other, "You cannot wrap fire in paper." Suppressed conflict will continue to smoulder and a small spark may ignite a destructive blaze. Chinese conciliators seem to see themselves as upholding traditional values and they may exert friendly but powerful moral pressures, encouraging senior members of the family to use their authority to settle marital and family squabbles for the good of the family and of society as a whole. In many cultures, the extended family has provided a forum for settling personal and family disputes, sometimes with the local parish priest, minister or rabbi acting in the role of conciliator. World history is littered with wars fought in the name of religion, but the main religions of the world preach that conflict should be settled by peaceful means. The Corinthians were sharply admonished by St Paul for their litigious tendencies: "Now therefore there is utterly a fault among you, because ye go to law one with another" (1 Corinthians 6 v. 7). Buddhism, too, preaches harmony and unity and warns against preoccupation with divisions and differences because this may prevent people from perceiving mutual interests and common needs. Christmas Humphreys (1984) wrote in relation to Zen Buddhism: "Most of our time is spent in analysing differences. Now concentrate on similarities, on what is common between two things which are habitually regarded as antagonistic opposites. In other words, look for the higher thirds above all opposites . . . look for this relationship, and you will be kinder to each of the pairs" (p. 158).

Conflict often results from failed communication rather than from incompatible needs and goals and conciliators generally seek to improve communication between disputants and to help them explain to each other the terms or changes they are looking for. Anthropologists (Gulliver 1971, 1979, Roberts 1979) have described the custom in many parts of Africa of calling a moot or meeting, where a respected senior tribesman may be asked to help settle a disagreement between individuals, families or villages. Gulliver (1971) described how the Ndendeuli in southern Tanzania would convene a meeting of kinsmen whenever a dispute arose between two members of the community. Both sides would outline their version of the dispute, sometimes with the support of relatives, and influential, neutrally placed members of the community would then look for possible settlement or compromise, appealing to the disputants not to disrupt the harmony of the community and reminding them of their social ties and obligations towards each other. Roberts (1979) concluded that the intervention of third parties as peace-makers seems almost universal in disputes between two members of a community. He quoted Grinnell's (1923) account of dispute settlement among the Cheyenne Indians where one of the recognised duties of a Cheyenne chief was that "he should be a peace-maker – should act as a mediator between any in the camp who quarrelled" (Grinnell vol. 1, p. 336).

Many minority ethnic and religious groups established their own particular methods of settling disputes, partly as a means of preserving their own cultural identity so as to avoid the imposition of the alien rules and norms of the society in which they lived. The Jewish Beth Din has existed for this purpose for many generations and in many different settings and the American Jewish community in New York City re-established its own conciliation forum, the Jewish Conciliation Board, in 1920 (Folberg 1983). Chinese immigrants to the United States set up the Chinese Benevolent Association to resolve disputes between individuals and families by means of conciliation, and early Quakers used conciliation and arbitration procedures, which are still maintained, as the principal means of settling marital and commercial disputes without resorting to litigation. Many of these schemes seem to have provided practical, down-to-earth methods of settling disputes but some of them seem to carry a rosy-tinted halo of idealism which tends to distract attention from their methods and results.

The Development of Industrial Conciliation

The more complex a society becomes, the more it develops elaborate institutions and rules to protect itself from internal dissensions. Formal legal systems relying on the presentation of evidence in ritualised ways to a professional judge tend to become longwinded and cumbersome, slow to respond to social change and financially costly to the disputants and to society as a whole. In contrast, conciliation can offer the advantages of easier accessibility, greater flexibility, the continuing autonomy of the parties and lower costs, compared with litigation. In industry and commerce, there may be strong incentives to settle disputes by agreement at an early stage because prolonged breaks in production can have damaging consequences for all concerned, as the miners'strike in 1984-85 demonstrated all too clearly. The systems of collective bargaining which developed between workers and employers in certain industries in the nineteenth century reflected a community of interest in reaching negotiated settlements without recourse to the law. These early collective bargaining activities began to be formalised in the 1860s with the creation of Boards of Conciliation. The best known early examples were in the Nottingham hosiery industry and in the North of England iron industry. The boards normally had equal representation of management and employees and an independent chairman acting as a conciliator. Two Acts passed in 1867 and 1872 enabled boards of arbitration, set up in conjunction with voluntary bargaining arrangements, to make legally binding awards, but these Acts were little used and were superseded in 1896 by a system whereby the state intervened only to assist and mediate in voluntary settlements (ACAS 1980). The Conciliation Act of 1896 was the legislative outcome of the 1891 Royal Commission on Labour. It empowered the Board of Trade to inquire into major industrial disputes where the parties had reached deadlock and to take steps to encourage them to meet together with an independent conciliator or board of conciliation. The Board of Trade also had a responsibility to aid and encourage the new voluntary joint boards which were responsible for most of the conciliated settlements in the years that followed.

This emphasis on settling disputes through conciliation and voluntary arbitration procedures, undertaken only with the consent of both parties to the dispute, was supported by successive governments during the twentieth century. During the second world war, the voluntary conciliation and arbitration service initiated by the government in 1896 was extended by further provisions which came to be known from 1960 onwards as the Industrial Relations Service and from 1969 as the Manpower and Productivity Service. Its terms of reference were revised in 1971 to concentrate on industrial relations and personnel matters, and in 1972 it was renamed the Conciliation and Advisory Service. "However, the constraints of the 1972-74 incomes policy made it difficult for the Service to operate effectively from within a government department, and in 1974 it was established on an independent basis . . . and renamed the Advisory, Conciliation and Arbitration Service (ACAS) in 1975" (ACAS 1980).

Independence of statutory authority and control is seen by ACAS as the linch-pin of its conciliation activities. Collective conciliation is defined as

> a means whereby employers and trade unions can be helped to reach mutually acceptable settlements of their disputes by a neutral and independent third party, ACAS. Its essential characteristics are that its use is voluntary and that agreements reached in conciliation are the responsibility of the disputing parties. Conciliation is to be distinguished from arbitration, whereby the parties jointly ask a third party to make an award which they undertake to accept (ACAS 1979).

ACAS also undertakes individual conciliation in disputes between individual employers and employees, for example over complaints of unfair dismissal. ACAS stresses that the parties to a dispute should be encouraged to pursue bilateral negotiations as far as possible and that the help of a conciliator should be sought only when negotiations appear to have failed to resolve the dispute, or where there are other indications that conciliation is needed. Although the job of the conciliator is to help employers and employees to settle their differences by agreement, if possible in a lasting way, ACAS recognises that this objective cannot always be achieved in full. "Sometimes the conciliator must be content to help the parties reach a strictly temporary accommodation or perhaps narrow the extent of their difference without resolving it. Sometimes he can do no more than clarify the issues in dispute" (ACAS 1979 par. 11).

ACAS conciliators work with

> certain broad assumptions, chiefly that in coming to conciliation the parties wish to reach agreement, so long as satisfactory terms can be found ... and that they will be generally co-operative ... The conciliator needs to win the acceptance of all parties to the dispute and establish a good working relationship with them. This depends on his gaining their trust and confidence which in turn depends on his personal qualities, knowledge, skill and effectiveness. The most fundamental of his characteristics is the conciliator's neutrality or impartiality. He must always remain above suspicion that he is biased in favour of one party or the other. His integrity should never be in doubt (ACAS 1979 paras. 13 and 15).

The conciliator's first task is to seek to understand the nature of the dispute, the goals of both parties, and their attitudes to each other, if hostile attitudes appear to be standing in the way of settlement. Although he may form his own views of the dispute and of the parties,

> it is not his role to pronounce on the merits of either side's case, nor to suggest how he thinks the dispute should be settled, although he may make suggestions at an appropriate stage. Where necessary he provides information, for example, about relevant legislation ... Those present are encouraged to talk freely to each other in confidence and no transcripts are made ... The conciliator is not a party to any agreements reached in conciliation and for this reason he does not normally sign any agreed document, except perhaps as a witness (ACAS 1979 paras. 17, 40, 48).

No report is made by ACAS conciliators to an industrial tribunal or court of law and if the parties proceed to arbitration or adjudication of their dispute, they are prevented by the rules of conciliation from exploiting the content of confidential discussions as a weapon against each other in an adversarial process. If, however, they agree to waive the confidentiality of their discussions, the content of conciliation can be put forward with their joint consent.

The ground-rules of conciliation observed by ACAS are more or less identical to those used by the International Chamber of Commerce (1977) in conciliation in international commercial disputes (except that ACAS provides a free service, whereas a conciliator appointed by the International Chamber of Commerce may charge high fees). The basic principles of conciliation in industrial and commercial disputes are clearly defined and applied within a nationally or internationally agreed framework of rules. The cornerstones of the process are the voluntary participation of both parties, their control over the outcome of their dispute and the conciliator's lack of statutory authority.

The Early History of Conciliation in Matrimonial Proceedings

In contrast to the practice of conciliation in industrial and commercial disputes, conciliation in matrimonial disputes developed in

England and Wales without clearly defined principles and in many instances without any firm boundary between the various processes labelled "conciliation" and the judicial process of the courts. Matrimonial disputes raise moral as well as legal, social and economic questions and conciliation in matrimonial disputes tends to get entangled with the prevailing values in society. There is also a semantic problem since the word "conciliation" was used historically in matrimonial cases synonymously with "reconciliation", indicating a preconceived aim to re-unite estranged couples whether they were seeking a reconciliation or not.

A Departmental Committee on Social Services in the Courts of Summary Jurisdiction (Report 1936) found that "conciliation" was very widely practised in matrimonial cases coming before the magistrates. In the county boroughs consulted by the Committee, "conciliation" was attempted in 71 per cent of matrimonial cases, generally before any formal application for a summons was made. In the Metropolitan boroughs, "conciliation" was attempted in 69 per cent of cases. The conciliator was often a probation officer, clergyman, policewoman or the clerk to the court. As Murch (1980) pointed out, many probation officers at that time held deep religious convictions and were motivated by "missionary zeal" (p. 186), seeing it as their moral duty to achieve a reconciliation wherever possible. The 1936 Report contains some startling figures showing the apparent success of these "conciliators" in deflecting wives from legal action against their husbands. Out of 6,222 applications studied in their 1935 sample, only 1,776 proceeded to a court hearing of the application. Reconciliation was assumed to have taken place if the applicant wife did not return to court within three months. The Departmental Committee viewed this amazing reconciliation rate with some disquiet:

> We cannot help feeling that under the present system there is a real risk that conciliation may be carried too far. The practice adopted in so many courts of allowing the probation officer to see all persons who come to them in matrimonial difficulties may well tend to lead to some denial of justice. It is not his function to determine whether on legal grounds the case should properly proceed to a hearing. There is a strong temptation to the zealous officer to settle as many cases as he can out of court and he may even be actuated by personal convictions as to the sanctity of the marriage tie (p. 12).

In spite of these misgivings, the Committee felt that it was justifiable to induce women to bear the ills they have, rather than fly to others they know not of[2] and they concluded that "there is no doubt whatever that some machinery for conciliation is an essential part of the administration of the Acts relating to matrimonial disputes" (p. 11). The Committee recommended that conciliators should have expert knowledge and training to deal with marital and psycho-sexual problems and they also recommended that no report from a conciliator should be communicated to the court unless the conciliator were sworn as a witness in the case. As a result of these recommendations, the conciliation work of the probation service, which had been carried out hitherto on an informal basis, became part of the service's statutory duties under the Summary Procedure (Domestic Proceedings) Act 1937. Under the Magistrates' Courts Act 1952, a probation officer or other conciliator was empowered to combine the process of conciliation with reporting to the court: "Where in any domestic proceedings ... a magistrates' court has requested a probation officer or any other person to effect a conciliation between the parties, the probation officer or that other person may, if the attempt has proved unsuccessful and he thinks fit in the circumstances of the case to do so, furnish to the court a report ... "[3].

The Finer Committee (1974) commented that "it is evident that the word 'conciliation' is here employed, at least primarily, in the sense ... of 'reconciliation' (par. 4.295 note 7). Moreover, a probation officer acting as a conciliator was invested with the formal authority of the court and there was apparently no attempt to check whether probation officers used this authority to impose the court's values on the parties or whether they were primarily concerned to help the parties reach their own decisions.

Reconciliation and Conciliation in the United States

In the United States, the word "conciliation" in matrimonial cases was also used originally in the sense of "reconciliation" and some American states introduced "conciliation" procedures which were a cover for very directive forms of paternalistic control. The Family Court of Milwaukee, Wisconsin, set up in 1935, was empowered from 1960 onwards to refer all divorce petitioners to the court's conciliation department, which could require both spouses to attend an appointment. This filter system apparently deterred many couples from divorce, since the court's records showed that 39 per cent of divorce proceedings were abandoned. In Toledo, Ohio, where a family court had been established in 1925, 40 per cent of divorce proceedings were discontinued, apparently as the result of conciliation. These family courts could adjourn divorce proceedings for six months while the position of children was investigated and they could order supervision by the conciliation department for six months or more. This use of conciliation smacks much more of coercive authority than of consensual decision-making by both partners and in fact the courts believed that they held a watching brief for the community to promote reconciliation or, if divorce was inevitable, to induce the parties to settle their affairs in an approved fashion (Sanctuary 1968).

By 1970, 24 American states were providing court-based conciliation services and the conciliation bureaux in New York State dealt with 4,912 referrals in 1969/70. Thirty-nine per cent of these referrals were reported to have resulted in reconciliation between the parties and 38 per cent in agreements on child custody, access, maintenance or property. Doubts were expressed, however, about the durability of the reconciliations that were apparently achieved and the Legislative Commission on Expenditure Review of the State of New York (Report 1971) reported that

> an overwhelming majority of matrimonial lawyers feel that the Conciliation Bureau is unsuccessful in reconciling married couples. The principal reason given for this failure is that a conciliation process which does not begin until a divorce action has been filed is too late to save the marriage ... [But] although most matrimonial lawyers believe that the Conciliation Bureau has been unsuccessful in reconciling married couples, a majority believe that the bureau has been successful in a significant number of cases in effecting consensual agreements on custody of children, visitation rights, and the amount of support ... Supporters of the bureau indicate that such settlements save the judge's time, save trial and other costs, and promote family harmony, despite the divorce (p. 13).

The rapid rise in the divorce rate in the 1970s was accompanied by a corresponding increase in matrimonial litigation, and as court waiting-lists lengthened, more dissatisfaction was expressed about the time-scale, expense and adversarial nature of court proceedings in divorce and other family matters. Conciliation was increasingly seen to be preferable to litigation, and the focus of divorce conciliation shifted from reconciliation counselling to divorce counselling and the settlement of disputes between divorcing parents over custody and access arrangements for their children (Folberg 1983). A number of professionals involved in these developments formed the Association of Family and Conciliation Courts, an interdisciplinary organisation founded in 1963 to promote the concept and practice of conciliation in family law. Additionally, some individuals with a background in law or industrial conciliation (Coogler 1978, Haynes 1978) began to offer divorce conciliation as a new form of private practice, using principles and methods derived mainly from industrial conciliation and applying them to all disputes connected with divorce, including financial and property issues[4].

The historical development of divorce conciliation in the United States and in Britain reveals its different and potentially conflicting antecedents and values. Over little more than half a century, its history reflects the fundamental changes that have taken place in public attitudes towards marriage and divorce, in which society's concern to protect the institution of marriage has been largely superseded by a more liberal approach to divorce, combined with a greater emphasis on the interests of children. In the last ten years, paternalistic social policies have been questioned more rigorously (Murch 1980) and there has been a move towards informalism, self-determination and the rights of individuals and families to manage their own affairs, without interference from the state. Conciliation has thus inherited different values and concerns in relation to divorce and remarriage, and the similarity between the words "conciliation" and "reconciliation" continues to cause confusion about its objectives. This ambiguity makes conciliation particularly vulnerable to external influences and pressures, and in Britain it is only gradually evolving an identity which is distinct from marital counselling, social welfare and arbitration. A growing number of professionals, and some members of the general public, now understand it as a structured method of settling disputed matters through negotiated agreements – a process for which collective conciliation in industrial disputes provides a useful model. ACAS conciliators encourage disputants to take part in private and informal negotiations, instead of getting embroiled in a formal confrontation in court, yet they operate within a framework of clearly defined rules. These rules distinguish conciliation from arbitration and adjudication, and also help industrial conciliators to avoid the pitfalls of paternalism and the disguised use of authority. In contrast, divorce conciliators in Britain are still in the process of clarifying their inheritance from the past, their function in the present and their directions for the future.

Notes

1. A brief account of the Family Court of Australia is given in chapter 9.
2. The quotation used by the Committee is from *Hamlet*, Act 3, scene 1.
3. Magistrates' Courts Act 1952, section 59.
4. See chapter 9 for further reference to the American experience of divorce conciliation and mediation.

4 THE DEVELOPMENT OF DIVORCE CONCILIATION IN BRITAIN

The first time that an English legislative procedure made provision for conciliation, as distinct from reconciliation, in the context of matrimonial proceedings was a Practice Direction on Matrimonial Conciliation issued on 27 January 1971 by the President of the Family Division of the High Court, with the concurrence of the Lord Chancellor. The Practice Direction provided that divorce courts could refer contested cases to probation officers (initially in the Greater London area) for "conciliation" – a task which was distinguished both from reconciliation and from the preparation of a welfare report to assist the court's decisions. The Practice Direction explained the new procedure as follows:

> (a) Where the Court considers that there is a reasonable possibility of reconciliation or that there are ancillary proceedings in which conciliation might serve a useful purpose, the Court may refer the case, or any particular matter or matters in dispute therein, to the Court Welfare Officer.
> (b) The Court Welfare Officer will, after discussion with the parties, decide whether there is any reasonable prospect of reconciliation (experience having shown that reconciliation is unlikely to be successful in the absence of readiness to co-operate on the part of the spouses) or that conciliation might assist the parties to resolve their disputes or any part of them by agreement.
> (c) If the Court Welfare Officer decides that there is no such reasonable prospect, he should report accordingly to the Court.
> (d) If the Court Welfare Officer decides that there is some reasonable prospect of reconciliation, or that conciliation might assist the parties to resolve their disputes or any part of them by agreement, he will, unless he continues to deal with the case himself, refer the parties to either (i) a Probation Officer; or (ii) a fully qualified marriage guidance counsellor recommended by the branch of the appropriate organisation concerned with marriage guidance and welfare; or (iii) some other appropriate person or body indicated by the special circumstances (for example, denominational) of the case.
> (e) The person to whom the parties have been referred will report back to the Court Welfare Officer, who in turn will report to the

> Court. These reports will be limited to a statement whether or not reconciliation has been effective, or to what extent (if at all) the parties have been assisted by conciliation to resolve their disputes or any part of them by agreement[1].

This Practice Direction is important in the historical development of conciliation in divorce proceedings for three reasons. First, it makes the distinction between "conciliation" and "reconciliation" which the Finer Committee on One-Parent Families (1974) was to draw more emphatically three years later[2]. Secondly, it recognised that welfare officers have a role in helping parents to reach agreement which can be separated from the task of making inquiries to assist the court. Murch (1980) showed that welfare officers were increasingly using a request for a welfare report as an opportunity to undertake short-term work with families and this Practice Direction identified the task of conciliation as one which could be properly undertaken without the constraints and duties of the reporting task. Thirdly, the Practice Direction provided that both reconciliation and conciliation should be legally privileged: that is, no information should be given to the court by the welfare officer except a statement as to whether the parties had reached any agreement or not.

This Practice Direction seems to have been ahead of its time and many judges appear to be unaware of it. According to the Finer Committee[3], little or nothing resulted from it and the Committee overlooked the important distinction that was being made between conciliation and reconciliation, since they commended New Zealand[4] on making a "pragmatic working distinction" between the two terms. In the Finer Committee's definitions, which are now widely accepted, "reconciliation" is "restricted to its proper meaning, that is, the action of re-uniting persons who are estranged; whilst conciliation is coming to denote, as it should, the process of engendering common sense, reasonableness and agreement in dealing with the consequences of estrangement" (par. 4.305). The Finer Committee explained that they were using the term "conciliation" to mean

> assisting the parties to deal with the consequences of the established breakdown of their marriage, whether resulting in a divorce or a separation, by reaching agreements or giving consents or reducing the area of conflict upon custody, support, access to and education of the children, financial provision, the disposition of the matrimonial home, lawyers' fees and every other matter arising

> from the breakdown which calls for a decision on future arrangements (par. 4.288).

This definition continues to be widely quoted as the most authoritative and comprehensive definition of conciliation in separation or divorce, but it is unsatisfactory for several reasons. In many cases, the breakdown of the marriage is not "established" in any formal sense, since statements made by one partner may be strenuously denied by the other. Disagreement about the divorce itself is very common and conciliation may be needed on this primary issue. Secondly, the Finer Committee's definition could apply to conciliatory advice from solicitors or other professionals, rather than to a formal process of conciliation undertaken by a neutrally placed conciliator. Some lawyers define "conciliation" as "a settlement of cases without recourse to contentious litigation, as an essential function of the lawyer practising in these matters" (Jackson 1983 p. vii). Many registrars and judges use a conciliatory approach not only at initial hearings or section 41 appointments but also in the context of contested proceedings in which judicial authority may be used to persuade the parties to accept a consent order. Some court welfare officers consider that in their statutory work for the court "the two processes of investigation and conciliation are ... inextricably interwoven and very largely interdependent"(Wilkinson 1981 p. 8). Partly as a result of the ambiguity in the Finer Committee's definition, "conciliation" has become a fashionable portmanteau word carrying whatever bundle of meanings and values its user chooses to pack into it. Many professionals see it as an intrinsic part of their work which can be combined with other tasks. Wilkinson (1981) stated that "the task of conciliation is implicit in all that the welfare officer undertakes" (p. 20) and he used the term synonymously with counselling by suggesting that the term "personal conciliation" could be applied to "the work undertaken with the person who is so depressed and debilitated by divorce that he is not only unable to cope with the separate demands of separate living, but is equally incapable of contemplating his single future as anything other than arid and meaningless" (pp. 20-1).

Conciliation may therefore be confused with divorce counselling, and lawyers may take it to mean bilateral negotiations between solicitors and/or the process of pacifying belligerent clients (Wilkins 1984). In 1985 the Family Law Bar Association set up a "Conciliation Board" (Johnson and Laurie 1985) to settle matrimonial disputes over maintenance and property. The Law Society (1985) objected that the proposed scheme could not be described properly as conciliation as it was "more in the nature of arbitration": the parties would have no direct contact with each other, merely receiving a recommendation via their solicitors of the proposed terms of settlement. This misuse of the term "conciliation" muddies waters which are already far from clear. Confusion would be reduced if its use were restricted to a clearly defined process (Davis 1983a, Roberts 1983) instead of being a kind of woolly blanket which is thrown loosely over a variety of approaches undertaken by different professionals in different settings.

The Finer Committee envisaged conciliation being developed in the context of a major reform of family law. One of the main functions of the unified and comprehensive family court proposed by the Committee would be "to provide the best possible facilities for conciliation between parties in matrimonial disputes" (par. 4.283 [3]), although the Committee was vague as to when and how these facilities would be provided. Objections were raised that the Finer Committee's proposals were too costly. The Working Party on Family Courts set up by the Law Commission in 1971 had been suspended indefinitely in 1973, ostensibly because the Finer Committee was covering the same ground. Objections to the family court on cost grounds may have disguised profound resistance to reform. As Murch (1980) pointed out, the contradictions and anomalies of the existing system allowed all kinds of vested interests to be served, while divorcing couples continued to be pitted against each other at considerable cost in emotional and financial terms, both to themselves and to the state.

Recognising that any major reform of divorce and family law was still a long way off, small groups of professionals in different parts of the country began to plan improvements at local level. The Finer Committee's proposals drew together many of those who were seeking change, who mobilised under the conciliation banner without any universally agreed definition of what it stood for but with a sense of common purpose and shared goals. Their apparent unity masked considerable differences in their objectives and values, some seeing conciliation as a lubricating oil that could be poured over the existing legal machine without redesigning it, while others were evidently seeking a radical overhaul. Some lawyers and court officials evidently hoped that conciliation would streamline the court's production line and reduce court waiting-lists and some saw conciliators as "charitable ladies" (as they were described in one part of the country, until they politely declined the description), who would pacify distressed and angry people and clear the way for effective action by solicitors or the court. Court welfare officers had long seen the need for conciliation with parents in conflict over their children and many felt they were well placed to develop their role as conciliators. The issues of a conciliator's accountability and overt or covert power in the context of an extremely powerful legal system received little attention initially. Practical problems, rather than ideological ones, preoccupied the groups of lawyers, probation officers, social workers and counsellors who began to work together to set up conciliation services of various kinds. To this end, a professional alliance was formed between members of the legal and social work professions but as the terms of the alliance were not spelled out, the objectives and function of conciliation remained open to different interpretations. There seem to have been a number of concerns which fuelled the rapid growth of conciliation schemes from 1975 onwards, which may be briefly summarised as follows:

1. Concern to provide an alternative to the adversarial system in the divorce courts.
2. Concern to protect children involved in their parents' divorce.
3. Concern to give people more control over their own affairs and reduce their reliance on formal institutions.
4. Concern to achieve greater administrative efficiency by processing contested cases more quickly.
5. Concern to reduce public expenditure, particularly on legal aid.
6. Concern to stem the rising tide of divorce.

1 An Alternative to the Adversarial System

The members of the Finer Committee were by no means the first to contend that an adversarially based legal system, in which lawyers confront each other as adversaries and fight out their clients' differences in court, exacerbates the hostility and bitterness which divorcing couples commonly feel towards each other (Friedmann 1964, Abel-Smith and Stevens 1968, Mortlock 1971). Critics of this system argue that it destroys any vestiges of goodwill and co-operation and reduces the likelihood of agreements being reached and maintained. As an experienced matrimonial solicitor (Mostyn 1976) put it:

> when domestic discord breaks out, it cannot rationally be the aim of the parties to smash each other to pieces ... They ... need advice and help, not fuel. The rational aim is for the lawyers on each side to cool it down, each to endeavour to restore a sense of balance to his client and then for both to look for a sensible solution which will enable the parties to withdraw from the marriage with dignity (p. 166).

The Lay Observer appointed under the provisions of the Solicitors Act 1974, s. 45, observed in his 5th Annual Report that "in so many cases, the inevitable unhappiness associated with most matrimonial proceedings has apparently been considerably magnified by the adversarial nature of the court proceedings and of the preliminaries thereto"[5]. Those who sought to modify the adversarial system in family law saw conciliation as a much better method of settling disagreements than hostile litigation, especially as divorcing couples often have mutual concerns and responsibilities as parents of their children, as well as conflicting individual interests. By focusing both parties' attention on finding solutions for the future rather than on blaming each other for the past, it was hoped that conciliation would reduce conflict between them and make the divorce process less painful and destructive.

2 Concern to Protect Children Involved in their Parents' Divorce

Research does not provide conclusive evidence about the effects of parental separation and divorce on children. On the one hand, there is a widespread belief that it is better for children to live with one parent than with two parents who cannot get on together[6] and on the other hand, deep concern that children often become the victims of parental battles which may be waged long after the marriage ends. A child psychiatrist (Black 1982) reported that children of divorce were referred to child guidance clinics twice as frequently as children from intact families and although it is not stated whether this statistic referred to a local or national sample, many child psychologists and psychiatrists have commented that children suffer greatly from the loss of a parent to whom they are attached and that the conflict of divided loyalties puts them under severe stress. Another child psychiatrist (Benians 1980) quoted his 22 years' experience in child psychiatric and child guidance clinics in protesting that "withholding of access is so often, and wickedly, used as a weapon in divorce settlements of income and property" (p. 424). A Proposed Visiting Code published by Justice, the British section of the International Commission of Jurists (1975) emphasised that children should be able to enjoy the love of both parents without being made to feel anxious and guilty through the jealousy or demands of either parent. The Code urged parents to remember that access visits are for the good of the child and are not a parental right: that perceptible acrimony between parents may ruin the visit for the child and that sensitive children may blame themselves for causing fights between the two people they love most.

One of the main arguments used by supporters of conciliation services was that children would benefit from parental agreement and co-operation over custody and access arrangements[7]. It was recognised that court proceedings often involve long delays and that children need the security of clear and reliable arrangements, not persistent uncertainty and argument. Conciliation may prevent or reduce long-running disputes over children and focus on their perceptions and feelings, possibly including them in discussions with their parents or at least encouraging parents to give them adequate explanations and reassurance. Murch (1980) warned however against a paternalistic approach aimed at protecting children from the predicted harm of divorce, quoting Jordan's caveat that the "prevention of disasters by social work intervention is at best a fairly unverifiable business" (Jordan 1976). An emphasis on the welfare of the child may carry the negative implication that divorcing parents are uncaring or irresponsible.

3 Concern to Give People More Control over their own Affairs

The Finer Committee (1974) stressed that "the individual in the family court must in the last resort remain the subject of rights, not the object of assistance" (par. 4.285) and supporters of conciliation argued that out of court discussions would provide a forum in which people could work out their own decisions instead of abdicating this responsibility to the court. There was evidence from research that many divorcing couples felt the need for this kind of private forum[8] and that decisions imposed on them by a remote authority figure, as judges were sometimes perceived, were not necessarily acceptable to either party. Joint decisions are more likely to be maintained if both parties feel committed to them. Conciliation may also enable them to deal with the emotional, practical and legal aspects of their situation at the same time, instead of splitting them artificially into separate compartments. Court welfare officers increasingly saw their primary role as assisting parents to resolve disputes over custody and access themselves, rather than resorting to courtroom battles (Howard and Shepherd 1982), arguing that they "should not collude with any system which allows parents to abdicate responsibility for their children's future. Decisions about the future are more likely to prove effective and workable if they are made from within" (Francis and Shaw 1981 p. 71).

At a broader level, the move towards out-of-court settlements was part of a larger movement to reduce reliance on impersonal and formal institutions controlled by professionals and experts. Freeman (1984) referred to many "delegalisation projects" of which those concerned with family dispute settlement made up only a small number but he shared Abel's (1982) suspicion that the trend towards greater informalism actually provides professionals with more subtle means of maintaining control, without the safeguards of open justice and accountability.

4 Concern to Achieve Greater Administrative Efficiency

The increase in divorce and the corresponding increase in contested proceedings threatened to bring a cumbersome legal system almost to breaking point. In the autumn of 1977, the President of the Family Division of the High Court told the Law Society's Annual Conference: "The number of ancillary proceedings has risen sharply and of late alarmingly. We are now at saturation point . . . One attempt at alleviation has been to increase the number of judges in the long vacation. They too have been swamped" (quoted by Murch 1980 p. 237). In the face of such congestion in the courts, it was hoped that conciliation would filter out many contested cases and prevent the system from clogging up completely. It would thus serve the interests of the courts by facilitating early and quick settlements, reducing court waiting-lists and the pressure on registrars and judges. From an administrative point of view, the speed at which contested cases could be disposed of was of more importance than the quality of the settlements reached.

5 Concern to Reduce Public Expenditure

The need to speed up the wheels of justice was closely linked with concern to reduce expenditure on matrimonial legal aid, which was increasing at a much faster rate than inflation[9]. The Lord Chancellor's Department was cautiously attracted by the possibility that conciliation might save money and an official in the Department remarked at a meeting in the Solicitor-General's office in February 1978 that the government was very interested in experimental conciliation schemes because they represented "a happy concatenation of economy and humanity". Economy rather than humanity seemed to be the main attraction, however, to a government looking for new ways of cutting public expenditure. In a climate of economic retrenchment, the claim that conciliation would cut legal aid costs was advanced as a foregone conclusion by some and rather more cautiously by others. The claim is not easily proved, since it is difficult to show how much would have been spent on litigation or to prove that apparent savings are attributable solely to conciliation and not to other factors as well. Taken to extremes, the cost-saving argument could be used to support a "short, sharp shock" method of knocking people's heads together, with scant attention to their feelings or to the needs of their children.

6 Concern to Stem the Rising Tide of Divorce

Some groups, such as the Society of Conservative Lawyers and the Order of Christian Unity, felt that divorce had become too easy and that people on the verge of divorce should receive counselling. These groups criticised "the false economy in reducing Legal Aid for divorce by the special procedures and devaluing the provision for reconciliation, thereby greatly increasing the rate of divorce and the overall cost[10]." They believed that "the nation as a whole is tired of the permissive society in general and tired of the high divorce rate in particular"[11] and they supported the call of the Justices' Clerks' Society (1982) for a National Reconciliation and Conciliation Service with branches affiliated to the local magistrates' court. This service would be largely voluntary and unpaid, although "it would contain a professional element"[12]. The magistrates' courts would become the first tier of a family court, "their principal aim being to encourage reconciliation and conciliation"[13].

It should be obvious from this brief summary that conciliation was expected to serve many different purposes, some of which were fundamentally incompatible with each other.

The Introduction of In-Court Conciliation

On 15 September 1976, the Presiding Judge of the Western Circuit, Lord Justice Dunn, called a meeting of local county court registrars to consider ways of reducing the number of defended divorces set down for a High Court hearing. Apart from the enormous cost of these proceedings, there were usually long delays before a High Court hearing could take place (sometimes as long as a year), by which time any respondent who managed to defend the divorce successfully was likely to have won a Pyrrhic victory. Following the meeting with the Presiding Judge, a registrar at Bristol County Court suggested a new system of preliminary appointments in defended divorce cases and this move coincided with a policy initiative by Avon Probation Service, in response to the Finer Report, to establish a separate team of welfare officers who would specialise in civil work, particularly in the divorce court. It was agreed that the welfare officers would staff preliminary court appointments in defended divorce cases and these became known locally as "conciliation appointments". Both parties and their solicitors were asked to attend before the registrar in cases in which the respondent had filed an Answer to the petition. After clarifying the issues in dispute the registrar might suggest that the couple should withdraw for private discussion with the welfare officer, to see if agreement could be reached. At the same time, the parties' solicitors often got together to negotiate over financial matters and other issues (Parmiter 1981).

These appointments were so successful in reducing the number of defended divorces set down for a High Court hearing that in 1978 they were extended to include some undefended divorces in which there was a dispute over custody of the children or access to children. The procedure in this latter category was termed "mediation", to distinguish these appointments from the defended divorce cases. In 1978-79, 27 contested custody and access cases (about a quarter of the total number of contested custody and access cases referred to Bristol County Court in that year) were selected for a preliminary mediation appointment and 56 per cent settled at this appointment. The following year, 51 cases were selected for mediation and 65 per cent of these were settled (Parmiter 1981).

After three years' experience of operating this system of in-court conciliation, the registrar principally concerned reported five particular advantages over the previous system:

> First, the experiments show conclusively the validity of the proposals set out in the Finer Report for conciliation as part of the family court process. Secondly, there are very clear benefits to the litigants arising from much speedier resolution of their problems as well as the elimination of bitterness. Thirdly, there are very clear and substantial benefits to the parties and their children. Fourthly, there are very clear advantages to solicitors and savings to the legal aid fund. Solicitors are, I believe, aware of the pressure to keep down rates per hour and anything which can be done which leaves more of the available fund to pay better rates per hour in the more deserving cases is, I suggest, to be preferred to spreading the available cash ever thinner. Fifthly, there are substantial savings to the welfare service which are desperately needed if present delays in welfare officer reporting are to be contained (Parmiter 1981 p. 196).

The new system may have been greatly preferable to fully contested proceedings, but settlements do not necessarily resolve conflict. The average welfare officer time per case over 25 cases was only 41 minutes in 1979-80 (Parmiter 1981) and it was assumed perhaps too readily that a consent order invariably benefited both parties and their children, although theoretically it could involve a parent agreeing to withdraw a claim for custody or access without the reasons for the original application receiving adequate attention. In the in-court scheme at Bristol County Court, parents with children of secondary school age were asked to bring them to the mediation appointment so that they could be interviewed by the welfare officer about their wishes and feelings. Observation of these appointments by Davis (1982c), a researcher at Bristol University, suggested that the children's views generally determined the outcome, certainly as far as access visits were concerned. Views expressed by children in such circumstances are unreliable, since they may simply say what they have been told to say or feel obliged to say. As far as financial savings were concerned, the senior court welfare officer estimated that "the combined savings in legal aid, litigant and court fees for the first two years of operation now stands at £121,000. This sum is the result of 147 cases worked with successfully" (Fraser 1980). This estimate assumed that, without conciliation, all these cases would have proceeded to a full judicial trial, whereas some of them might have settled in some other way, even at the door of the court. It was also claimed (Fraser 1980) that welfare officers' time was being used more efficiently, because successful mediation avoided the need for a full welfare inquiry. Davis (1982d) showed, however, that 67 per cent of the mediation cases in his research sample involved both a mediation appointment and a welfare report, undertaken before or after the appointment. These findings indicated that in-court conciliation promoted settlement but was often not sufficient by itself to achieve a full settlement.

From 1977, the county court registrar who introduced the in-court conciliation procedure at Bristol County Court undertook a systematic scrutiny of all divorce petitions, with the help of the senior divorce court welfare officer, to identify cases in which a welfare inquiry was needed. In about a quarter of these cases, the inquiry was limited to checking that the arrangements for the children were satisfactory; the majority involved disputes over custody or access. The inspection of petitions initially produced a large increase in the number of welfare reports called for, from 361 in 1976 to 607 in 1978, but in 1979 the number dropped to 403. This abrupt decrease may have been due to a number of factors: the senior court welfare officer ceased his scrutiny of petitions, leaving it to the registrars to decide when a welfare inquiry should be called for; solicitors may have developed a more conciliatory approach in cases involving children and the establishment of Bristol Courts Family Conciliation Service on a full-time basis from May 1979 may have enabled a proportion of contested cases to be settled without being referred to the court.

The Development of Out-of-Court Conciliation Services

The first practical initiative in Britain to provide an independent conciliation service for separating and divorcing couples was taken in Bristol by a small sub-group of the Bristol Finer Joint Action Committee. This group, consisting of a university lecturer known for his research on divorce, an assistant chief probation officer experienced in matrimonial work, a solicitor specialising in family law and a social worker with Bristol Council of Voluntary Service began to meet together from April 1975 onwards to plan a conciliation service for the Bristol area. The composition of this small group was a microcosm of the professions and agencies who have joined together to develop family conciliation services. The innovative feature of the Bristol group's plan was their concept of an independent service taking referrals from solicitors, generally before a contested case was referred to the court, unlike the Finer Committee's concept of a court-based service. There was strong local support for the scheme and a committee was formed which included representatives of Bristol Law Society, the Bristol Bar, two divorce court registrars, two magistrates on the domestic panel, the Chief Probation Officer for Avon, the Assistant Chief Probation Officer and the university lecturer, representatives of Bristol Council of Voluntary Service, Bristol Marriage Guidance and the Catholic Marriage Advisory Service. After a time, a local circuit judge became chairman of the Steering Committee of Bristol Courts Family Conciliation Service (BCFCS), as the scheme was somewhat misleadingly called to show that it was operating with the blessing of local courts although it had no formal connection with them. The launching of the scheme was delayed however by the considerable difficulty of obtaining funds. Early approaches to three major trusts had met with a negative response and the steering committee met periodically for over two years, with disappointingly little result. An unexpected breakthrough took place on 1 December 1977, when a committee member happened to hear the Solicitor-General, Peter Archer MP, being interviewed on the radio about the extension of the "special procedure" and the possibility that consequent savings in legal aid might release a little more funding for law centres. A letter to the Solicitor-General resulted in a meeting at the House of Commons on 9 February 1978 between the Solicitor-General, two officials from the Lord Chancellor's Department and three members of the BCFCS committee. The Solicitor-General and the officials from the Lord Chancellor's Department expressed great interest in the proposed scheme and the BCFCS representatives were advised that an application to the Nuffield Foundation would receive the backing of the Lord Chancellor's Department. In the same month that this meeting took place at the House of Commons, the BCFCS committee launched a small pilot project with a grant of £1,250 from the Van Neste Trust (BCFCS 1979). Seven conciliators who were qualified social workers or marriage guidance counsellors had been recruited via Bristol Marriage Guidance Council and a Bristol-based organisation for part-time social workers, the Third Hand. Bristol Council for Voluntary Service offered the use of a room and a small pilot scheme was undertaken in 1978-79. Although very limited (about 50 cases were undertaken), it provided valuable experience for the conciliators and helped to clarify their understanding of the conciliation task.

The primarily pre-court service provided by Bristol Courts Family Conciliation Service[14] was designed to complement the in-court conciliation at Bristol County Court in a number of ways: a) in its early availability, before an application was made to the court and even before a divorce petition had been filed; b) in its quick accessibility in crisis situations, without the delay of awaiting a court appointment or for legal aid to be granted; c) in its availability to unmarried as well as married couples; d) in its acceptance of self-referrals from couples who were anxious to avoid any court proceedings; and e) in its independence of statutory authority. Furthermore, the service was not subject to the time-limits of the in-court system and the conciliation usually extended over three one-hour appointments per case (BCFCS 1980). In December 1978 the Trustees of the Nuffield Foundation decided to make a three-year grant to BCFCS on condition that in the second year one-third and in the third year two-thirds of the service's funding would be provided by central government. In this way, the Nuffield Foundation hoped to persuade the government to support an experiment which in their view had important implications for family law reform. Unfortunately, central government responsibility for the legal aid system, the administration of the courts and the probation service is divided between the Lord Chancellor's Department and the Home Office and this resulted in applications for financial support being batted between the two departments rather like a pingpong ball at times, with occasional encouraging pats from ministers at the Department of Health and Social Security, who recognised the possible implications that conciliation might have for social security payments to one-parent families and the reception of children into care under matrimonial care orders[15]. The Nuffield Foundation's condition that central government funding must be obtained was met by an arrangement authorised by the Lord Chancellor's Department and the Law Society that a fixed fee of £20 per individual would be payable under an extension of the Green Form scheme, where a client was being advised by a solicitor under this scheme or was in receipt of legal aid. As the fee could not be paid directly to BCFCS by the Law Society, the service invoiced solicitors and sent regular reminders in many cases, as solicitors' claims to the Law Society were usually submitted on completion of their work which was often long after conciliation finished. As a means of financing conciliation, the system was inadequate and unsatisfactory, producing only a small proportion of the funds needed and much of this amount was spent on correspondence to collect the fees from solicitors.

The grants from the Nuffield Foundation and two other trusts enabled BCFCS to rent its own offices in the city centre from May 1979 and to employ a full-time co-ordinator who also undertook conciliation, a full-time secretary/receptionist and five part-time conciliators each working on average ten hours per week (BCFCS 1979). Referrals were accepted from the public and via other agencies as well as from solicitors, provided that the referral satisfied the following three conditions: first, that one or both parties believed that their marriage (or relationship, in the case of unmarried couples) had broken down irretrievably; secondly, that there was an actual or incipient dispute arising from separation or divorce; and thirdly, that both parties were willing or might be willing to accept conciliation. If they had already consulted solicitors, their permission was sought to contact their solicitors before the first appointment took place, because it was felt to be particularly important to work with the co-operation of solicitors and to have accurate information about the stage of the legal process and the nature of any existing court orders which might have a substantial bearing on conciliation. Unrepresented individuals were encouraged to seek legal advice from a solicitor specialising in matrimonial work and the BCFCS co-ordinator estimated that as many referrals were made to solicitors (using the directory compiled by Bristol Law Society) as were received from them. In 1981-82, 350 conciliation cases were undertaken in which both parties attended at least one conciliation appointment and 112 firms of solicitors initiated or concurred with these referrals (BCFCS 1982). In a sample of 290 cases, 207 couples were seen jointly by a conciliator at one or more appointments and in 83 cases they were seen separately; 138 cases (47.5%) were referred before a divorce petition had been filed, 92 (31.7%) after a petition had been filed, 48 cases (16.5%) after the decree absolute, while in 12 cases (4.1%) the parties were unmarried. In 240 out of the 290 cases, the conciliators recorded that one or more issues had been fully or partially settled, generally with advice and support to each party from their solicitors and usually with negotiations between the solicitors on financial and property matters. Access to children was the issue most frequently referred but an increasing number of referrals involved a dispute over the divorce itself. BCFCS reported that

> conciliation is accepted by many individuals who rule out reconciliation and refuse marriage guidance counselling, . . . some of

> them nonetheless have second thoughts about divorce, in the course of conciliation. This change is not due to pressure from the conciliator but to the increased ability of both spouses to listen and respond to each other. Early and skilled intervention is essential, preferably before a petition is filed and served ... Couples who stop divorce proceedings and attempt reconciliation are usually referred to a marriage guidance counsellor or family therapist. Approximately one in six cases changed direction from conciliation to reconciliation in 1981 (Parkinson 1983b p. 23).

When BCFCS was engaged in November 1981 in its annual struggle for further funding, the Council of Bristol Law Society passed a unanimous resolution that "the termination of BCFCS would be detrimental to the public, the legal profession, and to the work of the courts in family matters"[16]. In conveying this resolution to the Lord Chancellor's Department in support of the service's urgent plea for financial support, the President of Bristol Law Society wrote:

> To my mind, BCFCS is much more than another piece of social work. Its principal achievement, I believe, is to demonstrate that an informal system of conciliation can work in harmony with a judicial system, the one complementing and supporting the other. In my view, this achievement may well show a direction in which a reform of the whole family law system might proceed[17].

Both the in-court and out-of-court conciliation schemes were watched with interest by the Lord Chancellor's Legal Aid Advisory Committee who invited two representatives of BCFCS to meet with the Committee in May 1978. The Committee wrote in their *32nd Annual Report 1981-82*:

> as we said last year, we believe that a decision is long overdue on how such initiatives should be directed and funded. We continue to believe that the development and extension of appropriate conciliation arrangements and their incorporation as far as possible into matrimonial procedure are vitally important measures necessary to reduce the expense of litigation in this area and the amount of unhappiness which at present results from it (par. 105).

Referrals to BCFCS came mainly from solicitors and via the Citizens' Advice Bureau, sometimes at a rate of 6 referrals per day;

on one occasion there were 15 referrals in one day. Not all these referrals met the service's criteria for conciliation but where it seemed appropriate and the first party agreed to it, a carefully planned approach to the second party generally produced a positive response (see chapter 8). The number of "conciliated cases" almost doubled from about 180 cases in 1979-80 to 350 cases in 1981-82 (defined as those in which both parties took part in conciliation) but even 350 cases represented fewer than 10 per cent of the 3,000 divorces per year at Bristol County Court as the service was also used by couples who were separating but not divorcing, couples who were already divorced, unmarried couples and some couples from other areas. As Davis (1983a) pointed out, "it does not demand very much of solicitors that they support independent schemes. They can regard them as a benign fringe activity suitable for only a minority of their clients" (p. 13). There was however a good partnership in Bristol between the in-court and out-of-court schemes and the involvement of Avon Probation Service in the management of both schemes helped to link them without merging their identity and function. They attracted considerable interest from other parts of the country and a variety of conciliation schemes began to mushroom, with broadly similar objectives but with major differences in their organisation, staffing and funding.

The Family Conciliation Bureau at Bromley

This out-of-court service developed from July 1979 as a separate entity in the work of the Civil Work Unit of South-East London Probation Service. No additional funding was necessary as the Bureau was housed by the Civil Work Unit and co-ordinated by the senior divorce court welfare officer with the help of two administrative assistants. The Bureau is staffed on a sessional basis by welfare officers, social workers and marriage guidance counsellors who work as unpaid volunteers, generally in pairs. The conciliators are trained in a carefully structured method of working which is normally limited to a single meeting of 1-2 hours with both parties, in which each party has a short time alone with the conciliators to explain his or her point of view, followed by about an hour of joint discussion aimed at working out the terms of an agreement (Burrett and Gibbons 1981). Initially, the Bureau concentrated solely on access disputes. From July 1979 to March 1982, 24 per cent of the Bureau's 118 conciliation cases came from solicitors, 18 per cent from local courts, 27 per cent from welfare officers and social workers and 11 per cent from the parties themselves (Davis 1983b). This was a different referral pattern from Bristol, where 51 per cent of referrals in 1981-82 were made by one or both parties (either directly or via another agency such as the Citizens' Advice Bureau), 46 per cent by solicitors and 3 per cent by the courts (BCFCS 1982).

The out-of-court services at Bristol and Bromley both maintain a strict boundary of confidentiality between conciliation and the statutory work of the welfare service: information is not passed to an officer preparing a report for the court and at Bromley the same welfare officer would not be permitted to undertake both functions in the same case. The same rule was observed to some extent in the in-court Bristol scheme but in practice the same welfare officer often prepared the report, if the parties raised no objection.

The Conciliation Bureau at Bromley received increasing numbers of referrals from solicitors, the courts, other agencies and the public and the projected referral rate for 1985 was about 460 cases (Gibbons 1985). Links were established with the local magistrates' domestic court and with the Citizens' Advice Bureau and an information desk staffed by one of the conciliators at the entrance to the domestic court offers information on the range of services available from the Bureau, including a divorce counselling and advice service and the use of an access centre at weekends.

The Growth of Family Conciliation Services

From 1980 onwards, conciliation schemes developed rapidly but sporadically in statutory and voluntary agencies. There were many developments within the Probation Service (which will be discussed further in chapter 5) and a number of independent conciliation services were launched, including Sunderland in May 1980, Cleveland in January 1981, Surrey in March 1981, Coventry and Newham both in May 1981 and Swindon in June 1981. Most of these schemes were run by independent management committees of lawyers, senior probation officers, social workers and representatives of voluntary agencies and many were chaired by a local circuit judge. The support of the judiciary was particularly valuable to new services struggling for credibility and for an identity which was distinct from marital counselling. An initiative was also taken in Scotland in April 1981 to look into the possibilities of a pilot scheme in Scotland. The Scottish Council for Single Parents convened a steering group and held a conference on conciliation in May 1981, and by November that year a separate, independent committee was established to set up a service in Lothian (Forster 1982).

There was great interest among these pioneer schemes in learning from each other's experience and it was recognised that a co-ordinated conciliation movement could be much more effective than fragmented schemes in publicising the existence of conciliation services and putting pressure on central government to fund pilot projects. There was also concern to maintain support for conciliation by setting good standards of professional practice. The Clerk to the Bristol Justices and the co-ordinator of BCFCS wrote in September 1980:

> Conciliation services cannot be developed and maintained without the support of the legal profession and, accordingly, solicitors need to be assured of the qualifications and competence of the conciliators to whom they refer their clients. It is known that some areas are proposing to use unqualified volunteers, with a view to reducing the costs of the newly created service ... The co-ordinator and conciliators employed by BCFCS are well qualified social workers or accredited marriage guidance counsellors who have substantial experience of marital and family work and additional specialist training. Although these conciliators do not give legal advice, they work within a legal frame of reference and must be familiar with the relevant legislation and court procedures. They have a new and specialist role, not identical with counselling or social work. The eagerness therefore in some areas to meet the undoubted need for conciliation must be tempered by a real understanding of the work and what is required of the workers (Parkinson and Sullivan 1980, p. 568).

The Origins of the National Family Conciliation Council

The idea of forming a national association of independent schemes to share knowledge and experience and to promote good professional practice developed from a meeting in Bristol in October 1978 between two court welfare officers from Surrey and the co-ordinator of BCFCS. When enough projects were under way to make a national association a viable possibility, the BCFCS co-ordinator sought the Law Society's permission to hold a few initial meetings at the Law Society's headquarters in London. This request was intended to show that conciliators saw their role as complementary to that of solicitors, not as substitutes for them, and that links with solicitors were welcomed. The first meeting took place on 16 January 1981, with representatives from eleven areas and apologies from three others. The eleven representatives of new conciliation schemes included a Chief Probation Officer, four Assistant Chief Probation Officers, two senior divorce court welfare officers, the secretary to Manchester Legal Services Committee and social workers representing three other independent services. A brief statement from each member of the group revealed that each area was at a different stage of development and proceeding on rather different lines, some relying on their local probation service to provide accommodation and administrative back-up, whereas others were setting up completely independent services. All agreed, however, on a common definition of conciliation as "helping separating and divorcing couples to reach agreed decisions on matters arising from the breakdown of their marriage, especially matters concerning children"[18]. At the second meeting in April 1981, mention was made of 24 operational or projected schemes and further meetings of the Conciliation Services Co-ordination Group, as it was called initially, led to a national conference in Birmingham in October 1982, when a steering committee was elected and given the tasks of drafting a constitution, drawing up criteria for affiliation, preparing a training programme for conciliators and applying for charitable status. It was agreed that the association should be called the National Family Conciliation Council. Its aims were ambitious, especially as its executive committee depended on voluntary effort given by its members in addition to promoting and developing their own local service. Administrative expenses were met by a small grant from the Nuffield Foundation and a retired court welfare officer agreed to become the Council's Information Officer and to edit the quarterly newsletter. The National Family Conciliation Council was formally inaugurated in March 1983, with Bruce Pearce as Chairman and Ken Leuillette as secretary, and by the end of that year 21 out-of-court services (some of them managed mainly under the wing of the divorce court welfare service, as at Bromley, Cardiff, Colchester, Leeds and Surrey) were affiliated to the Council and about six more schemes were seeking affiliation. During 1983, a tripartite working party consisting of representatives of the NFCC, members of the Law Society's Family Law Committee and officials from the Law Society met to draw up a code of practice for family conciliation services to provide some guide-lines on the objectives and function of conciliation in matrimonial disputes and on communications between conciliators and solicitors (NFCC 1984).

In addition to the scattered growth of out-of-court services run separately from or jointly with the probation service, other county courts (Wandsworth, Yeovil, Newport) introduced in-court conciliation appointments on the Bristol model (Davis 1982c and d) and the Principal Divorce Registry in London operated a form of conciliation procedure in financial and property applications, during 1980 and 1981. This scheme was deemed a failure and abandoned, but Davis (1982e) argued that the conclusion that conciliation would not work in disputes over maintenance and property was based on a false premise. Inevitably, it takes time for new ideas and new ways of working to be tested properly and follow-up research was needed to find out whether agreements were maintained and how far they benefited both parties and their children. By degrees, the assumptions underlying the objectives and practice of conciliation began to be questioned more rigorously. At a conference held at Bromley in July 1984, Judge Jean Graham Hall emphasised that conciliation is an important adjunct to the court system, preferably to a family court system. As she graphically put it, "it is essential that everyone involved in conciliation knows who the players are, who the ballboys are, and what rules the umpire is applying"[19]. Despite the efforts of the National Family Conciliation Council to define the boundaries of conciliation, the conciliation "game" was being played according to a variety of rules in different parts of the country and many different professionals were trying to hit the ball, as the following chapter sets out to describe in more detail.

Notes

1. Practice Direction on Matrimonial Conciliation, 27 January 1971 [1971] 1 All ER 894 [1971] 14 WLR 223.
2. Finer Report (1974), par. 4.288.
3. Ibid. par. 4.294.
4. Ibid. par. 4.305.
5. 5th Annual Report of the Lay Observer (1980) HC 507.
6. See the survey of divorced people conducted for *Woman* magazine, 27 February 1982, pp. 23-6.
7. See for example Burrett and Gibbons (1981).
8. See Davis, MacLeod and Murch (1982b).
9. See the Lord Chancellor's Advisory Committee on Legal Aid, *32nd Annual Report 1981-82*, Appendix B, Part 2, par. B(2) 12.
10. The Order of Christian Unity, *Reconcilation and Conciliation in the Context of Divorce* (Winchester, 1982), p. 13.

11. Ibid. p. 14.
12. Ibid. p. 19.
13. Ibid. p. 27.
14. For accounts of the history and development of BCFCS, see BCFCS 1979, 1980, 1982, 1984, Parkinson 1978, 1982a, 1983b, Parkinson and Westcott 1980 and research reports by Davis (1980, 1981).
15. The *Second Report of the House of Commons Social Services Committee* (HMSO, London, 1984) stated that "contrary to popular wisdom, the greatest proportional growth in recent years in children coming into care is not . . . as a result of criminal proceedings, but . . . under orders made as a result of divorce or matrimonial proceedings, or following disputes between parents . . . once in care, those on matrimonial care orders are more likely to stay there" (par. 144).
16. Quoted with the permission of J. Westcott, former President of Bristol Law Society.
17. Ibid.
18. Minutes of the first meeting of the group which formed the National Family Conciliation Council.
19. Quoted in L. Parkinson, "Mediation – A Wider View", *Family Law*, vol. 14 (1984), p. 267.

5 CONCILIATION: SYSTEMS AND METHODS

The term "conciliation" is being applied in Britain to various kinds of interventions aimed at settling disputes in different ways. Not surprisingly, this is causing confusion. A Director of Court Counselling in the Family Court of Australia (Madison 1982) has suggested that the terms "conciliation" and "mediation", which are often used interchangeably, could be used to distinguish processes of different range and complexity. In Madison's definition, "*mediation* is the least complicated method of effecting change to the presenting problem, and is confined to one aspect or dimension of the problem between the couple. It does not depend on the counsellor understanding, assessing or working with aspects of the individual's personality, or the couple or family relationships" (p. 2). If, on the other hand, the aim is to resolve conflict at a deeper level, so that people can manage to negotiate directly with each other and settle future difficulties by themselves, the intervention may be a more complex process relating to the problems of perception and communication which often underlie overt disputes. Madison suggests that "*conciliation* requires an assessment of the interaction between the couple, as a means of understanding the presenting problem. The counsellor works conjointly with the couple and facilitates their own efforts to reduce conflict, communicate and problem solve. The aim is to help the couple reach their own agreement with regard to the dispute and elements of their relationship that promote disputes between them. The method requires expertise in both the area of relationship skills and negotiation" (p. 2).

These definitions would not be appropriate in the United States, where "conciliation" generally applies to court-based and publicly funded schemes which concentrate on issues involving children, whereas "mediation" is the term used by practitioners in private practice, who are concerned with the emotional as well as practical aspects of divorce settlements. It does not seem possible at present to get a global consensus on terminology, but Madison's distinction between dispute-settling processes provides a useful starting-point for examining the different forms of conciliation which are being practised in Britain. It may be possible to highlight significant variables by exploring the following questions in relation to different systems and methods of conciliation:

1. The objectives of the process. Who sets it in motion, and whose needs is it primarily serving?
2. The location of the process. Does the physical location help to establish its identity or confuse it with other processes carried out in the same place?
3. The role of the conciliator. Is this role potentially in conflict with other roles carried by the same person?
4. The management of conciliation. Who controls the structure, rules and duration of the process? Are the parties free to decide what should be discussed and who should be involved in the discussion, or do they have no say in these matters? Can the content of the discussions be reported to the court, or used by one party to gain some advantage over the other?
5. The methods of conciliation. What methods are used, and what are the limitations and problems of these methods?

It may be easier to consider these questions if different processes which are loosely referred to as *conciliation* or *mediation* are placed in certain broad categories. In view of the variety of distinctions drawn between them, the two terms will be used interchangeably, to avoid increasing the confusion over terminology. The categories which will be considered are: 1) shuttle mediation, 2) brief structured conciliation, 3) in-court conciliation and 4) a settlement-seeking approach to welfare inquiries. These categories should not be seen as discrete nor as a comprehensive classification: some areas have developed hybrid schemes using a combination of systems and methods, whereas others adhere to one clearly defined model. Whether the term "conciliation" should be applied to all of them is debatable.

1 Shuttle Mediation

Shuttle mediation involves the use of a neutral third party, or mediator, acting as a go-between who shuttles to and fro beween the parties, providing them with a channel of communication without involving them in face-to-face negotiation. The mediator's role differs from that of solicitors in that the mediator is in direct communication with both parties without being aligned with either of them and the mediator is likely to be concerned with non-legal as well as legal aspects of the dispute. The mediator may offer to meet each party at a place of their own choosing or may invite them to separate meetings on neutral ground. The parties retain control over the extent to which they participate and are generally free to define the issues and set their own agenda, even though each party may have a different agenda.

Shuttle mediation is the method traditionally used by ACAS conciliators.

> Where conciliation is undertaken, the first step is usually a discussion of the dispute between the conciliator and each party separately, either at a briefing meeting or, if that is impracticable, by telephone ... The conciliator's prime objective in his preliminary briefing is to gain a clear understanding of the issues in dispute and the attitudes of the parties. He therefore seeks as much information as he needs and can obtain at that stage ... Preliminary briefing meetings usually provide the basis for an early assessment of the nature and dimensions of the dispute, the scope for conciliation and the best way to proceed (ACAS 1979 paras. 23 and 24).

Some mediators in the United States used this go-between method, carrying proposals or conditions backwards and forwards until a settlement was reached or until the effort was abandoned. Haynes applied his previous experience as a "'labor mediator" to divorce mediation (Haynes 1978, 1981):

> When the mediator meets with each party privately, he probes to determine what is possible. Frequently, one side uses the mediator to try out ideas that would be too risky to confront the other party with directly. The mediator then attempts to translate to each party what substantial areas of disagreement need to be resolved before a settlement can be reached ... As the mediator shuttles between the two parties, he creates an atmosphere of trust that permits either one to try out an idea without losing face ... it leaves both parties with their individual dignity intact (Haynes 1978 pp. 6-7).

It is interesting to learn that Haynes (1984) abandoned this shuttle mediation model because of the often insuperable problems he encountered in handling confidential information entrusted to him by one or both parties and because of problems relating to the parties' unequal bargaining power.

In England and Wales, court welfare officers and social workers have traditionally adopted the go-between role when making welfare inquiries and this is still common practice, especially in relation to matrimonial supervision orders. Many conciliators in independent schemes also showed an initial preference for shuttle mediation, possibly because this model was familiar to the social workers and counsellors involved in these schemes. Davis (1983a) suggested that

> many social workers habitually respond to conflict by being drawn into alliances. Hence the temptation to see the parties separately. This may give the feeling of support to both sides and avoids the tensions experienced by the mediator who has the much more difficult task holding the ring. The parties may also fear confrontation and so prefer to see the mediator separately. But in this way little can be achieved (p. 10).

The configuration in shuttle mediation can be represented by a simple triangle:

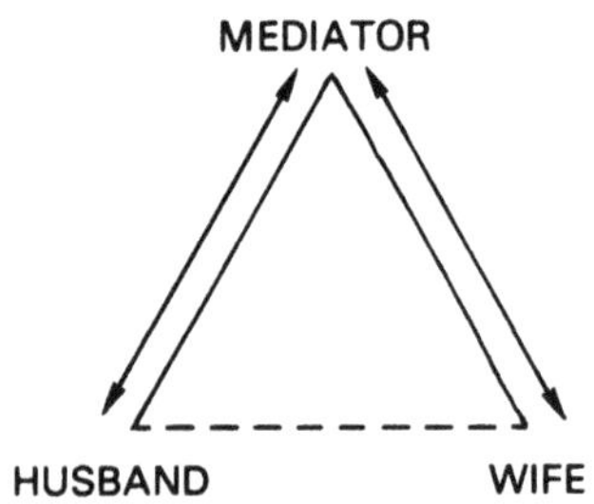

Case Example

Alan and Maureen Brown were referred to a conciliation service by their solicitors regarding Alan's access to his eight-year-old son, Roddy. Maureen had divorced Alan a year previously, on the basis of "unreasonable behaviour"; she had ended a previous marriage in the same way. It appeared that the two daughters of her first marriage, both now in their twenties and one of them married, had lost contact with their father, when he left home. Maureen complained that Roddy was upset by Alan's pressure to go out with him regularly, and that Alan often behaved carelessly and unreliably. She saw no value in the access visits, and did not want any contact with Alan, if it could be avoided. She accepted an appointment to see the mediator on her own, but was very resistant to the suggestion that this could be followed by a joint discussion with Alan.

In his separate appointment with the mediator, Alan said that he saw himself in a no-win situation, in which compliance with Maureen's conditions was his only chance of retaining contact with Roddy. He said that he had left the matrimonial home mainly to avoid the harm to Roddy of growing up in an increasingly bitter atmosphere in which he was torn between his parents. The house had belonged to Alan before his marriage to Maureen, and he now lived in a caravan near the site on which he was working. He complained that Maureen was repeatedly refusing his fortnightly access to Roddy, on one pretext or another. He was reluctant to apply to the court for a defined access order, partly because he feared incurring legal costs (he was not eligible for legal aid, and thought he would be at a disadvantage in trying to put his own case if Maureen was legally represented), and partly because he feared that Maureen would become even more hostile, if he applied to the court.

Maureen had raised a number of specific points, which the mediator put to Alan. One of these was that it was dangerous for Roddy to ride in the front seat of Alan's van, wearing an adult seat-belt, especially as Alan was allegedly a reckless driver. Alan denied the charge of reckless driving, but agreed to fix up a secure seat in the back of the van. He was particularly anxious to take Roddy to visit his parents in the Lake District during the Christmas holidays, and had asked Maureen to confirm the proposed dates. Maureen said, however, that she was taking Roddy with her to her married daughter in Kent and the dates unfortunately clashed, but in any case it was unwise to consider driving to the Lake District at the New Year, when the weather and road conditions were so unpredictable. Alan was infuriated by this reply, and by his powerless position. Even if he could obtain a court order in time, he suspected that Roddy would be "ill" at the last minute and "unable to travel". Maureen was not prepared to meet Alan to talk about these arrangements and she did not want Roddy involved in any way at all. Inevitably, in these circumstances, she and Alan had diametrically opposed views of Roddy's wishes and feelings.

After further discussion with the mediator, Maureen said that she would agree to the New Year trip if Alan and Roddy travelled by train. Alan objected to her controlling his travel arrangements, but finally gave in, seeing it as the price that had to be paid for having Roddy with him for several days. As Maureen usually refused to speak to him when he telephoned and normally said that it was not convenient for him to speak to Roddy either, the mediator managed to negotiate a time once a week when Alan could telephone Roddy and confirm weekend arrangements, without disturbing Roddy's tea or bedtime. In this way, some limited agreements were reached, but Maureen's co-operation was grudging, and the barriers may have gone up again when the mediator withdrew.

If the apparent outcome of mediation in this case is considered, the following conclusions might be drawn:

1. The mediator was not able to equalise the unequal bargaining positions of the two parties. Maureen had sole custody, care and control of Roddy, the occupation of the matrimonial home, and a maintenance order (which Alan was paying), while Alan was living in a caravan, on a greatly reduced income. Both parties preferred mediation to going to court but their inability to co-operate resulted in Alan being trapped in a catch-22 position, in which he felt obliged to concede to Maureen's demands, or risk losing access altogether. He did not have any confidence that a court order for defined access or even a matrimonial supervision order would ensure that his access to Roddy would take place, unless there was a change of attitude on Maureen's part.

2. If "settlement" is equated with "success", this case might have been rated as successful, as some limited agreements were reached and there were no contested court proceedings. Both parties were able to air their grievances to the mediator and this may have given them some relief, but they were no more able to negotiate with each other at the end of mediation than they had been at the beginning.

3. Roddy's actual feelings and anxieties were unknown to the mediator and it was not possible to assess how far he benefited, if at all, from the limited agreements that were reached.

One of the limitations of shuttle mediation is that the mediator's neutrality may be compromised by seeing each party separately. Acknowledging the validity of one party's point of view may be interpreted as support for that point of view, and any attempt to put a contrary point of view may be seen as bias towards the other party. A female mediator may be accused of having been taken in by a plausible husband, and a male mediator may be seen as easy prey for a scheming wife. If the two parties are not seen together, there is no means of demonstrating the mediator's evenly balanced position to both of them at the same time and each may have anxieties or fantasies about what has been said behind their back. A mediator who shuttles between two conflicting positions may be triangulated into the conflict, either being used by the dominant partner to press his or her demands on the weaker partner or becoming aligned with the weaker partner against the stronger one. The mediation triangle could then be re-drawn more realistically to show the dominant partner at the apex, controlling the process, with the mediator and the weaker partner at the base, apparently or actually aligned. Alternatively, the mediator may side with the more powerful party in encouraging the weaker one to give up.

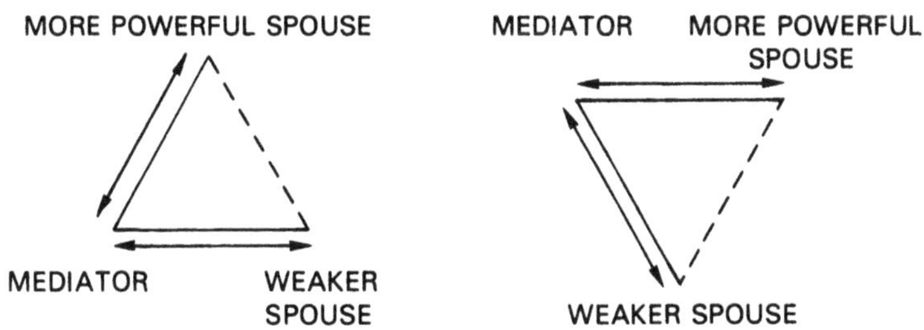

Davis and Bader (1985) reported that in 1981-82 when their research on in-court conciliation was undertaken, court welfare officers at Bristol and Newport tended to use shuttle mediation. Many conciliators in out-of-court services also used this method, at least initially. It is considerably easier to see both parties separately as they can avoid the stress of seeing and listening to each other and each can monopolise the mediator's attention and concern without having to share the mediator with each other. BCFCS reported that the preferred practice in 1983-84 was to begin by seeing each party alone. "Initially, couples are offered separate appointments ... It is unrealistic to believe that one can throw 2 people into a constructive discussion, when the very reason they need help is because their relationship has broken down" (BCFCS 1984 p. 9). One disadvantage of seeing the parties alone initially is that they may use this separate contact as a defence against meeting each other and communicating directly and the mediator is liable to be drawn into a counselling role of listening and empathising, instead of establishing a dialogue between the parties on particular issues or concerns.

Shuttle mediation may be a useful gateway to joint meetings with both parties, but, once begun, it may be harder to transfer to other ways of working. In a sample of 42 couples seen by BCFCS in March and April 1984, one-third were not seen together at any stage (BCFCS 1984) and the service acknowledged that "there are severe limitations to the work the conciliator can do if the couple are unable to agree to come to a joint appointment. The conciliator then has to negotiate at arm's length and the neutral position is much more difficult to sustain. When passing messages, it is difficult to distance oneself from the content of the message" (p. 9).

If mediators become trapped in the go-between role, there is a risk of them responding to the parties' conflict in an ad hoc, unstructured way, accepting urgent requests to telephone first one party and then the other, and getting drawn into long, emotional telephone conversations in which one party goes over familiar complaints or raises fresh objections in order to defer decisions. Apart from the possibility that the mediator is being used by one or both parties to prolong the conflict and provide a comfortable buffer at the same time, there is the practical consideration that shuttle mediation is an extremely expensive way of working. Mediators may expend a lot of time and effort without achieving significant change, and administrative and telephone costs are likely to be heavy. In certain circumstances, such as cases involving marital violence, physical illness or extreme stress, it may be appropriate to start mediation by seeing each party alone, but it is questionable whether this should be the method of first choice in all cases.

2 Brief Structured Conciliation

Brief structured conciliation is a process in which both parties agree to meet together with one or frequently two conciliators, who help them to clarify and if possible reach agreement on issues which they might otherwise contest in court. The practice of brief structured conciliation/mediation was developed in the United States by Coogler (1978) Haynes (1978, 1981) and others and in various parts of Canada (Irving 1980). Coogler (1978) advocated a very controlled process with detailed rules specifying the amount of time that could be spent on each stage of the discussions. Some commentators (Forster 1982) find Coogler's approach too rigid and impersonal and fear that it may act as a strait-jacket which prevents the parties from expressing strong feelings and concerns. A particular difference between the United States and Britain is that mediators in the United States deal to a very large extent with financial and property settlements (Haynes 1981, 1984), whereas British conciliators, both in private and court-based schemes, concentrate mainly on custody and access disputes. American mediators seek statements of income and expenditure from each party, help them draw up budgets and work out their tax liability and negotiate over the redistribution of the family's income. The knowledge and expertise needed for this type of mediation are extensive and raise broader questions about mediators' competence and accountability than those raised by current practice in Britain.

Allowing for differences in the nature and range of issues undertaken, structured conciliation involves a sequence of basic steps or stages of work. The sequence need not be followed mechanically and the time spent on each stage can be adapted to the level of conflict, the complexity of the issues and the emotional state of each party. These basic steps may be summarised as follows:

1. Engaging people in conciliation: obtaining a preliminary agreement from them to attend a joint or, if appropriate, family meeting to discuss decisions or difficulties, with the recognition that they may have different points of view but also a mutual interest in settling their affairs. Before inviting them to explain their respective positions and concerns, conciliators need to give them certain information, including the objectives and proposed duration of the meeting/s, the conciliator's role, the extent of confidentiality provided and the need for consent to liaise with their solicitors. Folberg and Taylor (1984) call this initial stage "creating trust and structure". A friendly, clear introduction to the process helps to reassure people at the outset that conciliators are sufficiently confident and competent to help them manage their anger, confusion and distress.

2. Gathering relevant facts. Basic information about the composition of the immediate family and living arrangements, the date and stage of separation/divorce, and any current applications to the court or existing court orders may have been provided by solicitors on a referral form but in any case its accuracy should be briefly checked. Certain details, such as the address of one party, may need to be held in strict confidence from the other party. Skill is needed to clarify essential facts in a non-authoritarian manner, before the parties become embroiled in the details of particular disputes.

3. Planning an agenda. This involves clarifying what is agreed and what is not agreed; the decisions that are needed and the time-scale for making them; whether anyone else who is not already present (children, new partners, grandparents) should be directly involved in working out these decisions; negotiating what issue/s should be given priority and whether some issues are being left entirely in the hands of solicitors. This stage helps conciliators to assess the emotional state

and needs of each party and of the family as a whole, in helping them to plan a practical and realistic agenda.

4. Exploring alternatives and options. Both parties should have an equal opportunity to explain their point of view and what they want to achieve. Conciliators help them to take stock of their options by asking questions, seeking clarification, providing neutral and non-directive information and suggesting other possibilities. The focus is on the present and the future, rather than the past and conciliators seek to identify mutual concerns and interests, particularly the position of children and aspects of parent-child relationships.

5. Negotiating possible agreements. Sometimes a short-term or trial arrangement may be worked out which helps people to overcome more fundamental blocks to agreement. This limited agreement may begin to restore their trust in each other so that they begin to co-operate on other issues. Negotiation skills and the need for separate legal advice to each party before final decisions are reached will be discussed further in subsequent chapters.

6. Summarising provisional agreements, or, if no agreement has been reached, considering the pros and cons of further conciliation. An interim or final summary of the outcome of conciliation should be drawn up with both parties, with copies sent to their solicitors (see the code of practice recommended by the National Family Conciliation Council's executive committee, Appendix A).

7. Reviewing agreements. It is helpful to anticipate difficulties that are likely to arise in practice, and if children have not so far been involved, conciliators should discuss with both parents whether the children should come to a family meeting at which the proposed arrangements can be explained to them in a reassuring way. People should also be encouraged to re-refer themselves if agreements break down or circumstances change, and the existence of community support groups, counselling services and other sources of help should be mentioned. If both parents feel adequately supported, agreements are more likely to be kept and children will feel less burdened by the need to support one parent.

Case Example

Pat and Colin Archer were referred for conciliation by their solicitors because Pat was opposed to Colin having access to their three-year-old daughter, Kelly. They accepted the offer of a joint appointment, with encouragement from their solicitors, who advised them to try to settle their dispute through conciliation before referring the matter to the court. Pat and Colin had been separated for three months; Pat had filed a divorce petition based on Colin's "unreasonable behaviour".

After introductions and preliminary explanation of the conciliation process, the conciliator checked the brief factual information provided by solicitors, establishing that there were no other children involved on either side. Pat was living alone with Kelly in the matrimonial home and Colin was living with his parents. The conciliator then invited Pat and Colin to talk about their particular concerns and priorities in relation to the access problem: they were asked not to interrupt each other, even if they disagreed with what was being said. Pat said, with mounting anger, that she thought Colin's access to Kelly was mainly for his mother's benefit and that Colin had never bothered much with Kelly and Kelly did not miss him if she did not see him. She also complained that Colin was not paying any maintenance for Kelly and she did not see why he should have access if he was not paying maintenance.

Colin was less angry and less articulate than Pat and did not find it easy to put his point of view. He acknowledged that his mother tended to take over Kelly, and that he had not insisted on looking after Kelly himself. He said that he was willing to give more time to her and that he was also willing to pay maintenance: he had been waiting for this to be sorted out by his solicitor. Pat's anger began to subside, as she realised that Colin was more co-operative than she had expected, and the conciliator commented that they both seemed concerned to put Kelly first and work out what they both thought would be best from her point of view. After discussing various possibilities regarding access, it was agreed that Colin would take Kelly out for a couple of hours on Saturday afternoons, which would allow Pat some time to do some shopping or see a friend, and that he would have Kelly for the day on alternate Sundays. On these Sundays, he would spend at least part of the time at his parents' home, sharing the care of Kelly with his mother but not handing over sole responsibility to her.

These proposals were summarised by the conciliator in wording which was agreed with Colin and Pat and a copy of the summary, marked "Without Prejudice", was sent to their solicitors. The solicitors then negotiated a maintenance agreement and applied for a court order with the consent of both parties, so that Colin could claim tax relief on the payments. Both Colin and Pat seemed to benefit from these agreements, as they produced practical advantages and reduced anxiety and stress. The outcome supported Deutsch's (1973) theory that the constructive settlement of a dispute can be mutual gain (win/win) for both parties, instead of mutual loss (lose/lose), or gain for one party and loss for the other (win/lose). The timing of the settlement is also extremely important, because empirical research indicates that it becomes progressively harder to establish regular access, once a child loses contact with the parent who leaves home (Wallerstein and Kelly 1980, Mitchell 1985).

McCrory (1985) suggests that the fundamental principles of conciliation are:

1. The voluntary nature of the process. The parties participate voluntarily and are free to accept a negotiated solution or to pursue their dispute in another way.
2. The impartiality of conciliators who have an equal and joint responsibility to both parties and to no other decision-making authority or process.
3. The confidentiality of the process. Negotiations take place on a "without prejudice" basis and the content of discussions is not reportable to the court or to anyone else without both parties' consent, unless the court orders disclosure. (The limits of confidentiality and the legal privilege attaching to conciliation will be discussed further in chapter 6.)
4. The informality of the process, within a basic framework. Discussions may be structured to a greater or lesser extent to facilitate direct communication and an informal exchange of views.

The techniques used by conciliators, the advantages and disadvantages of co-working and the problems and limitations of conciliation will be considered in more detail in subsequent chapters. The location also needs careful consideration. Some services operate from a medical setting which may imply that divorcing couples are sick people in need of some form of treatment. Medical specialists may be perceived as authority figures and these perceptions may decrease the autonomy and self-confidence of those referred to them for conciliation, especially if there are expectations of diagnosis and treatment.

3 In-Court Conciliation

There are important differences between an entirely voluntary process of conciliation initiated by the parties or their solicitors and a semi-mandatory form of conciliation initiated by the court. Although the courts have no power to order conciliation, the parties can be directed to attend a preliminary court appointment at which conciliation may take place and they may fear some penalty or disadvantage if they decline a recommendation of conciliation made by a registrar or judge. The parties may therefore participate under duress, without necessarily wanting conciliation or believing that it is likely to benefit their position. Moreover, research findings suggest that the location of conciliation in the court itself in the context of a formal hearing may confuse the process with adjudication, as far as the parties themselves are concerned (Davis and Bader 1985). Roberts (1983) expressed strong doubts about the desirability of linking conciliation explicitly with the authority and symbolism of the law:

> To me this represents a confusion that can sap the vitality both of negotiation and of the courts. The symbols of the law lie in terms of a hierarchical organisation of external authority, of imposed decisions, of coercion. All that is totally at odds with the spirit of negotiation which lies in the bargain, the agreement, the compromise. We simply cannot jack up conciliation by linking it in symbolic terms to the majesty of the law because it is an effort to get away from, to do without, the law (pp. 4-5).

(Roberts seems here to be using "the law" primarily in the sense of adjudication.)

Courts have a legitimate interest in promoting settlement and the success of the Bristol in-court conciliation scheme in settling a high proportion of contested cases without a full judicial hearing led to similar in-court schemes being introduced at other county courts and at the Principal Divorce Registry in London. A Practice Direction issued by the Senior Registrar on 2 November 1982 explained how the new procedure at the Principal Registry would operate:

> As from 1st January 1983, the Principal Registry of the Family Division will operate a pilot scheme of conciliation in contested applications in matrimonial proceedings for custody, access and variation thereof. The object of the scheme is to give an opportunity for agreement to be reached without the bitterness and exchange of recriminations which often develops between the parties when these issues remain in dispute. It may sometimes result in considerable saving of time and expense both to the parties and the court ... It is emphasised that it is extremely important that no affidavit should be filed or exchanged until after an unsuccessful concilia-

> tion appointment or until the registrar has so directed ... It is essential that both the parties and any legal advisers having conduct of the case attend. The nature of the application and the matters in dispute will be outlined to the registrar and the welfare officer. If the dispute continues, the parties and their advisers will be given the opportunity of retiring to a private room together with the welfare officer to attempt to reach agreement. These discussions will be privileged and will not be disclosed on any subsequent application ... If the conciliation appointment is successful, the registrar will make such orders as are agreed between the parties. If the appointment does not result in agreement being reached, any other subsequent application to a registrar will normally be dealt with by a different registrar and any further enquiry by a court welfare officer will be made by a different officer ... The party who has living with him or her any child aged 11 years or over, in respect of whom the dispute exists, should bring that child to the conciliation appointment, because it will sometimes be appropriate for the child to be seen by the registrar or the welfare officer. Any party upon whom a summons is served and who wishes to apply for legal aid should do so immediately. The Law Society will consider applications for emergency certificates in appropriate circumstances (*Family Law*, vol. 13 (1983), p. 5).

The aim of this procedure is to help the parties to settle matters by agreement but the court decides who should be present and the amount of time allowed and the process is under the court's control, rather than the parties' control. The content of the conciliation is not reportable to the court but the welfare officer's statutory role and attendance with the registrar confer an authority which could be used to press the parties to adopt the solution favoured by the welfare officer. Roberts (1983) has pointed out that a mediator who holds some formal status need not adopt a directive approach or use his authority to impose a solution, but "whatever posture the mediator of superior rank or specialist skill chooses to adopt" (p. 550 footnote), his intervention can never be seen by the disputants in the same light as that of a mediator who carries no formal status or authority. During 1983, almost one thousand conciliation appointments were held at the Principal Registry (more than one appointment is sometimes held in the same case). Two welfare officers were normally in attendance on the two days per week on which these appointments were held and each welfare officer was expected to undertake six or seven appointments per day, each lasting up to 45 minutes. The Senior Registrar reported informally that many contested cases were settled at these appointments and that requests for welfare reports were reduced substantially[1].

The aim of in-court conciliation is to settle contested cases as expeditiously as possible and avoid lengthy and bitter litigation, especially in divorces involving children. This is a worthwhile aim but research into the Bristol and Newport schemes (Davis and Bader 1985) suggested that the parties' satisfaction with the outcome was likely to depend to a large extent on the amount of time allowed for discussion of their respective concerns, on the skills and sensitivity shown by individual welfare officers and on the degree to which the parties participated in the decision-making. Some county courts adjourn cases to allow for one or more conciliation appointments of reasonable length (such as 1-2 hours) possibly away from court premises, rather than expecting conciliation to be completed on the spot, during a court session. A clearer boundary is then maintained between conciliation and adjudication, allowing the parties more time to put their point of view without the pressure and formality of the court setting (Price, Bilmes and Day 1985). This flexibility is preferable in many ways to a rigid division between in-court and out-of-court conciliation, though the fact that it is initiated by the court obviously gives it more status and power than a purely voluntary and independent scheme.

The Principal Registry scheme in London was extended by Registrar's Direction of 23 September 1983 to include section 41 appointments referred by a judge to a registrar for further inquiry and by a further Direction dated 31 October 1984[2] to include contested custody and access applications in guardianship and wardship proceedings (other than those in which a local authority is involved). This Practice Direction also lowered the age at which children should attend the conciliation appointment from eleven years to nine years and stated that if only one of two or more children is above the age of nine years, the younger child or children may also attend. The desirability of involving children in conciliation appointments at the court raises important questions. The pressure on children may be increased if inappropriate weight is given to their views and "wishes", especially if one or both parents brief them on what they should say. Davis and Bader, in their observation study at Bristol County Court (1982c), commented that

> it is of course extremely difficult to override the children's views

> in these circumstances if they are imparted directly. In a few cases, we observed the aftermath of these discussions where the child had clearly indicated that he or she did not want to see the non-custodial parent. It seemed to us that these occasions were extremely distressing for the rejected parent and that, potentially at least, they involved considerable costs for the child (p. 16).

If children are seen briefly at court by a welfare officer who has statutory responsibilities to protect "the best interests of the child", the principles of conciliation may become blurred with welfare principles and the lines of the welfare officer's accountability may get tangled.

It is questionable, therefore, whether attempts to reach a settlement during a court appointment should be called "conciliation" because the coercive element may be too strong (Davis 1983c). If the court considers that conciliation is appropriate and both parties agree to it, it should be separate and distinct from the judicial process. The terms "in-court" and "out-of-court"are confusing because they confuse process with location and blur important questions of authority and legal privilege. The court can promote conciliation by providing gateways which disputants can go through at different stages of the legal process. But there should be safeguards against a veiled or arbitrary use of the court's authority. The Practice Direction on Conciliation (1971) provided a formal basis for referrals to a court welfare officer for conciliation, without calling for a welfare inquiry at the same time. The conciliation could be undertaken either by a court welfare officer or by a conciliator working for a recognised voluntary agency. Reading County Court uses independent conciliators who work on a voluntary basis for Berkshire Family Conciliation Service and who are available at the court to take referrals from the registrar in appropriate cases. Most of the conciliation work is carried out in a room provided by the court but it may be continued if both parties accept the offer of further appointments at another location. About 70 conciliation cases were undertaken by the Berkshire service in 1983-84 and the registrar was reported to be very pleased with the way this system was working[3]. Other courts including some magistrates' courts are increasingly making referrals to conciliators, who may be welfare officers or part-time workers employed by an independent service. The question of paying independent conciliators for their work has not yet been resolved and the practice in some services of charging fees to the parties is problematic if the parties are referred to the service by the court, even if the fees are waived for those who cannot afford to pay.

Court-related conciliation in Britain has developed so far without any national framework of principles and rules, in contrast to countries such as Australia (see chapter 9), where the various functions of court counsellors are defined in different sections of the Family Law Act 1975.

A Settlement-Seeking Approach to Welfare Inquiries

There has been considerable controversy in England and Wales as to whether "conciliation" can be combined with reporting to the court. This has not been an issue in Scotland, where there is no separate divorce court welfare service staffed by probation officers: reports for Scottish courts are prepared by social workers or lawyers. In England and Wales, some county courts have allowed welfare officers to undertake conciliation and then make recommendations to the court if no agreement is reached. This practice is not supported by the President of the Family Division of the High Court (Arnold 1983), who has expressed the view that if a conciliation attempt fails, the parties should not find themselves in a position in which disclosures made in all good faith during conciliation are "thrown back in their teeth as part of the confrontational process in court" (p. 3). The Booth Committee also emphasised the differences between conciliation and welfare inquiries in a Consultation Paper published in 1983: "Conciliation encourages the parties to take the responsibility of making decisions themselves; the preparation of a report recognises that such decisions must instead be taken by the court and for this purpose it is the task of the welfare officer to investigate and assess the proposals of the respective parties" (1983 par. 4.10). There is certainly a strong argument that the principles of conciliation are violated if admissions or other information derived from conciliation are used subsequently to assist the court's decisions. Even if the parties raise no objection to a report being made, they may not have grasped that the welfare officer who acted as a conciliator was also making assessments and evaluations which might be detrimental to one or both of them, since the welfare officer has a statutory duty when making an inquiry to report all relevant matters to the court.

When a welfare inquiry is ordered by the court and used by the welfare officer to help parents reach agreement, there cannot be any question of confidential discussions, but much depends on the welfare officer's method of approach. Two court welfare officers (Francis and Shaw 1981) wrote that

> in Leicestershire the divorce court welfare officer's report which was once a request for information has now become an opportunity to mediate. The parties are drawn together to work jointly on their responsibility for their children's future, the work goes on during the "enquiries" and ideally the welfare report merely becomes a retrospective summary of what has been achieved. The parties are not permitted to use the request for a welfare report from the court to relinquish their parental responsibility into the hands of outsiders (p. 72).

Eekelaar (1982) found that welfare officers helped parents to reach agreement in 36 per cent of contested custody cases, 59 per cent of contested access cases and in 46 per cent of cases where custody and access were both in dispute. He concluded from this evidence that welfare officers have an important part to play in facilitating agreements, even when the referral to the welfare officer takes place at a late stage in the legal process. A senior court welfare officer (Taylor 1984) emphasised that a welfare inquiry should be "a whole family welfare investigation that has a conciliatory approach" (p. 302) and his use of the words "welfare" and "investigation" show that although the aim is to help parents reach agreement, the statutory context must be recognised. Parents are often helped by welfare officers to work out their own solutions and a settlement-seeking approach by welfare officers may reduce the number of cases requiring a judicial decision to a very small number indeed (Price, Bilmes and Day 1985). However, the court has no powers to compel disputants to take part in conciliation and if the request for a welfare report is used to force people into a conciliation process against their will, we run the risk of the "rampant interventionism" of which Freeman (1984) has warned.

Apart from the lack of clarity about the welfare officer's primary function, there are differences of view about the methods that should be used in the context of a welfare inquiry. Welfare officers who believe strongly in the value of a family systems approach (see chapter 6) argue that instead of colluding with parents who are trying to hand over their authority and responsibility to the court they enable many parents to work out difficult decisions themselves (Taylor 1984). Other welfare officers question the assumption of parental competence and rationality implicit in these methods, pointing out that "if we were to allow a blanket assumption of parental competence to supersede the long established values of child welfare, and where necessary child protection, we would at the last find the baby had vanished with the bath water" (Pugsley and Wilkinson 1984 p. 92). Pugsley and Wilkinson believed nonetheless that "conciliation can continue within the legal process. The report itself can be an instrument of conciliation" (p. 91). They saw no fundamental conflict between the role of conciliator and that of report-writer, because "it is our experience that the parties often accept our descriptions and our opinions, even when they are not supportive of their application" (p. 91). Pugsley and Wilkinson's interpretation of "conciliation" seems to mean steering the parties towards an outcome defined and approved by the welfare officer, showing that those who warned that conciliation might become a disguised form of paternalistic control were justified in voicing their fears. King (1981) cautioned that

> however much one might agree with these efforts to minimise the conflict, what is being offered is hardly "participant justice". Solutions are still being imposed by professionals, if not directly, then indirectly through persuading and cajoling. It is really not much less paternal than the present system, for despite . . . talk of "openness" and "shared decisions", it is values of the professional advisers and decision-makers which will prevail in most cases and not those of the participants (p. 44).

The increasing number of welfare officers using a family systems approach, working with parents and children together in a neutral, non-judgemental way, deny that that they urge parents to accept their views of what is "best" for the children. Taylor (1984) ruefully observed that the neutrality of the welfare officer using this approach is not fully understood by those not familiar with it. The use of techniques derived from family therapy has led to further confusion and conflict among professionals about who is doing what to whom, under the label of "conciliation". Davis (1982a) argued that "consideration of individual rights and of justice between the parties could be subverted by notions of treatment and therapy . . . [and] the conduct of the legal process should not be based upon couples' willingness to undergo any kind of treatment" (p. 127). This comment echoed the Finer Committee's view that "the court must not see the men, women and children with whom it is concerned as 'clients' and still less as 'patients' for whom the court process is one form of . . . 'treatment'" (Report 1974 par. 4.285). But Davis may not have appreciated that some techniques derived from family therapy can be used with families without submitting them to therapy as such. He has also provoked debate by accusing welfare officers of "stealing" conciliation (Davis 1985) by laying claim to it as part of their statutory reporting task. It is ironic that the term "conciliation" should have given rise to so much controversy: like so many marital disputes, this is partly due to muddle and misunderstanding as well as to a conflict of principle. The dispute over the custody, care and control of conciliation could be settled if its principles and methods are clearly defined and if it is agreed that similar settlement-seeking methods can be used in different contexts, provided that there is clarity about the roles and responsibilities applicable in each context. Moreover, the evidence that some welfare officers and some conciliators in independent services steer people in certain directions (Davis and Bader 1985, Dingwall, in press) does not prove that conciliation invariably "becomes a cloak to let yet another group of professionals take over" (Freeman 1981). Shepherd and Howard (1985a) argued in a sharp riposte to Davis (1985) that their methods of working – which have not been researched so far – increase parents' autonomy instead of undermining it: they deny banging people's heads together and telling them what to do. Nonetheless, their statutory authority as welfare officers gives them a different role and "image" from that of the independent conciliator.

The status and powers of conciliators need further clarification, to establish their independence of statutory authority and control. However, this freedom from external control makes internal monitoring and supervision all the more important. Questions of conciliators' accountability may be particularly unclear in relation to in-court conciliation appointments, which may be staffed by statutory or voluntary workers or by conciliators from both sectors working in a combined team. Whatever organisational structure is used, difficult balances have to be maintained between public and private interests. It is in the public interest to provide a cost-effective system of settling disputes, provided that economic pressures do not result in conciliation becoming a thinly veiled form of arbitration in which professionals engineer quick settlements without much concern about either justice or welfare. On the one hand, there is anxiety about too much authority being exercised by conciliators, and on the other hand, a fear that they may not be able to protect the weaker party from being bullied into surrender by the stronger one. The very real problem of inequalities of bargaining power between the parties will be considered in chapter 7.

Notes

1. L. Parkinson, "Conciliation – The English Experience", paper given at the Solicitors' Family Law Association seminar on "Conciliation – The Australian Experience", Royal Courts of Justice, London, 15 May 1984 (1984a).
2. Practice Direction on Custody of, and Access to, Children: Conciliation 31 October 1984, *Family Law*, vol. 15 (1985), p. 20.
3. Berkshire Family Conciliation Service, *Annual Report, 1983-84.*

Suggested Reading

Booth Committee *Consultation Paper*, Lord Chancellor's Department, 1983, and *Report* (HMSO, London, 1985).
G. Davis, "Conciliation – A Dilemma for the Divorce Court Welfare Service", *Probation Journal*, (December 1982), and "The Theft of Conciliation", *Probation Journal*, vol. 32 (March 1985).
J. Howard and G. Shepherd, "Conciliation – New Beginnings?", *Probation Journal*, September 1982.
S. Roberts, "Mediation in Family Law Disputes", *Modern Law Review* (September 1983).
G. Shepherd and J. Howard, "Theft of Conciliation? The Thieves Reply", *Probation Journal* (June 1985).

6 THE ROLE OF THE CONCILIATOR IN SEPARATION AND DIVORCE

This chapter considers some questions concerning the selection and training of conciliators in separation and divorce and the kinds of knowledge and skills they need. It includes some discussion of the confidentiality of conciliation in the event of subsequent litigation, as different categories of legal privilege are not always familiar even to experienced solicitors, let alone inexperienced conciliators. Although some disputes may settle relatively easily, the complexity and potential pitfalls of conciliation should not be underestimated: if they are played down, disillusion may replace enthusiasm and support for conciliation may wane.

Anthropologists such as Gulliver (1971) and Roberts (1983) have shown that the role of conciliator is well established in many cultures and may even be universal. In the societies they describe, conciliators perform their task without formal training and this has led some commentators to question why conciliators in Britain need formal qualifications or specialist training. The anti-elitist view of conciliation is that an ordinary person with sufficient goodwill, common sense and life experience and some basic negotiation skills may be just as effective as a highly qualified professional and probably more acceptable to couples in difficulty. Davis (1983a) shares Abel's suspicion (1982) that insistence on specialist training for conciliators may be a means of creating an exclusive occupational group which can corner the market and build up its status. "Informal justice . . . spawns its own specialists who, not surprisingly, become its strongest boosters. They ensure that informal institutions foster dependence on paraprofessional mediators, counsellors, and advocates, notwithstanding the rhetoric of disputant participation and self-reliance" (Abel 1982 p. 303).

There is truth in this charge. On the other hand, it can be argued that conciliation among the Ndendeuli in a dispute over the payment of bridewealth (Gulliver 1971) is a very different matter from conciliation in Britain in the shadow of a powerful legal system which can determine parental rights and re-allocate private income and jointly owned property. Britain is a complex multi-cultural society whose laws and social institutions impinge on family life in numerous ways. Conciliators are not (or should not be) agents of social control who persuade or coerce people to conform to established norms but they cannot operate in a vacuum, ignoring the legal, financial and social context in which divorce takes place. One of the conciliator's main tasks is to help the parties consider the options available to them and to weigh up the relative merits of different options. To do this, conciliators must be aware of potential risks, such as the fact that housing departments regard people as voluntarily homeless if they sell the matrimonial home and then apply for council accommodation. The responsibility to advise individuals lies with solicitors, not with conciliators, and people should obtain legal advice before entering into agreements. However, some individuals remain confused or resist seeking advice and a conciliator who is as much at sea as they are in unfamiliar legal procedures and terminology would not only be of no help to them but, worse still, might encourage them to give undertakings and sign disastrous agreements which could turn out to be legally binding.

Separating and divorcing individuals are particularly vulnerable to pressures of all kinds and the decisions they take in the crisis of separation are often the basis of long-term arrangements which are not easily modified or reversed (Mitchell 1985). People should therefore be safeguarded as far as possible from the risks of being coerced into agreements without understanding the probable consequences and from the malpractice to which they might be exposed if there were no recognised system of accreditation for conciliators. The National Family Conciliation Council grew out of the awareness of these risks and from concern that individuals with unresolved problems related to personal divorce might seek to grind a particular axe by setting themselves up as conciliators. In recognition of the responsibilities incumbent on conciliators and their employers, the National Family Conciliation Council (1982) drew up a list of criteria which must be met by services granted full affiliation to the Council. These criteria include requirements that:

1. The Management Committee of the service must include members of the social work and legal professions. If possible, there should be a solicitor specialising in divorce and family work, who also represents the local Law Society.
2. The Management Committee must ensure the proper selection, training, supervision and accountability of its staff and provide adequate accommodation, secretarial support and other facilities. If the service is provided under the wing of another organisation or if premises are shared with another service, the conciliation ser-

vice must be managed separately so that it has a separate identity and the confidentiality of its records is safeguarded.
3. Conciliators appointed to the service must have relevant qualifications and subsequent experience in marital or family work and must be willing to accept further training. Their work must be supervised by a person with a professional qualification in social work.

These criteria are almost identical to those followed by the Law Society (*Legal Aid Annual Report 1981-82*, section 16) when authorising an extension under the Green Form scheme which allows a £15 fee to be paid via a solicitor to an approved conciliation service, where the solicitor has referred a "Green Form" or legally aided client to the service for the purpose of "clarifying the issues between the parties". Previously, the fee payable to certain conciliation services under a "blanket" extension had been £20. The Law Society's criteria specify that conciliators should be qualified social workers or probation officers, "although, for example, a suitably trained marriage guidance counsellor might also be appropriate" (p. 15). The criteria also stipulate that initial and continuing training must be provided for conciliators and that both parties must be seen in any case in which a fee is applied for under the Green Form scheme.

The questions as to whether conciliators must be qualified professionals and if so, what qualifications should be accepted are controversial, and may distract attention from equally important questions concerning the personal qualities and values of conciliators. Zetzel (1985) pointed out that everyone carries an intangible but bulky collection of ideals, images and values about family life, and we need to examine how conciliators' values might intrude in their work, consciously or unconsciously. Those with responsibility for recruiting and selecting conciliators need to screen out applicants who show signs of dogmatic attitudes, personal grievance or prejudice, or zeal to impart some message to divorcing couples. The personal values of prospective conciliators should be explored with them because disputes arising from marriage breakdown and divorce raise all kinds of controversial moral and social issues, on which society as a whole may be deeply divided. For example, family conciliation services, like the courts, support children's right to have access to both parents, but this principle may be alien to the cultural norms of some parents and there may be risks of doctrinaire views being imposed on families in an authoritarian way. Conciliators should not arbitrate, but parents may try to make them do so, and they may be faced with particularly controversial situations where for example the homosexuality of one parent is used by the other in an attempt to win a battle over custody or access. In these potentially stormy waters, conciliators need a reasonably watertight structure of basic rules and principles to help them steer their way without capsizing.

Conciliation is contained by three different kinds of boundaries which are designed to structure the process and protect it from abuse. First, there is the physical boundary of neutral territory which should be reserved exclusively for conciliation and not also used for different activities which might confuse people's perceptions and expectations of conciliation. Antagonistic couples who refuse to meet on each other's home ground may need a private, neutral place, free from distressing associations and interruptions, which offers some degree of protection. This safe area of common ground has both practical and symbolic value, and reception and seating arrangements need to be planned with care. Secondly, there is a time boundary, since conciliation is a time-limited process and its duration should be agreed with both parties at the outset and extended only by mutual consent. Awareness that time is limited can help people concentrate on the main issue/s and explain their position concisely instead of exhaustively, but if the time is too brief they are liable to feel pressurised and devalued. Solicitors need to be kept informed of the projected time-scale for conciliation, since time itself may be an important factor if adjudication is necessary, especially in a custody dispute. Thirdly, there is the boundary of confidentiality which prevents conciliators from disclosing information about either party without their consent and from giving personal evaluations which might be used to influence a judicial decision.

The structure of the conciliation process helps people to deal with highly emotional questions in a non-adversarial way, with a focus on collaborative effort. The rationality of the structure is important, but rationality alone can be chilling and the personal qualities of conciliators may be at least as important to those who approach them as their professional expertise. Generally speaking, the most important qualities for a conciliator (not listed in order of importance) seem to be:

1. Personal warmth: the ability to engage anxious and angry people and gain their trust.
2. Maturity, preferably including personal experience of marriage and bringing up children.

3. Sensitivity to distress: the ability to relate to varying degrees of distress and to gauge whether an individual is in need of help other than conciliation.
4. Impartiality and even-handedness: a respect for the validity of different points of view.
5. Firmness in establishing the ground-rules of conciliation and keeping sufficient control.
6. Flexibility in selecting a method and pace of work appropriate to the level of conflict and in choosing words which make sense to the couple or family concerned.
7. Down-to-earth common sense in identifying practical options and anticipating probable difficulties.
8. Clarity in noting salient points in a jumble of confusing information.
9. Open-mindedness in laying aside personal values and avoiding dogmatic or stereotyped responses.
10. Sufficient dynamism to help counteract the depression of divorce and to act as a catalyst for constructive decisions.
11. Humour: used sensitively, humour can help restore equilibrium and common sense.
12. Patience: the ability to tolerate frustration and disappointment.
13. Humility in lacking answers to problems and being able to recognise when another person or agency might be more helpful.
14. Attention to detail. Some agreements may hinge on fine details of time, exact place or apparently minor matters which are charged with emotional significance for one or both parties. Conciliators need to be accurate, reliable, and well-organised in keeping concise factual records of dates of meetings, main issues discussed and any provisional arrangements. (These notes should act as an aide-memoire, without containing subjective opinions or assessments.)

Although conciliators cannot be paragons who display all these qualities in equal measure, those who appoint them should consider what qualities they are seeking, since conciliators' personal style and manner of approach may enhance or restrict their skills in negotiation and conciliation.

Training for Conciliation

Voluntary conciliation services in Britain have generally taken the view that conciliators need additional specialist training, however knowledgeable and experienced they may be in related disciplines. Many of the early training programmes provided by individual services aimed to give prospective conciliators an adequate grasp of divorce law and procedure and some knowledge of the roles and responsibilities of solicitors, registrars, judges, magistrates and court welfare officers. This legal orientation is essential, but it needs to be combined with teaching the ground-rules of conciliation and the practical skills required. Attention should also be given to the considerable strains of conciliation work and the need for professional support and supervision. As Zetzel (1985) says, conciliators are regularly faced with situations which challenge their equanimity, and rather than assume that they can automatically function in a neutral, dispassionate way, we should recognise that their personal reactions need to be taken into account. The opportunity to share feelings spontaneously with a colleague immediately after a stressful session may be just as important for conciliators' sanity as provision for regular supervision.

Training for conciliation can be usefully divided into three main sections: A) basic principles and ground-rules, B) necessary background knowledge and C) practical skills. Many independent services in Britain began by running a short basic training programme for prospective conciliators totalling about 20 hours, but in the United States 40 hours is often considered the minimum even for people with previous professional training in related disciplines. Knowledge and experience derived from social work, counselling, law, psychology etc. may be very useful, but conciliators need to be able to lay aside habits and assumptions fostered by their profession of origin. Folberg and Taylor (1984) suggest that this involves a shift in the internal map which we rely on to guide us as we move from one task to the next. The map of a therapist or counsellor may trace underlying causes and interconnections, whereas a conciliator's map needs to lead more directly to mutually identified landmarks. The territory may be fundamentally the same but a conciliator moves over it in a different way from a counsellor or therapist and with different objectives.

A. Basic Principles and Ground-rules of Conciliation

The first stage of training should include defining the conciliation task and clarifying the boundaries between conciliation, the legal process and counselling or therapy. The code of practice recommended by the National Family Conciliation Council's executive committee (Appendix A) should be considered carefully, because conciliators move in relatively uncharted professional waters and need to be alive to the hazards. Solicitors may switch abruptly from a conciliatory stance to adversarial action and tricky questions can arise in practice from the various triangular communications which take place between solicitors, conciliators, each party and the court (Parker and Parkinson 1985). Conciliation services normally give assurances of confidentiality, but this needs to be distinguished from the legal privilege that may attach to conciliation as a process.

English law has long recognised the value of "without prejudice" negotiations in encouraging the settlement of disputes. The legal privilege attaching to such negotiations derives from the public interest in the settlement of disputes, so that neither party need be deterred from attempting to reach a settlement by the fear that admissions or other information disclosed during discussions could be used to one party's advantage in court. If the negotiations produce an agreement, the protection of the "without prejudice" privilege falls away and the terms of the agreement and the way it was arrived at can be examined in court. The Morton Commission (1956) recommended that this privilege should be extended to marriage guidance counselling and a bill was promoted in 1963 that a marriage guidance counsellor should not be a compellable witness in court proceedings. This bill never became law and there is no legislation in England and Wales or in Scotland which provides a specific ruling on the privilege attaching to matrimonial conciliation. Case law has however established that where parties to a matrimonial dispute consult a third party with a view to possible reconciliation their discussions are legally privileged, on the grounds that there is a public interest in the stability of marriage. In the case of McTaggart v. McTaggart (1948)[1], the Court of Appeal held that statements made to a probation officer in this context were privileged and Lord Denning had no doubt that "the rule as to 'without prejudice' communications applies with especial force to negotiations for reconciliation" (p. 755). The privilege was also upheld in the cases of Mole v. Mole (1950)[2] and Theodoropoulos v. Theodoropoulos (1963)[3], where it was held that the privilege belonged to both parties jointly and could be waived only with their joint consent. In the case of Pais v. Pais (1970)[4], Lord Justice Baker took a similar view, holding that the privilege attaching to matrimonial conciliation attaches to the process and not to the type of professional involved.

These rulings may prevent one party from using the content of conciliation discussions to his or her advantage in subsequent litigation but they do not protect the conciliator from being called to give evidence if both parties choose to waive their privilege (McCrory 1985). Arguably, the privilege should belong to all participants so that it can be waived only with the conciliator's consent as well as that of both parties[5]. In considering extensions of legal privilege in relation to the case of D. v. NSPCC[6], Lord Hailsham said that "the categories of public interest are not closed, and must alter from time to time ... as social conditions and social legislation develop" (p. 605). The President of the Family Division of the High Court in England and Wales (Arnold 1983) has expressed the view that legal privilege should be extended to conciliation on child-related issues, and his advice was sought on the drafting of the National Family Conciliation Council's Code of Practice (Appendix A). The privilege is unlikely to be treated as absolute[7], however, because in exceptional cases where a child's interests might be jeopardised by excluding evidence of something said during conciliation, the principle of privileged negotiations might be overridden by the "best interests of the child" principle, if the two were found to be in direct conflict. In practice, it is unlikely that a conciliator would be ordered to give evidence because the court would normally call for a full inquiry by a welfare officer, without reference to earlier conciliation.

A few unreported cases have already arisen in England in which one party (or a solicitor) has attempted to gain some advantage by reporting to the court information allegedly derived from conciliation. The courts have generally upheld the concept of privilege by ruling that such evidence, including evidence of non-attendance at a conciliation appointment, is not admissible. A precedent on the applicability of the rules of privilege in the context of conciliation is urgently needed to clarify this grey area of the law. In Scotland a case has also arisen in which a conciliator was called as a witness but she was not finally required to give evidence (Ross 1985a). The category of privileged evidence in Scotland is very restricted and recent decisions by Scottish courts suggest that a conciliator would be regarded as a competent and compellable witness in certain circumstances (Doran 1984).

B. Background Knowledge for Conciliation

Areas of background knowledge which are helpful to conciliators and arguably essential may be sub-divided into three parts: i) legal knowledge, ii) knowledge about marital and family interaction and iii) knowledge of adult and child development.

i) Legal knowledge. For those without legal qualifications, training for conciliation should provide a rudimentary grounding in matrimonial law and procedure. This should include knowledge of divorce and other matrimonial legislation; knowledge of legal procedures and the Matrimonial Causes Rules (particularly Rule 76A, which deals with applications for a consent order); knowledge of the various provisions relating to domestic violence; and knowledge of the availability of the Green Form scheme and legal aid. Conciliators need to understand the duties and responsibilities of solicitors, registrars, judges, magistrates and court welfare officers, as this understanding helps them to be clear about their own role and its boundaries. They also need to be fully aware of the legal implications of custody and access decisions and of an unforced decision to leave the matrimonial home, so that they can explain the need for legal advice from a solicitor on such matters. Conciliators are not substitutes for solicitors, but it is essential that they have a sound grasp of the legal frame of reference in which decisions are taken in separation and divorce.

ii) Knowledge about marital and family interaction. Some of the most difficult disputes between separated, divorcing or divorced couples are those in which one or both partners cannot let go of their relationship, however painful it may be, perhaps because of deep fears of being totally alone. Conciliators need to be aware of the ambivalent feelings harboured by many couples and the tendency for marital conflicts to spill over into other family relationships, affecting all those involved in different ways or degrees. Every family is unique, but families experience particular stresses at turning-points in what has been termed the life-cycle of the family (Carter and McGoldrick 1980) and conciliators benefit from having at least some general knowledge about the ways in which predictable or unpredictable events (such as children being born or leaving home, illness in the family, the onset of disability or the death of a grandparent) may trigger a breakdown in an already fragile marriage. Communication problems may be exacerbated by worries about money or employment and although conciliators cannot alter these social pressures, they need to be sensitive to their effects.

The disputes which couples bring to conciliation may arise from internal and/or external pressures and conciliators may be more effective if they recognise these contextual issues even though they do not deal with them directly. The roles of men and women in society are seen differently today from the way they were seen in our parents' and grandparents' generations and some of the conflicts over child custody and access to children arise from confused expectations of parenting roles. These problems often come to a head when one parent acquires a new partner or remarries and the conflict may then centre on the role of this third party. Children may be given conflicting messages to accept or reject this newcomer in their lives and may suffer profound bewilderment and isolation (Mitchell 1985). Conciliators need to understand the differences between nuclear families and step-families (Visher and Visher 1979, Hodder 1985), helping parents in new marriages to feel secure without necessarily discarding parent-child relationships from a previous marriage.

iii) Adult and child development. Unresolved emotional problems within individuals can fuel conflict and act as a block to agreement, and conciliators should therefore be aware of the experience of bereavement and loss for adults and children and the stages which individuals need to work through in order to cope with loss (Bowlby 1973, Parkes 1975, Kaslow 1981). Although conciliators do not counsel people through the often lengthy process of grieving for the lost marriage, as a counsellor or therapist may do, the level of emotion cannot be ignored because the physical presence of both partners may unleash powerful feelings of anger, vulnerability and distress. The element of irrationality in these feelings needs to be recognised even if it is not the focus of work: some feelings may need to be released before any constructive negotiations can take place. Some couples may vent their feelings explosively, whereas others may suppress or deny them. Conciliators need to make some assessment of the stage each partner has reached in disengaging from a broken relationship, in order to help them plan the agenda for discussion and a realistic time-scale for reaching decisions.

Conciliators also need to have some basic knowledge of child development and child psychology, not because they set themselves up as experts who know better than parents what their children need, but for a number of other reasons. A conciliator's understanding of the way children of different ages and stages of development react to parental conflict and family break-up may enable them to throw helpful light on children's reactions, which are often interpreted differently by estranged parents. The Justice report on parental rights and duties and custody suits (1975), referred to in chapter 4, listed the contradictory ways in which custodial and non-custodial parents may interpret their children's distress before, during or after access visits. For example, the custodial parent may attribute the distress to fear, dislike of, or anger with the absent parent, whereas the visiting parent may be convinced that the distress is due to indoctrination by the custodial parent and the child's fear of losing his or her approval. Without putting either parent down, conciliators may help them to see their children's difficulties in a different light. Children are not inanimate objects to be collected and deposited like parcels: a focus on their perceptions and feelings may lead to co-operation between parents, whereas arguing over adult claims and rights increases hostility and competition.

C. Practical Skills in Conciliation

Rather than compiling a long and possibly superficial list of the skills applicable to conciliation, it may be more helpful to look at a few basic skills and comment briefly on how they may be used in practice. Welfare officers, social workers and counsellors have not necessarily received training in conjoint work with two or more distressed and angry people, nor are they necessarily experienced in managing family meetings. Conciliators need particular skills in working with couples and families, especially in relation to conflict management, and training courses should include experiential exercises as well as other teaching methods. Role-playing different scenarios helps conciliators to gain practical insights into people's reactions, including their own, and to practise basic skills such as: i) clarifying and defining issues and options; ii) reframing; iii) confronting; iv) managing open conflict; v) negotiating.

i) Clarifying and defining issues and options. When one parent's application for custody or access is contested by the other or when a respondent seeks to defend the petition, the issue in dispute has been identified to some extent (although the "real issue" may turn out to be different when the parties come to court). Referrals for pre-court conciliation often take place before a divorce petition has been filed and these situations may be very unclear. In many cases the dust of one partner's sudden departure has not settled at all and the air may be thick with confused impressions and uncertainty. The first stage of finding out what is agreed between couples and what is not agreed involves gathering relevant facts (American mediators call this "data collection" – Haynes 1981), some of which may have been supplied by solicitors on a referral form. Apart from basic information about the composition of the family and where parents and children are living (actual addresses may need to be kept in strict confidence), it is important for conciliators to know whether legal proceedings have been started, whether a dispute has already been referred to the court (and if so, to which court), and whether there are any existing court orders. One of the reasons for asking permission to contact solicitors is that the parties themselves are often unclear about the stage of the legal process and even about existing court orders. If there is a non-molestation order in force or a matrimonial supervision order, this may have substantial implications for conciliation and should be known at the outset, if possible.

If separation is recent or has not yet taken place, conciliators need to be particularly careful not to assume that a permanent separation, with or without divorce, is inevitable. Solicitors often refer cases in which one party's decision to separate or divorce is opposed by the other and it should be explained that although conciliators do not set out to achieve a reconciliation, neither are they promoting divorce: the outcome of conciliation must be open-ended or one party will feel disadvantaged from the outset. The aim of the process is to help both parties take stock of their respective positions and alternatives, and if possible reach mutually agreed decisions. Because people may be afraid of losing face or admitting their mixed feelings, conciliators need to use what Haynes (1982) described as "third ear listening", picking up hesitations, ambivalence or contradictions which may not be stated explicitly. Some individuals start divorce proceedings not because they want a divorce, but because they believe there is no other solution to the breakdown in their marriage. If they have grounds for divorce – and they are easy to find – divorce proceedings may be started very quickly and both parties may then lose the opportunity to consider other possible courses of action. The conciliator's task in clarifying each party's position and the practical alternatives differs from the task of counsellor or therapist. Without exploring feelings in depth, the conciliator should try to identify any fundamental misunderstandings between the couple, as well as drawing their attention to possibilities they may not have considered. It is important to distinguish a dispute over the divorce itself or the principle of access from a "when and how" dispute over the timing of the divorce or the frequency and duration of access visits.

Conciliators need to be alert for assumptions which may be due to lack of information or inadequate communication. In one extreme case, a wife had filed an inflammatory divorce petition, believing that it was unlawful to live apart from her husband. He was preparing to defend the divorce. However, when the conciliator explained to them both that a judicial separation or deed of separation might be possible, the wife sought further legal advice on separation, and an acrimonious divorce was then avoided. In some cases, a dialogue may open up between the couple which suggests that they want to explore ways of changing their marriage instead of ending it. If the focus then shifts from divorce to possible reconciliation, conciliators usually encourage referral to a marriage guidance counsellor. In this way a boundary can be maintained between conciliation and marital counselling without positive options being ruled out prematurely. These options are unlikely to emerge if conciliators take initial statements at face value and neglect to clarify whether the action embarked on is the action both partners actually want to take. The clarification of options in relation to separation, divorce or possible reconciliation is particularly important in Britain, where relatively few couples referred for conciliation have previously sought marital counselling or therapy, whereas in the United States many couples have seen a counsellor or therapist and are therefore more likely to have explored and ruled out other options by the time they see a divorce mediator.

ii) Reframing. In simple terms, reframing (also known as "positive connotation" – Haley 1976) consists of offering people another way of looking at things, in a way which encourages more positive attitudes. This is a useful technique in conciliation, because some couples habitually read a hostile intention into every word or gesture from each other and this hostility may be only one facet of a complex interaction between them. An adversarial approach to a custody dispute may result in a destructive contest as to which parent is the "good" parent, whereas both may be equally competent and caring. The polarising question: "Which of you is the better parent?" can be reframed by conciliators as "How can both of you jointly support and care for your children, in spite of the ending of your marriage?" Differences can then be explored in terms of mutual concerns instead of competitive interests. For example, conciliators' recognition that one parent's opposition to the other's contact with the children may be genuinely protective and not necessarily selfish or vindictive can acknowledge the custodial parent's concern without making any judgement about its reasonableness. Roberts (1983) was suspicious that "many mediators will see it as necessary to a settlement that the disputants' view of their predicament be transformed; and so deliberately set out to do this, offering evaluations of past conduct or future options and identifying what they consider to be the appropriate outcome" (p. 549). He seemed to think that in reframing or translating one party's position to the other the conciliator's own views are imposed, whereas an accurate translation should present different facets of the parties' own perceptions, not the conciliator's perception of the way things ought to look. Reframing may convey an underlying reality which has been overlaid by angry or defensive reactions.

In some cases, one parent accuses the other of brainwashing the children and the second parent retaliates with tit-for-tat allegations. Conciliators can sometimes help both parents to see that they are each supporting the children in different ways and that it is possible to trust each other. Reframing can help to validate each party's position in an impartial and encouraging way, and some couples can use the positive connotation of their different views as a plank on which they can tread warily together as they weigh up practical possibilities. A mother often doubts the father's competence as a parent, especially if he has played little part in the day-to-day care of the children, but with some reframing of their respective roles she may accept that he has a valuable part to play which need not undermine her own central role. The same can apply in reverse, where a custodial father questions the mother's access to the children.

iii) Confronting. Confronting disputants with the reality of their position may be necessary to overcome a particular "block" or to help them see that they are clinging to a fantasy. A conciliator can confront a person forcefully without being aggressive or dictatorial: a powerful statement may reach the person precisely because it is voiced in a warm and caring way, whereas an accusatory tone may only increase resistance. In some circumstances, soothing and placating may be the opposite of what is needed and conciliators may have to be direct and firm while offering people enough support to help them face a very painful reality.

Often the confrontation is between the two former partners and conciliators need skill and confidence to allow it to happen while maintaining enough control and security. Bente and Gunnar Oberg (1982), who co-work in Sweden as divorce mediators, argue that "confrontation is the only means of emotional release and preventing aggression from becoming destructive" (p. 37). They see the avoidance of confrontation as one of the main causes of incomplete emotional divorce. The skilled conciliator can assess how much confrontation can be coped with at any one time, intervening when necessary with a positive "reframe" or to deflect the discussion into less heated channels. Confrontation may temporarily increase the pressure on one parent's ability to cope and it is important to check how much support is available from relatives and friends. Individuals who seem very isolated or desperate may accept a suggestion to contact another agency or self-help group: information can be provided about local agencies, not necessarily in the presence of both parties but without jeopardising the conciliator's impartial position. Support from a sympathetic member of Gingerbread or Families Need Fathers may be particularly helpful to a separated person who feels very lonely, overburdened or uncontrollably angry, and conciliation services should establish good working relationships with various community groups so that referrals can be made appropriately.

iv) Managing open and violent conflict. The structure of conciliation discussions and the presence of conciliators may enable some couples to manage their conflict in a way they have been unable to do on their own. For many couples, clarifying what the dispute is about, reframing its function, and focusing on children's needs may lower the temperature and permit more rational discussion, but others may be in the grip of more powerful conflict. Physical violence is very common in the crisis of separation, and the fear of losing control may deter such couples from risking face-to-face contact with each other. Conciliators can help them to deal with this fear by referring to it directly when proposing a joint meeting with both parties. Sometimes a wife may trust the conciliator's ability to keep control in the meeting but may fear, perhaps with good reason, that if she speaks frankly her husband may waylay her afterwards, attacking her in the street or following her home to pursue the fight there. It may be necessary to structure the meeting in meticulous detail beforehand, obtaining the husband's firm commitment to stay behind with the conciliator for an extra twenty minutes or so, so that the wife can leave safely and keep her address secret. Personal experience of making such arrangements is very positive: husbands readily accepted these terms because they held out the only hope of direct communication with their wives and both partners often observed that the conciliator's presence enabled them to talk to each other in a way they could not manage on their own and that this helped to defuse tension. However, this is not to say that conciliation is a panacea for domestic violence, only that it may enable some couples to gain control of violent feelings. In planning with both parties whether conciliation is acceptable to them and how it can be managed, it is particularly important to be aware of the difference between an isolated outburst of violence, in which both partners have lashed out at each other, and the regular abuse of one partner by the other, which is often associated with an alcohol problem. Sometimes both parents agree about access in principle but cannot accept any direct contact at the time of access visits. The parent who feels threatened may agree to use an access centre or some other mutually acceptable place where children can be delivered and collected safely, at agreed times, without the parents having to see each other. If both parents are sufficiently relaxed about access visits, the stress on the children is greatly reduced.

It is difficult to obtain accurate statistical information about the incidence of physical violence in association with marriage breakdown and separation, as there seems to be a tendency to underestimate its occurrence and severity (Pahl 1985). Researchers in Bristol (Borkowski, Murch and Walker 1983) found that 20 per cent of the women petitioners in their sample used evidence of their husband's violence to support a petition based on unreasonable behaviour and a further 20 per cent claimed that there had been episodes of violence in their marriage, although they had chosen to base their petition on other evidence. Most of the statistics on violence come from the records of agencies from whom women seek help, and although it has been suggested (Booth Committee 1983) that allegations of violence are sometimes used as a tactical manoeuvre to obtain sole occupation of the home, research (Levinger 1966) suggests that serious violence is frequently not reported, especially when it occurs between middle-class couples. A quarter of all crimes of violence reported in England and Wales in 1979 involved domestic violence (*Guardian* 4 March 1985) and experience of conciliation suggests that physical fighting, rather than sustained assault by one party on the other, occurs very frequently between couples on the brink of separation.

Two English lawyers (Bottomley and Olley 1983) expressed great concern that in some American states a woman seeking protection from her husband's violence may be compelled to go through a mandatory conciliation procedure instead of being allowed direct access to the court. In these schemes, a lawyer acting as conciliator may control the applicant's access to the court and may thus deprive her of the court's protection. Personal protection orders may in any case fail to give adequate protection, as was seen in the tragic case of Mary Khelifati (Irving and Cuthbertson 1985). Conciliation should not be used as an alternative to an application for an injunction if either party is in danger but it may be appropriate in conjunction with court proceedings and with separate legal advice to each party. In some areas, civil work teams of welfare officers offer conciliation at emergency applications for injunctions and the results are said to be encouraging. It is important, however, that threats of violence are not glossed over and that conciliators do not collude in any way with the continuation of violence. If the risks are confronted openly and directly, some violent individuals may be able to acknowledge their fears of losing control and plans may then be formulated which avoid replicating the situations in which violence tended to occur.

Example. A husband was referred to a conciliation service by the Citizens' Advice Bureau, ostensibly because he and his wife were arguing whether one of them should divorce the other. The wife accepted the offer of conciliation, and in the course of a stormy meeting both admitted to acute fears that they might seriously injure or even kill each other. Each accused the other of provocation, and recent incidents were mentioned in which the husband had thrown furniture and the wife had grabbed a kitchen knife. The wife slept in a separate bedroom, with the door barricaded. Both partners had been divorced previously and the wife had a twelve-year-old son from her first marriage who was a focus of conflict between them. The high level of anxiety made it easier to reach several short-term agreements. Both partners undertook to avoid provocative arguments over the next few days and to obtain separate legal advice before returning home. It was agreed that both solicitors would be requested to contact the conciliator, so that their advice to each party could be linked with further conciliation. The combination of conciliation with legal advice from solicitors led in due course to an agreed separation, without further violence occurring in the home, and to agreements about the matrimonial home and maintenance. The wife remained in the council-owned property with her son and her husband went to live with his elderly mother. Although this was very painful for them, they both felt that they had brought insoluble problems from their first marriages into the second marriage and that this had put an intolerable strain on themselves and on their relationship which could be eased only by separating from each other. The irrational fears and anger which had culminated in primitive outbursts of violence became more manageable in the presence of a neutral third person who provided a safe and sufficiently controlled environment where irreconcilable needs could be looked at more calmly and rationally.

v) Negotiating. Negotiation is sometimes equated with quid pro quo bargaining in which the parties make some trade-off or concession in order to secure some improvement in their position (Bellow and Moulton 1981). Conciliators may encourage compromise or token exchanges (Haynes 1984) but it should not be assumed that settlement of a dispute necessarily results in loss or disadvantage to either party. On the contrary, conciliation may mobilise a more efficient and co-operative use of available resources, so that less wastage occurs (of money or emotional energy or both), benefiting both parties even if they do not feel entirely satisfied. Conciliators may suggest fresh options which carry some mutual advantages for each party and the children, and they frequently suggest that a new form of access arrangements should be tested out and reviewed before any firm undertakings are given.

It is often helpful to apply methods derived from task-centred casework (Reid and Epstein 1972) which usually involves drawing up an agenda before negotiation can take place on specific issues. As a step towards solving a major problem, conciliators may ask each parent to suggest some task which the other could undertake as tangible evidence of co-operation. For example, the visiting parent could undertake something that the other finds a particular chore, such as taking the children for a check-up at the dentist. This can reduce the pressure on the parent with day-to-day care of the children and help her (or him) see the other parent as a source of practical help and support and not merely as a giver of treats. In response, the care-taker parent might be asked to share school reports and any significant information about the children's health. Negotiation may also be needed about who should be involved in and responsible for decisions about the children. This may result in parents agreeing to restrict interference from a grandparent or cohabitee, or alternatively agreeing to include them in their discussions, provided that each parent feels equally supported. If both of them have new partners, conciliation with both couples together can work very well, but if only one has a new partner it is usually preferable to meet first with the natural parents and then, if appropriate, with the new partners, rather than attempting an unbalanced and stressful meeting with all three adults together.

Theoretical Frameworks for Conciliation

Short training courses cannot cover extensive amounts of theoretical material, and in any case it may be questioned whether conciliators need to be aware of any particular theories, and if so, which ones. Sutton (1981) has argued convincingly that "theories have risen and fallen . . . our accumulated knowledge may show very effectively that certain common assumptions are wrongly founded, or that established practices are very different in their results from what their advocates intended" (p. 51). Theories about individual and family functioning are notoriously prone to vary according to current fashion and prevailing beliefs[8], and one argument for an acquaintance with different theories is that it encourages a healthy scepticism. Slavish reliance on any single theory may result in a blinkered approach and stereotyping, without recognising the unique characteristics of individuals and situations. However, provided conciliators review and question received wisdom from any source, their awareness of different theories can extend their perspectives and encourage a flexible, wide-ranging approach with access to a variety of methods and skills. This approach is likely to be eclectic (or as Kaslow (1981) suggests, "diaclectic" – a term coined from "eclectic" and "dialectic"). The following brief references to extensive bodies of theoretical literature and clinical practice draw attention to some concepts and techniques which may be relevant to conciliation, although they need to be carefully adapted so that the conciliation task is not lost sight of and merged with other kinds of intervention.

A. Conflict Management Theory

Conciliation is essentially a method of managing conflict in order to settle disputes and there is a great deal of literature on dispute settlement (see for example Deutsch 1973, Fisher and Ury 1981, Folberg and Taylor 1984) which is relevant to conciliation in separation and divorce. American authors, in particular (Haynes 1981, Epstein, Bishop and Baldwin 1982, Moore 1983), have identified the sequence of steps or stages which conciliators follow in settling disputes in a planned and logical way and the progression that is needed to move from one stage to the next. Their theories emphasise the importance of structured and ordered discussions, rejecting the stigmatising assumption that a failure to agree implies pathology in individuals or families. People are assumed to be competent to take decisions and a systematic reviewing of their goals and priorities helps to increase their autonomy and self-reliance and may unravel tangled problems. However, if conciliators are excessively matter-of-fact in negotiating parental care and practical support as though they were mathematical equations, they may increase people's anger and distress. Conflict management theory tends to underestimate the force of irrational feelings and the influence of third parties and social factors. The issues that are at stake in separation and divorce are as explosive as dynamite and conciliators need more than formal negotiation skills to manage these highly charged situations.

B. Communication Theory

Paolucci and colleagues (1977) suggest that family members who communicate dysfunctionally or not at all are likely to have great difficulty in settling their differences and working out agreed arrangements. These are the families who are most likely to be referred for conciliation, because they lack the negotiation or verbal skills to settle problems on their own. Conflict may arise from blocked or misdirected communication rather than from incompatible goals, and techniques derived from communication theory (Watzlawick, Beavin and Jackson 1967, Watzlawick, Weakland and Fisch 1974, Crowe 1982) may be useful in helping people to articulate their problems more clearly and constructively. These techniques need to be adapted to the language and style of communication used by the individuals concerned and conciliators need to monitor their own linguistic habits and check on their intelligibility. Translating legal language into ordinary language is often helpful. One husband comes to mind who brought a letter from his wife's solicitor which he could not understand at all. When the proposals in it were explained to him in simpler language, he said that he agreed with them. Even highly intelligent people may need to have things said very slowly, sometimes more than once, because their normal powers of comprehension may be numbed by acute anxiety and distress.

C. Theories of Marital Interaction

Theories of marital interaction (Dicks 1967, Mattinson and Sinclair 1979) use insights derived from psychoanalytic theory to explain the dynamics of marital relationships. They offer ways of understanding the ambivalence which separated couples often show towards one another, both in words and behaviour. However, conciliators are concerned with conscious rather than unconscious processes and it is not usually appropriate to explore the marital relationship in any depth. Moreover, disputes relating to separation and divorce commonly involve triangular relationships and larger systems which extend well beyond the rather narrow focus of psychodynamic theory.

D. Family Systems Theory

Marital counselling and conciliation in industrial disputes both concentrate mainly on the two partners or protagonists, whether husband/wife or employer/employee. This perspective overlooks two insights which are familiar to family therapists: 1) that an integral aspect of family life is the interdependence of its members, and 2) that problems and tensions affecting one or more members of a family generally affect the other members as well (e.g. Minuchin 1974, Bentovim, Gorell Barnes and Cooklin (eds.) 1982, Irving and Benjamin 1984). Although many writers on conciliation emphasise that it should be distinguished from family therapy (Folberg 1983, Kelly 1983, Haynes 1984), it has also been pointed out (Saposnek 1983, Lemmon 1985, Robinson and Parkinson 1985) that disputes over child custody and access to children are "typically created out of a complex of interactional family dynamics" (Saposnek 1983 p. 29). If children have become closely involved in their parents' conflicts, it may be unhelpful to focus solely on the adults' concerns without taking account of other relationships in the family. Family systems theory provides a useful framework for understanding the disputes associated with separation, divorce and remarriage, particularly where there are coalitions between family members which may be perpetuating the dispute (see for example Haley 1976, Gorell Barnes 1984). Family therapists (such as Minuchin 1974, Minuchin and Fishman 1981) have pointed to the significance of maintaining generational boundaries and to the burdens on children who take the place of an absent or non-functioning parent. Strategic therapists, especially a team of therapists based in Milan (Palazzoli, Boscolo and Prata 1978, Palazzoli 1985) have contributed significant ideas and techniques which are relevant to the ways in which conciliators engage and work with split families. Training in a family systems approach helps conciliators to relate simultaneously to couples who are in conflict with one another, while keeping track of the roles assumed by or assigned to third parties (children, grandparents, solicitors and conciliators themselves), especially where an alliance has been formed with one person or system against another. Systems thinking is also relevant in the sense that conciliation is an organisational system of decision-making which mediates between the family's private decision-making system and the public system of statutory decisions by the court, acting as a bulwark to the former and reducing the latter's intrusion to the minimum needed to validate agreements.

Professional opinion is divided about the use of a family systems approach in conciliation (Davis 1985, Shepherd and Howard 1985a) but those who question it cannot claim with any certainty that traditional methods are more valid or successful, either from the court or the family's point of view (see Sutton 1981). The argument may subside if there is more clarity about the context in which certain methods of working are being used and further analysis of the skills that are needed to practise these methods effectively.

E. Crisis Theory

Separation is a major life crisis for most couples (Kaslow 1981) and the Chinese character for crisis denotes both "danger" and "opportunity", indicating that people in crisis are less resistant to change but that the risks of personal breakdown, even suicide, may be high. Conciliators can be catalysts for constructive planning during this crisis period (Parkinson 1983a) and it is helpful if they are aware of the emotional stages people pass through in reacting to crisis. Skill is needed to help them reach considered decisions, despite high levels of stress. The crisis theory of mental health (Caplan 1961, Parad (ed.) 1965) suggests that if sufficient support is available, the crisis can be an opportunity for positive change and does not inevitably cause damage in the longer term. This positive view of crisis can help people tolerate the depression or despair they experience, so that they can see some light at the end of the tunnel. Caplan (1985) identified a number of preventive interventions in crisis situations which combine methods that are central to conciliation practice with others drawn from clinical practice. For example, it is often helpful to emphasise that the emotional turmoil people experience is normal, not abnormal, and by anticipating points of high stress, such as handing over the children before and after access visits, it may be possible to work out in advance how to cope with them.

F. Attachment Theory

Attachment theory evolved from studies of the ways in which infants and young animals reacted to separation from their mothers. It rests on the belief that the continuation of strong attachments between parents and children is important for children's healthy development, that the disruption of these bonds can cause acute and prolonged distress to children, and that their development may be impaired if subsequent experience fails to compensate for the loss (Bowlby 1969, 1973, 1980, Rutter 1981). More recently, studies of child development and children's experience of divorce have emphasised the importance of fathers as well as mothers. Wallerstein and Kelly (1980) found that from the children's point of view the psychological importance of both their parents did not diminish during the five years of their study, regardless of which parent had custody. Other research evidence (Richards and Dyson 1982) suggests that maintaining links between children and both natural parents contributes to good relationships between children and step-parents, thus strengthening the stability of step-families instead of undermining it, as is commonly feared. The assumption that a step-parent is a replacement for the other natural parent tends to encourage harmful rivalry for children's affections. The roles of natural parent and step-parent can be complementary, not competitive, and conciliators can help parents to negotiate these roles in practice. However, it is easy to stray into the role of child advocate in conveying children's views and needs to their parents. The task of investigating and assessing what may be in the best interests of the child is not part of the conciliation task, and conciliators may find themselves in a serious dilemma if they encounter parents who seem totally unaware of or unresponsive to their children's needs (see chapter 8).

Comment

An appreciation of theoretical concepts can help conciliators approach their work in an organised and coherent way so that they can explain it to themselves and to others, but there are often discrepancies between theory and practice – and there may be discrepancies between what conciliators claim they do and what they actually do. However experienced they may be in other settings, they need training to clarify and define what is expected of them and to learn appropriate methods and skills. Considerable commitment is required, as the work can be extremely demanding and stressful. It is important that management committees of independent services draw from the experience that has now been accumulated so that suitable candidates are selected and adequate training provided. Some services pay only travel expenses, but even where conciliators work as unpaid volunteers a renewable contract is needed to clarify the terms on which they are providing their services and the nature of their accountability. There must be a commitment to accept continuing training and supervision and there should be provisions for the agency or the conciliator to terminate the contract. Failure to define the responsibilities of conciliators, co-ordinators and supervisors has caused problems in some services and the fact that a few complaints have been made by dissatisfied customers or their solicitors shows the need for professional indemnity insurance and a complaints procedure. Conciliators should also be prepared to accept monitoring of their work by independent researchers, to test whether the role they aspire to is tenable in practice and what results are achieved by different methods. Without this scrutiny of their practice, the fear will remain in some quarters that conciliators are welfare wolves disguised in the soft sheepswool of conciliation, holding out promises of "party control" but in reality exerting considerable power over people and the decisions they make.

It is no exaggeration to say that disputes associated with separation and divorce carry high risks of physical or psychological collapse or even homicide. Conciliators need considerable skills to help people contain high levels of internal or inter-personal conflict, while focusing on specific decisions and difficulties. Haynes (1982) concluded that conciliation should not be practised by just anyone with a common-sense approach to problem-solving, and that it would be a mistake for any single discipline to attempt to monopolise this emerging field of work. One of conciliation's main strengths is its interdisciplinary character: it should not be taken over by any single discipline, and more work is needed to fuse relevant knowledge and skills drawn from different disciplines. We also need to be clearer about the base-line that trainee conciliators should start from, so that training packs can be designed for use both at initial and advanced levels of training.

Notes

1. McTaggart v. McTaggart [1948] 2 All ER 754.
2. Mole v. Mole [1950] 2 All ER 328.
3. Theodoropoulos v. Theodoropoulos [1963] 2 All ER 772.
4. Pais v. Pais [1970] 3 All ER 491.
5. Parker and Parkinson, *Family Law*, vol. 15 (1985), pp. 270-4.
6. D v. NSPCC [1977] 1 All ER HL, pp. 589-619.
7. The recommendation of the Booth Committee (Report 1985) that an absolute privilege should attach to conciliation will be referred to in chapter 10.
8. For example, Goldstein, Freud and Solnit (1973) argued on the basis of a particular theory of child development that the custodial parent should make all decisions concerning the children, including deciding whether the other parent should have access to them. This theory has come under attack from other experts (Wallerstein and Kelly 1980) who based their contrary views on empirical evidence of the ways in which parents and children adjusted to divorce over a five-year period.

7 UNEQUAL BARGAINING POWER IN CONCILIATION

In conciliation jargon, a conciliator "empowers" the parties to work out agreements which take account of each party's needs and concerns, as well as meeting the needs of their children. In an ideal world, two people who have equal resources in economic, psychological, legal and physical terms and who are motivated to settle their differences may work out arrangements which would be rated fair and reasonable on objective criteria. In the real world, however, each partner's resources are rarely equal. Each may hold some "cards" which give them some advantage over the other party and stalemate may result if neither is prepared to share their cards with the other or work towards a fair deal. Sometimes one party may hold all the important cards and the other may feel powerless to negotiate a different set of terms. What is the conciliator's role in this power game? Should conciliators try to shuffle the pack and deal the cards equally or, if their main goal is to obtain a settlement, do they effectively collude with the stronger party by encouraging the weaker party to capitulate? Studies of community mediation schemes in other countries (Merry 1982) suggest that "with few exceptions, a mediated settlement reflects the status inequalities between the disputants" (p. 32) and that "a mutually acceptable solution tends to be one in which the less powerful gives up more"(p. 33).

Questions about the ability of British conciliators to handle inequalities of bargaining power in matrimonial cases were raised in an editorial in the *Legal Action Group Bulletin* in November 1982:

> One spouse may be in urgent economic need, ignorant of his or her rights, inarticulate, frightened of the other or fearful of losing contact with the children. Are the conciliators to adopt a strictly neutral role or can they attempt to equalise spouses' bargaining power? How far should conciliators seek information that has not been volunteered, or verify that information? Should conciliators warn a party if a proposed agreement appears unfair? Should conciliators raise issues that parties themselves have not thought of or advise them on points of law? Should conciliators see the children and how far should they seek to check that any agreement reached by parents really is in the interests of the children? Finally, how far are conciliation proceedings confidential or privileged? (p. 2).

These are very important questions and solicitors may be justifiably wary of referring their clients to conciliation services until some satisfactory answers are provided. An American study (Kressel 1972) of conciliation in industrial disputes found that discrepancy in the parties' relative bargaining power was one of the main problems encountered by conciliators. Other common problems were the scarcity of divisible resources, high levels of internal conflict in one or both parties and their inexperience and anxiety in coping with face-to-face negotiations. In an industrial dispute, one party may have less cause than the other to fear the consequences of a strike, and the employer may have substantially greater financial resources or political power, or greater access to crucial information. Kressel and colleagues made a further study (Kressel, Deutsch, Jaffe, Tuchman and Watson 1977a) which compared conciliation in industrial disputes with conciliation in divorce, and which showed that conciliators in both contexts experienced similar difficulties in balancing inequalities of bargaining power. Industrial disputes are often strongly charged with emotion but they do not always disrupt all aspects of an individual's personal life and relationships as profoundly and traumatically as divorce is apt to do, and industrial disputes may not affect arrangements for children as directly as personal disputes between their parents. In industrial disputes, the conciliator's aim may be to reach a fair settlement without necessarily restoring good relations between the parties, whereas divorced couples may be obliged to maintain contact and access to the children may depend on their ability to co-operate.

The power relationships which separating and divorcing couples bring to conciliation are very complex. If lasting agreements are to be reached which take account of the needs of the adults and children concerned, conciliators need some understanding of the ways in which power is distributed between family members. This power may be visible to outsiders (for example, financial power, or the higher social status of one party), but conciliators also need to understand the ways in which couples allocate power subjectively to each other or to another adult or child. The following categorisation of different power relationships relevant to conciliation does not claim to be complete but it may help to clarify the kind of disputes which commonly arise in separation and divorce, some of the dilemmas experienced by conciliators and the methods they may use to balance unequal power without becoming partisan.

Haynes (1981) identified three primary power relationships:

1. the power to control financial resources;

2. the power to reject the other partner;
3. the power to resist a settlement.

Of these three kinds of power, Haynes considered the power to control financial resources the most complex power relationship. Many divorcing couples in Britain have little income to control and they may exercise power over each other in other ways, including the following:

a) the power conferred by legal advantage;
b) superior knowledge, social status, or greater intellectual or verbal ability;
c) the power of emotional dominance and emotional blackmail;
d) the physical power of actual or threatened violence;
e) the delegation of power to children or other family members;
f) invoking religious or moral authority, possibly with support from a religious leader or senior members of the community.

1 The Power to Control Financial Resources

American researchers (Kressel, Deutsch, Jaffe, Tuchman and Watson 1977a) reported that the imbalance of power in divorce conciliation generally stems from the disadvantaged position of the wife who has often given up her employment or career to look after the children.

> Moreover, although husbands were frequently uninformed about financial matters, they were paragons of financial expertise in comparison to their wives. Husbands had almost exclusive control of important financial documents and were aware of financial arrangements of which their wives were ignorant. The ignorance of the wives combined with their heightened anxiety at their poor post-divorce prospects created strong pressures on the mediator to shore up the wives' side of negotiations (p. 11).

This imbalance applies particularly to mediation in North America, where divorce mediators negotiate financial and property settlements, reporting that conflict over money is much more common than conflict over children (Camozzi 1984, Haynes 1984). Mediation in financial and property disputes assumes that the mediator is competent to deal with these issues and that the parties can trust each other to make a full disclosure of their income and assets. In private mediation schemes in the United States (Haynes 1981), each party undertakes to make a full disclosure of means in a detailed questionnaire. These schemes cater mainly for middle and upper-income couples in professional occupations (Pearson, Ring and Milne 1983) and it is assumed that wives either have sufficient knowledge of their husbands' income to assess the accuracy of their financial statements or that they can obtain professional advice from accountants. The possibility of unintended or deliberate deception practised by one party on the other is nonetheless an uncomfortable reality which cannot be discounted.

Some feminists believe that women are disadvantaged in conciliation (Bottomley and Olley 1983) but there is no British evidence so far which substantiates these fears. Conciliation in this country has concentrated so far on custody and access disputes where mothers are generally in a stronger position than fathers, and although feminists may fear that women will be urged to agree to joint custody or more generous access arrangements, positive reactions to conciliation both from women and men suggest that conciliators are not automatically biased towards either sex and that bullying tactics by either partner are kept in check if the conciliation process is managed properly.

As far as financial matters are concerned, the code of practice drawn up by the National Family Conciliation Council's executive committee in consultation with the Law Society's Family Law Committee and the Solicitors' Family Law Association (Appendix A) provides that where issues over finance or property are inseparably linked with the primary issues of the divorce itself and/or children, there should be only preliminary discussions about finance and property, and couples should be restrained from entering into firm agreements without obtaining separate legal advice. Some commentators (Dingwall, in press) have seen this willingness to leave financial and property matters in the hands of solicitors as a diplomatic move, designed to encourage solicitors to refer custody and access disputes to conciliators. In fact, its main objective is to provide adequate safeguards for both parties and for conciliators themselves, who might otherwise find themselves charged with professional negligence in relation to unsound financial settlements. Dingwall has pointed out, however, that conciliators' effectiveness may be limited if financial and property issues are excluded, because this restricts the bargaining counters that can be brought into play. Milne (1983) sees both advantages and disadvantages in separating arrangements for children from other issues. "Separating the mediation of parent-child issues from financial and property issues allows children to be treated as an issue in their own right, and it lessens the potential for using them as pawns in the negotiation process. However, separation of issues can segment a divorce agreement artificially when property, finances and children are indeed related and when decisions made in one area affect decisions made in the other areas" (p. 19).

Negotiations over finance and property may involve complicated questions about joint business interests, taxation and pension rights and it would be irresponsible to encourage couples to rely solely on conciliators, without emphasising the need for adequate legal advice: both the weaker party and a conciliator might be hoodwinked into accepting arrangements which a more sophisticated partner had calculated to his or her advantage. Even the due process of law does not always guarantee justice to both parties, since property and business valuations made by the husband's accountant may be accepted by the wife's solicitor and by the court, although an accountant acting for the wife might have valued the assets differently. At present, few conciliators in Britain are qualified in law or accountancy, and they should not be seen as substitutes for solicitors, but as an additional source of help. The joint involvement of conciliators, solicitors and in some cases accountants may enable couples to arrive at an equitable distribution of their resources which takes account of their children's needs while balancing each parent's position as fairly as possible.

2 The Power to Reject the Other Partner

Seven out of ten divorce petitions filed in England and Wales are filed by wives (Central Statistical Office, Social Trends 1985) but the petitioner is not necessarily the partner who initiated the separation. The loss of a partner through separation and divorce has often been compared to loss through death (Bohannan 1970, Brown 1976), but there are also important differences between these experiences (Kaslow 1981). Although a bereaved spouse may feel irrational anger towards the partner who has died, this kind of anger is different from the deep pain and resentment inflicted by a spouse's apparently deliberate choice to leave the marriage, often for someone else. The rejected partner often accuses the other of being irresponsible, selfish or misled, and the rejecting partner may counter-attack by blaming his or her partner for the breakdown (Weiss 1975). Passive rejection and denial can be as aggressive as active rejection, but if this is not recognised, one partner may be left with all the anger and resentment which actually belong to them both and which need some mutual acknowledgement. This emotional gulf may result in one partner remaining stuck in negative reactions to loss, while the other moves on to acceptance and adjustment. Reactions to loss may be conceptualised as three related stages, of which the first is shock/denial, the second anger/depression and the third understanding/acceptance. Anger may give way to depression if the rejected partner feels humiliated or personally destroyed and if there appears to be no way forward.

The decision to end a marriage is not usually a mutual decision (Hart 1976, Davis 1981, Burgoyne and Clark 1984) and the fact that 99 per cent of divorces are undefended does not prove that the respondent accepts the need for divorce. Kressel and Deutsch (1977b) found that the non-mutuality of the divorce decision was associated with conflict on other issues and with poor post-divorce adjustment. "The single most frequently cited predictor of a difficult divorce was one spouse's eagerness to end the marriage, coupled with reluctance to do so on the part of the other" (p. 423). If the decision to separate or divorce has been taken unilaterally by one spouse, often without discussion with the other, the two partners may be at very different stages in letting go of the marriage (see chapter 8) and this may greatly restrict their ability to negotiate effectively. The partner who feels rejected and demoralised may be very vulnerable to pressure and might relinquish a valid claim through lacking the confidence and emotional strength to pursue it. Conciliators need to be sensitive to each party's emotional state although this is not the main focus of their work, so that they can detect when apparent consensus is due to depression or despair rather than genuine agreement. In such circumstances, they should assess with both parties whether conciliation should continue and if so, what additional forms of help might be appropriate.

3 The Power to Resist a Settlement

Haynes (1984) warned that conciliators should watch out for the power of the apparently passive partner. The partner who blocks decisions and agreements is usually the one who feels rejected, but occasionally both partners block decisions because of deep feelings of ambivalence about each other and about the ending of the marriage. The filing of a petition enables applications to be made on other issues as well and this may be deeply threatening to an unprepared partner whose familiar lifestyle is suddenly in jeopardy. Delaying tactics in filing affidavits may be used as a means of postponing the final settlement, and a resistant partner may avoid paying maintenance or refuse to co-operate over access arrangements. Neither conciliators nor the court may be able to overcome this resistance unless the blocks to agreement are resolved at a much deeper level.

It is naive to assume that couples who accept a referral for conciliation are necessarily seeking a settlement. Their motives vary, and one party's apparent acquiescence with the referral may disguise a profound determination to resist any agreement and/or an emotional inability to take any decisions at all. Conciliation may be seen by one or both partners as a means of perpetuating their involvement with each other, rather than letting it go (Parkinson 1983a) and conciliators should beware being sucked into the conflict and being used as a means of maintaining it.

Case Example: the Problems of Rejection and Resistance

Mrs Smith's solicitor advised her to seek help from her local conciliation service. When she telephoned the service it was explained that her husband would need to be involved as well and at first it seemed unlikely that Mr Smith, from whom she had been separated for nearly a year, could take part as he was based in Germany. However, he was due home shortly on leave and Mrs Smith agreed to the conciliation service approaching his solicitor. In fact, she welcomed this suggestion, saying she was extremely worried about unpaid bills and about her husband's access to their youngest child, Stephen, who was upset by his irregular visits. Stephen had been sent by the local authority to a boarding school for maladjusted children and Mrs Smith was anxious that he should not be unsettled again. Her two daughters, aged 15 and 17, lived at home with her and she was worried about them too. An older son was working away from home.

Mr Smith's solicitor thought that conciliation on the question of access to Stephen might be very helpful. He undertook to seek Mr Smith's consent to the referral and to explain to him that although Mrs Smith had contacted the service by telephone, the service had not sought to obtain her account of the difficulties until it was known whether Mr Smith would agree to participate. The acceptance of the referral was thus a four-stage process involving contact with both parties and both solicitors. Once Mr Smith's co-operation had been ascertained via his solicitor, it was agreed that an initial appointment would be arranged with Mrs Smith and that this would be balanced by a separate appointment with Mr Smith when he was back in England.

The conciliator would have preferred to see them both together from the outset but Mrs Smith sounded distraught and the reports of the children's reactions suggested that help was needed without delay.

The following account of the conciliator's intervention is very condensed and comments about the children's perceptions and reactions are omitted in order to focus on the power-struggles between their parents. Mrs Smith saw her husband as a dominant, Machiavellian character who had tied her in knots, emotionally, financially and now legally. She had left him because he was having an affair with another woman in Germany, but she did not want to "give" him a divorce. Her financial affairs seemed to be in total disarray and she felt that her husband would always get the better of her, as she was "stupid" and he was very clever and able to manipulate any system in his favour. There were problems about cashing the cheques he sent her and the allowances he was supposed to send the two older girls were overdue. He was insisting that Mrs Smith should sell the matrimonial home and move into a smaller house but Mrs Smith was afraid of incurring the Law Society's statutory charge and did not want to make any move until she knew how much money she would have to live on. She was extremely distressed, jumping from one problem to another and becoming more and more hysterical as she did so. She seemed to need personal counselling and support which could not be provided by means of conciliation, yet her fears and distress were bound up with the practical problems of her broken marriage and these pressing problems would not be resolved by personal counselling alone. Although she evidently saw herself as the victim of her husband's selfish and unprincipled behaviour and felt deeply betrayed and sexually humiliated by him, she was resistant to legal and financial orders being made which might leave her worse off than she was already. It seemed as though her remaining sense of identity was bound up with being victimised and distraught and that if her life were somehow straightened out, there might be nothing left to live for. One of the girls had been showing some suicidal tendencies and it was possible that her mother identified with them. Mrs Smith's doctor was aware of the family's problems, having been consulted by her on numerous occasions and when the possibility of personal counselling was mentioned it emerged that she had been to a counselling agency a number of times. She gave the impression of going round in circles, literally as well as emotionally. "Doing the rounds" of different agencies can be a way of blocking any positive or decisive action and the conciliator felt that although Mrs Smith might be unable to negotiate with her husband in a rational way, this should at least be attempted, as it might improve communications between them and help to reduce the confusion.

Discussion with Mr Smith when he returned revealed that although he was exasperated by his wife's personality and behaviour, he was more concerned to help her and the family settle down than she had believed him to be. He was angry with her for refusing to start divorce proceedings and for prevaricating over his access to Stephen. He said that although he was impatient to remarry, he was not trying to avoid his responsibilities to her and the children. He felt that Mrs Smith was very confused about their financial position and that the house she was living in was unnecessarily large and expensive. He admitted holding up some payments in an attempt to force her to take some action. He knew very well that she was relatively powerless financially but she was powerful as the mother of their children and he felt she was trying to turn the children against him.

Mr and Mrs Smith were thus locked in a struggle which had produced a deadlock in all areas of their relationship. The conciliator found however that it was possible to begin some careful negotiation because they each wanted access to the area of power controlled by the other. Liaison between the conciliator and both solicitors resulted in a much more conciliatory approach by the solicitors instead of a strongly partisan approach focusing on each party's demands and grievances. With their help, progress began to be made on financial matters and after Mrs Smith's solicitor had advised her slowly and carefully on her legal position, she decided that she wanted to divorce her husband and said that she felt much less confused about the legal and financial consequences. In relation to Mr Smith's access to Stephen, she preferred arrangements being made between the conciliator, Stephen's headmaster and Mr Smith without involving her directly because she recognised that her own very disturbed feelings about her husband tended to upset Stephen. The headmaster said that Stephen was very attached to his father and that he would benefit greatly from seeing him, provided that he was reassured that he was not being disloyal to his mother. The conciliator therefore suggested to Mrs Smith that it would help Stephen if she could refer to his father's visit in a letter, making it clear that it was taking place with her knowledge and consent.

In this far from straightforward case, different forms of power were used by each party to block and threaten the other. Competition was reduced by exploring the potential gains of relinquishing a monopoly of power in one area in order to achieve desired changes in another area. This was not a mere trade-off because the atmosphere of greater trust and co-operation seemed to benefit both parties. Their consent to the conciliator's liaison with other professionals (solicitors and teachers) extended the conciliation process without the conciliator assuming responsibility for solving all the family's problems. Although the level of emotion and irrationality at the outset precluded a straightforward bargaining process, the conciliation which took place during five appointments over a three-month period focused on specific issues without moving into personal counselling or therapy. Mrs Smith was encouraged to seek further counselling, but it is not known whether she did so or not.

4 The Power Conferred by Legal Advantage

There is substantial evidence that most decisions connected with divorce are taken by one or both parties and rubber-stamped by the court (Eekelaar and Clive 1977, Dodds 1983) and this evidence suggests that the court's control of divorce decisions is more nominal than real. It would be misleading, however, to discount the court's influence because anticipation of the court's decisions may exert a powerful influence over the parties' own decisions. An unsatisfactory compromise over access may be accepted if a court order might result in even less access or if one party feels that the odds are stacked so heavily in the other's favour that defeat is inevitable. Mnookin and Kornhauser (1979) used the term "private ordering" to describe the process in which divorcing couples sort out their affairs and submit their decisions to the court for ratification. They suggested that the primary function of contemporary divorce law is to provide a framework in which couples determine their respective rights and responsibilities, emphasising that they

> do not bargain over the division of family wealth and custodial prerogatives in a vacuum. Instead, they bargain in the shadow of the law. The legal rules governing alimony, child support, marital property and custody give each parent certain claims based on what each would get if he or she simply went to court and had the court impose some allocation. In other words, the outcome that the law would impose if no agreement is reached gives each parent certain bargaining chips – an "endowment" of sorts (p. 78).

In the nineteenth century, the custody of minor children was normally given to their father but this policy gradually changed during the early part of this century to a presumption in favour of the mother, on the grounds that it is generally mothers who are the primary caretakers and "the welfare of the infant"should be the court's first and paramount consideration (Guardianship of Infants Act 1925, s. 1). Research into custody allocation in England and Wales during the 1970s showed that it was granted solely to the mother in the vast majority of cases. The Keele study (Maidment 1976) found that sole custody was awarded to the mother in 87 per cent of cases and the Oxford study (Eekelaar and Clive 1977) based on the records of ten courts in England and Wales found that 91.3 per cent of sole custody orders were made in favour of the mother and 8.7 per cent in favour of the father. In uncontested cases, this allocation of custody may reflect the preference of the parents themselves but it has been suggested by Maidment (1981) and by Richards (1982) that some fathers do not ask for custody because they are convinced that their application would be unsuccessful.

Both the Keele and the Oxford studies showed that the most significant factor in relation to custody decisions is the "residential status quo". In other words, the parent with whom the children are living at the time of the proceedings continues to be the custodial parent in 99 per cent of cases. In the small proportion of fully contested custody cases, the status quo factor generally seems to determine the court's decisions, reflecting the judicial view that a child's relationships, environment and schooling should not be disrupted unless there are powerful reasons for doing so. Some judges hold the view that young children should live with their mother unless she is manifestly unfit to look after them, and controversial judicial decisions are reported from time to time which have resulted in a child being removed from the father's apparently satisfactory care (see the case of B. v. B., reported in *Family Law*, vol. 15 (1985)). Although the Court of Appeal reversed the trial judge's decision in this case, ruling that the child should remain with his father, Maidment (1981) found in a small sample of contested custody cases referred to the Court of Appeal that in 14 out of 19 cases (74%) custody was transferred from the father to the mother for no reason as far as she could see except a presumption in favour of the mother. Recent decisions in appellate cases suggest however that this bias towards mothers may be diminishing. In one case, the father was "awarded" care and control of two boys aged six and eight and a leading article about this decision in *The Times*

(16 September 1985) remarked that "the contest between the 'full-time mother' and the 'part-time father' is not quite as one-sided as it used to be". It is sad that equally valid claims from two caring parents may be seen by the courts and by society generally as a two-sided contest in which the children's interests are identifiable with the cause of either husband or wife, so that choosing one parent implies a rejection of the other. The roles of parents after separation and divorce should not be seen solely in terms of providing physical care and financial support, since research studies (Wallerstein and Kelly 1980, Walczak 1984, Mitchell 1985) show that children generally want both parents to continue being psychological parents, regardless of how the physical caring is allocated. The continuing security of having two psychological parents is very important for most children, and if this fact were better appreciated by parents and by their legal advisers, there might be fewer destructive battles to "win" the children.

However, de facto custody is a very powerful bargaining counter and parents who are fighting each other for the possession of their children are generally very aware that whoever "wins" them is likely to win the occupation of the matrimonial home as well. Fathers tend to feel disadvantaged by the prevailing assumption that children should be looked after by their mothers – an assumption which may be reinforced by the publicity given to some judicial decisions. Parents who feel that the stakes are loaded unfairly against them may react by trying to disqualify the other parent, making real or unsubstantiated allegations about their care of the children, and/or about their sexually promiscuous behaviour, homosexuality or addiction to alcohol or drugs. The real questions about the children's emotional attachments and material needs may then be obliterated in the cross-fire of accusations and counter-accusations which inflict a great deal of pain and damage without solving the main problem. If the allegations cannot be substantiated, the status quo is likely to prevail but the parent who has lost an adversarial bid for custody may then find that he or she has effectively lost access as well.

Time is a very important factor in these situations and one parent may literally play for time if he or she recognises that if nothing else changes, time itself may weight the scales substantially. This is another reason for beginning conciliation as early as possible, before time and the status quo have given powerful advantages to one parent. If both of them are still together in the matrimonial home, with equal parental status, the scales are much more evenly balanced than if one is in sole possession of the home and the children. Although the level of tension and distress may be very high at this early stage, parents may be more able to negotiate because there are more options to consider and because they may not yet be in totally entrenched positions.

Case Example: Fighting for the Children and the Home

Brian and Carol G. were referred for conciliation by their solicitors, after Brian instructed his solicitor to draw up a petition based on Carol's adultery. They were both still living in the matrimonial home with their children, Matthew aged eleven and Sarah aged seven. Brian's solicitor noted on the referral form that there was no dispute over the divorce itself nor over custody of the children, as Carol would be moving out to live with her boyfriend, who had a home of his own. The issue that was identified for conciliation was Carol's access to the children, after she left home. However, when the conciliator began to check what was agreed and what was not agreed, Carol said vehemently that custody was far from being agreed as she was asking her solicitor to put in a counter-application for custody. Brian looked appalled when Carol said this. It emerged that both parents wanted care and control of the children and the matrimonial home, and each felt that "right" was on their side. Brian was potentially in a strong position if he made Carol feel so guilty about her adulterous relationship that she fled from the matrimonial home. Once she left, time would be on his side, and it would be harder for her to reclaim the occupation of the home and the care of the children. Both the status quo and her "conduct" in leaving home might influence the court in his favour. Carol's trump card was that she was the children's mother and so far their primary caretaker. As long as she looked after them, Brian's claim to sole custody was very insecure. Brian and Carol were thus faced with a very painful and threatening contest which was already putting them both under acute stress. The conciliator proposed that joint discussions could help them to weigh up their priorities and consider the practical alternatives available to them. They agreed to the conciliator contacting their solicitors who were assured that their clients would seek further advice from them before taking any final decisions.

The conciliator next explored whether Brian and Carol had considered all the options available to them. It transpired that neither of them knew (or perhaps had failed to understand) that it was possible for them to hold custody jointly, with day-to-day care and control in the hands of one parent. They had both assumed that custody was a win-or-lose situation, with the children and the home as the "prize" for the "better parent". The conciliator helped them to separate the issue of Carol's new relationship from the parental issue of how the children should be looked after – physically, emotionally and financially. As parents they were invited in turn to explain their priorities and practical proposals and their attention was focused not on the past but on a future in which neither parent need lose the children altogether. They both felt that the children were very attached to them both and their mutual concern to support the children and minimise their distress emerged as a substantial area of common ground. Parents who are caught up in their own personal crisis may fear that the children's attachment to them may disappear when one of them leaves home. Research shows however that children's feelings for both parents are strongly and deeply held, even if they are not shown openly because of anxiety and stress. Wallerstein and Kelly found that "within the post-divorce family, the relationship between the children and both original parents did not diminish in emotional importance to the child over five years, . . . regardless of the legal allocation of custody and responsibility" (pp. 307-8).

Once Brian and Carol began to focus more positively and optimistically on their continuing joint parental task of looking after the children, it became clear that Carol did not envisage her boyfriend replacing Brian as the children's father. This may well have been Brian's main fear – that he might lose his wife, children and home to an unknown man who might cut him out of the children's lives altogether. The easing of this fear made it possible for him to acknowledge that he would find it difficult in practice to look after the children on his own, even if his parents helped him out during school holidays. Conciliation often involves some "reality-testing" of each parent's proposals and in this case Brian was not at all sure how he would manage when one of the children was unwell, as he did not want to give up his job. He was also unsure who would look after them in school holidays, at half-terms and when they came home from school in the afternoons. His idea that various neighbours would help out had not been looked at carefully from the children's point of view and the reality of how he would keep house for all three of them needed to be thought out in more detail. The way couples share or divide parental roles and domestic chores naturally varies a great deal and conciliators should try to help parents work out arrangements which fit in as far as possible with their familiar pattern of life and expectations of each other.

Carol's boyfriend was an unknown quantity to Brian and as such, a powerful figure who might disrupt whatever Brian and Carol worked out together. The conciliator suggested that it could be helpful if she met with Carol and her boyfriend, if he was willing, to prepare the ground for a possible meeting between the two men. Carol had made it clear that she intended to remarry and she and Brian recognised that access arrangements would be very difficult if he and the future stepfather saw each other as rivals for the children's affections. David (the boyfriend) accepted the offer of a joint meeting with Carol and the conciliator and this proved to be extremely useful. David said that he was apprehensive whether the children would accept him and that he did not know what would be expected of him, especially as he had no children of his own and no other experience with children. He did not see himself as a rival or a substitute for Brian as far as the children were concerned and he hoped that Brian and Carol would be able to co-operate with regard to the children. This discussion helped to dispel some of the fantasies which Brian and David had begun to construct about each other and they agreed to meet in a pub, with Carol. Although this degree of co-operation is unusual, it is by no means unique: a great deal depends on the motivation of all concerned and on establishing some co-operation at an early stage, before a series of acrimonious incidents poisons the atmosphere.

Conciliation took place in conjunction with legal advice to each party and with some contact between the conciliator and both solicitors. The outcome was that Brian and Carol agreed to hold custody jointly, with Carol having care and control of the children and Brian having regular and frequent access. In the more positive atmosphere which developed, the solicitors were able to negotiate a further agreement that a lump sum payment would be made to Brian (from David) to buy out his share of the matrimonial home so that he could buy a flat in the same area. Brian did not feel resentful that he had been forced to surrender his claim for custody because he felt that he had come to this decision himself and his position was not one of total loss, as he had feared it might be. He and Carol were intrinsically much more co-operative than Mr and Mrs Smith in the previous example, but they had also been lining up for a bitter fight when conciliation began. Firmly structured discussions were needed to contain the escalating conflict and to help them draw on their own strengths, which had been giving way under the acute strain. The co-operation of their solicitors with the conciliation process was also a major factor.

As in the previous example, the issues and problems were too complex to be tackled in a single session and a sequence of joint appointments, plus two separate appointments, gave Brian and Carol time to reflect between discussions. At one stage, when the situation was potentially explosive, the conciliator made an interim agreement with them that they would have no discussion at home because of the likelihood that it would get out of hand. Their next appointment was only a few days later and this direction from the conciliator was accepted as a means of controlling the structure of their discussions but not imposing an outcome.

There may be anxiety, especially on the part of a father and/or his solicitor, that a female conciliator may be consciously or unconsciously biased towards a mother having care and control of the children and that she therefore steers parents in this direction. Conciliators should refer explicitly to their gender as each parent may suspect them of being biased for or against their own sex. In the case in question, the conciliator took care to mention that she had worked with couples who had decided that the father should have care and control of the children as well as with couples who preferred that the mother should have day-to-day care. Conciliators also need to be aware of the powerful social pressures on mothers not to give up the care of their children even to a caring and able father. Women who decide, usually at considerable personal cost, that their children will be happier or more settled with their father tend to suffer not only from the loss of their daily contact with the children but from the uncomprehending condemnation of relatives, friends, teachers and others. Some mothers feel compelled to put up a token fight for custody so that they cannot be accused of lacking maternal feelings. The existence of a new self-support group, MATCH (Mothers Apart from Their Children), specifically for mothers who do not have custody of their children should be more widely known as the members of the organisation report receiving a great deal of support and understanding from each other and this can help counteract the negative attitudes of society in general towards non-custodial mothers.

The inequalities of bargaining power experienced by divorcing couples derive from the force of established social conventions as well as from legal conventions. A parent who feels completely powerless may grasp at conciliation as a drowning person might clutch at a straw, hoping unrealistically that a conciliator will somehow exert power in the desired direction. But as Borkowski, Murch and Walker (1983) have warned, "where the power of the parties is unequal, impartiality by outsiders does not correct the balance" (p. 192). The passive neutrality of conciliators may make no difference at all to the allocation of power between the parties and conciliators therefore need to consider what balancing strategies they can use without acting as arbitrators.

The structure of conciliation helps to balance power, and within this structure people can explore whether they have something to gain from reaching agreement and less to lose than they had imagined. In custody and access disputes, the parent who is most resistant to any concession is often afraid of losing the children to the other parent, who may be perceived as having better accommodation, more resources or a stronger relationship with the children. Paradoxically, the only way of enabling the resistant parent to negotiate at all may be to increase their sense of security, not threaten it. Reassurance generally has to come directly from the other parent and the most significant shifts often occur after one parent says to the other: "I am not trying to take the children away from you." If, on the other hand, this is precisely what he or she is trying to do, this intention and the reasons for it need to be examined as openly as possible. The parent who is looking after the children often needs reassurance that his or her relationship with the children is likely to be strengthened, not undermined, by the other parent's contact with them. Tangible evidence may still be needed however and trial access arrangements may be agreed on an interim basis before any firm commitment is made.

A tight grasp of power may be a sign of deep-seated fears of losing it and conciliators also need to be aware of third parties who may have a vested interest in the balance of power lying in one direction. A conciliation strategy which concentrates on bilateral negotiations between the two principals in the dispute is likely to fail if the power has been tacitly handed to someone else, who may have reasons for keeping the power where it is and sabotaging any agreement reached through conciliation. If parents have been at odds with each other for some time, another adult or child has often taken over the vacant space between them and this person may have become very powerful in manipulating the situation. Wallerstein and Kelly (1980) found that when unresolved conflict drove parents apart, children aged between nine and twelve were particularly likely to form an alliance with one parent against the other. Conciliators are unlikely to redress this unequal balance if they fail to understand the distorted hierarchy of power within split families. Understanding the family's dynamics within a short space of time calls for considerable expertise, including the ability to pay attention to many things simultaneously. It is for these and similar reasons that many conciliation services use two conciliators in each case, rather than one.

Advocates of co-working (Burrett and Gibbons 1981, Howard and Shepherd 1982, Guise 1983) argue that it maximises the potential value of conciliation and facilitates genuine agreement. Two workers, particularly if one is male and the other female, can provide a model of rational negotiation and reduce the gender-based transferences which may be projected on to a single worker (Hunt 1985). Against this, it has been argued that the use of two workers may lead to problematic coalitions and that the worker pair is not immune to being sucked into the family's conflicts. If the two workers are unsure of each other's way of working, they may fail to pick up each other's signals and direction. Any signs of confusion or hesitation will probably be detected by the family who may then play the game of "Let's show them our problems are insoluble." Some services use a male-female pair and find that this works very well, but there is a shortage of male conciliators in independent services and the use of two workers of the same sex risks compounding existing imbalances. Waldron and colleagues (Waldron, Roth, Fair, McDermott 1984) found some evidence from a small sample of cases that a male-female pairing of conciliators was more successful in terms of recorded agreements than pairing two female conciliators with each other.

There are different methods of co-working which need fuller examination than they can be given here. The use of two paired workers does not guarantee that inequalities between parents and other family members can be compensated for and a number of specialist divorce court welfare teams are using a live consultation model within a family systems approach, in preference to paired working. In this model, which is derived mainly from the work of family therapists in Milan (Palazzoli, Boscolo and Prata 1978), one worker engages in discussion with the couple or the family while one or more colleagues remain outside the discussion, observing the non-verbal communications, underlying dynamics and the function of the dispute in relation to the family as a whole. This allocation of tasks needs to be explained in simple terms to the family so that they understand the reasons for it. In practice, families seem to appreciate that the complexity of the problems they bring can overwhelm a single worker, whereas two workers are less likely to miss a significant statement and may perceive fresh possibilities. The conciliator who engages directly with the family can concentrate on gathering relevant facts and clarifying the surface issues, while the consultant may perceive the nub of the dispute and offer a possible way forward. Although it may seem extravagant to use two workers per session plus additional time to plan and review the work, conciliators with experience of working singly and jointly believe that joint working is nonetheless economic, because more progress can be made in one or two sessions than a single worker may achieve in a number of sessions, using traditional methods (Shropshire Probation Service 1983, Fisher 1984).

Another form of co-working involves what has been termed an interdisciplinary or "transdisciplinary" approach (Palazzoli 1985), in which workers with different professional training and experience (such as a conciliator qualified in law teamed with a conciliator trained in psychology) draw on knowledge and skills from both disciplines. This model may be particularly useful if there are complex legal and nonlegal issues. Carefully structured co-working can offer a means of balancing power while negotiations take place, if knowledge and expertise are combined in ways which support the weaker party without the stronger one feeling overpowered. However, co-working in an ad hoc way can increase existing imbalances, and two workers who rely on their instincts rather than on a planned approach may be dismayed to find themselves working at cross purposes. There is a risk of unstructured co-working being used in conciliation mainly to bolster the workers' confidence, without real benefit to the couples or families concerned.

Space does not allow further exploration of the various inequalities of bargaining power in separation and divorce, nor is it possible to consider in any depth the techniques which are being developed to balance these inequalities. Video films of live and role-played sessions may provide a better way of studying conciliation techniques. Sometimes there is a serious imbalance between the parties due to mental handicap, a major language difficulty or a physical or psychiatric condition, and in such cases conciliation is probably inappropriate. Creative ways may be found to overcome some problems: for example, the illiteracy of one spouse need not be an insuperable obstacle, and conciliation can take place effectively with a profoundly deaf person or couple, using a special worker for the deaf (who may need some training as a conciliator). Conciliators should be alert, however, to inequalities between the parties which they are unable to handle and which may need consideration by the court without delay. As conciliators may occasionally fail to perceive these inequalities themselves, it is important that their work is adequately supervised. There is sometimes a tendency to be overly concerned with equality and justice, without recognising that these are not always the primary values of divorcing couples themselves. Particularly where children are involved, parents may choose arrangements which are manifestly unfair to one of them, because their main concern is their children's wellbeing. Having made apparently "unfair" arrangements, they may find that these arrangements work out fairly after all, because co-operation is increased and each parent gives more, literally or symbolically, than the other had expected. Conciliators should seek to provide space and support so that people can work out arrangements which take account of their own private values and concerns, without having doctrinaire views forced upon them, or legal or social conventions imposed on them which may be ill-suited to their needs.

8 SOME DIFFICULTIES AND CONTRADICTIONS IN CONCILIATION

There is a tendency to assume that a voluntary referral to an independent conciliation service "implies a readiness as well as a willingness for conciliation" (Day, Jones and Owen 1984 p. 202). This does not accord with the experience of conciliators, who may find that neither party is ready or willing to reach a settlement with the other. Individuals may seek to enlist a conciliator as an ally rather than as an impartial negotiator and even if the conciliator's role is acceptable to both parties their conflicting claims may impede a straightforward negotiation process. The practice of conciliation raises many questions about the boundaries between conciliation, divorce counselling and therapy on the one hand and between conciliation and legal advice on the other. This chapter looks at some of the questions and difficulties which conciliators frequently encounter, such as the disparate needs of the two parties, the reservations solicitors may have about referring their clients to a conciliation service, and appropriate ways of involving children.

The theory of conciliation rests on the premise that people caught up in disputes are capable of rational discussion and negotiation with each other. The reality may be otherwise, in some cases at least. Numerous research studies (including Chester 1971, Hart 1976, Murch 1980, Ambrose, Harper and Pemberton 1983) have documented the physical ill-health and mental stress which are associated with marriage breakdown and separation. Chester (1971) found that most wife petitioners experienced a serious deterioration in their health, especially in the early stages of separation, and three-quarters of them consulted their doctor about stress-related symptoms. Admission rates to psychiatric hospitals are lowest for married people and highest for the divorced and separated, and the impact of separation on mental health seems even greater for men than for women (Grad and Sainsbury 1966). McMurray (1970) showed that the motor vehicle accident rate of divorcing people doubled in the year of their divorce. The personal stress experienced by each partner in a failing or broken marriage is often associated with communication problems which make it difficult or impossible for them to address major questions together: whether they should separate informally or divorce without delay; who will continue to provide the day-to-day care of the children and financial support; who will be responsible for the mortgage or rent and the upkeep of the matrimonial home; how often and for how long the parent leaving home should have access to the children; whether decisions concerning the children's education and other important aspects of their lives will be taken by one parent alone or by both parents jointly; and whether the division of jointly owned property and possessions should be undertaken straight away to achieve an immediate "clean break" or whether the division should be deferred. Marriage breakdown implies that there are irreconcilable differences, and conflict commonly results in a flight-or-fight reaction from one or both partners. The last thing either of them may want to do, or feel able to do, is to sit down quietly together to take "joint decisions". How realistic is it to expect antagonistic, deeply hurt people to negotiate practical arrangements with each other, especially in the early stages of separation?

The provision of legal advice and assistance to each partner separately, without any structured procedure to encourage joint decision-making, tends to drive estranged couples even further apart from each other. Each partner may harbour real or imagined grievances about the past and they may have contradictory views of their present situation and very different hopes or expectations for the future. As the gulf between them widens, it becomes increasingly difficult to bridge it: words that are shouted across it may convey angry threats to which the other partner reacts with counter-threats. Feelings of wounded love, grief and fear often remain unspoken. This pattern of destructive communication, or of no communication at all, takes an enormous toll of each partner's reserves of emotional energy, leaving them little strength to look for alternative ways of coping with their predicament, or even the strength to believe that alternatives exist. Even if they separate physically, some couples remain locked in conflict from which neither is able to disengage emotionally. Those who dare not express their powerful feelings directly to each other, because of deep fears of inflicting and suffering pain, may avoid direct confrontation and seek other indirect means of making demands or attacks on each other.

Physical separation is often a hasty act in the heat of a particular crisis, but the alienation it expresses may be the outcome of a much longer process of emotional withdrawal by one or both partners. Bernard (1973) has suggested that there are two different experiences of marriage in every actual marriage, and this is true to an even greater extent in marriage breakdown, where each partner is likely to construct different perceptions and interpretations out of the same events and conversations. The partner who apparently initiated the separation is often, but not invariably, the one who leaves home (Burgoyne and Clark 1984), and this proactive partner has commonly experienced the most stress before taking the decision to leave. The passive partner, on the other hand, is likely to experience most stress after the separation takes place, because the shock of separation is magnified by the intense pain and anger of rejection. Hart (1976) found that only 5 per cent of her admittedly non-representative sample of divorced people had taken a mutual decision to separate, and Burgoyne and Clark (1984) found in their study of remarried couples in Sheffield that only 6 out of 64 divorced men and women had agreed with their former partners that a divorce was necessary. Both these studies suggest that the emotional experience of the proactive partner is very different from that of the reactive partner and that these differences "are closely intertwined with emotional, physical and health outcomes" (Burgoyne and Clark 1984 p. 78). In the United States, Kressel and colleagues (1980) found similarly that the non-mutuality of the decision to separate or divorce had a very significant influence on other decisions. A partner who feels not only rejected, but excluded from major decisions about the marriage and about future arrangements for the family, may become stuck in the role of victim and may experience prolonged difficulty in regaining self-esteem and personal autonomy.

The more the two partners become out of phase with each other as they move, or fail to move, from one stage of marriage breakdown to the next, the more difficult it becomes to engage them both simultaneously, with an offer of help which relates to their discordant needs. The partner who wants to end the marriage may want help in dealing with legal and practical matters as swiftly and painlessly as possible, whereas the partner who feels rejected may look desperately for some means of hanging on to the marriage. Some couples may dread facing each other at all, and their unresolved feelings may make it impossible for them to negotiate over practical issues. One or both may be strongly resistant to the idea of joint discussion, and in the initial stages of shock and disorientation there may be a risk of them making ill-judged concessions or hasty agreements which they may later regret. In some cases, one partner may be pressing the other into hasty decisions which call for reflection and discussion, whereas in others, one partner may be blocking urgent decisions unreasonably. Conciliators need sensitivity and skill in planning the pace of work with both partners: the pressure can be considerable when husband and wife are pulling frantically in opposite directions.

Bohannan (1970) identified six "stations" or dimensions of the divorce experience, which he called the emotional divorce, the legal divorce, the economic divorce, the co-parental divorce (signifying the continuation of parenthood despite the dissolution of the marriage), the community divorce (meaning the loss of joint social activities and shared friendships), and the psychic divorce (meaning the ability to manage one's own life independently, without clinging to a relationship that no longer exists). The position of each partner in each of these dimensions may diverge widely and the dimensions may be unsynchronised with each other. For example, the legal divorce may take place long before the emotional divorce has been completed and the couple may divorce each other not only as spouses but also as parents, because unresolved conflict is easily transmitted from one area of their relationship to another.

Conciliation services should try to make it clear both in explanatory leaflets and in accepting referrals whether help is being offered on all the inter-related issues connected with separation and divorce or only on some of them. There may be confusion as to whether the objective is to help the parties reach a limited settlement of a concrete issue or whether it is to help them deal with underlying conflicts and problems. Some separating and divorcing individuals may accept only the former, whereas others may feel dissatisfied and angry if conciliation fails to resolve their conflicts at a much deeper level. If conciliators attempt to deal with the individual needs and underlying conflicts which fuel long-running disputes, they may stray into counselling or therapy and lose track of the conciliation task. They may be accused in any case of practising undercover therapy, especially if they claim that effective conciliation has therapeutic effects. If angry feelings are defused in the course of working out mutually acceptable arrangements, the couples concerned may express considerable relief, but the process which produced these "therapeutic" results was not necessarily "therapy". There are differences between conciliation and therapy in the expectations, function and roles of those involved in each process and it is important not to confuse them, especially as some practitioners work in more than one setting or agency. Similar distinctions need to be made between conciliation and divorce counselling. Although thousands of people divorce each year, divorce counselling as a clearly identified, specialist form of counselling seems to be in short supply. Marriage guidance is trying to broaden its marriage-saving image and some counsellors provide separation and divorce counselling as well as marital counselling, but there is evidence from research (Brannen and Collard 1982, Hunt 1985) of a tacit assumption on the part of many marriage guidance counsellors and their clients that counselling has to end, if the marriage ends. This unfortunate assumption may be changing but there still seems to be a shortage of divorce counsellors offering longer-term supportive counselling to individuals who need help with a slow and painful recovery from devastating shock and grief. Information should be readily available from advice agencies and other sources (as recommended by the Booth Committee 1985) about divorce counselling and conciliation services, including divorce experience courses if they are available locally. Some explanation is also needed to clarify the differences between superficially similar kinds of help, so that people can approach the agency of their choice with realistic expectations of what it may be offering. A clearer understanding of the differences between conciliation and divorce counselling is needed both by professionals and by the general public. Some of these differences may be summarised as follows:

Divorce Counselling	**Conciliation**
May be offered to one partner only.	Essentially involves both partners or ex-partners, and possibly children and new partners.
May be long-term.	Short-term (often 1-3 sessions)
Helps client/s to gain insight into personal difficulties; to express and gain control of feelings; to improve relationships, and/or the capacity to cope with stressful circumstances.	Helps both parties to reach mutually acceptable decisions, and to co-operate as parents in relation to their children.
May seek connections between the present and the past.	Focuses on the present and the future.
Usually independent of and separate from the legal process of divorce.	A socio-legal process involving contact with solicitors and understanding of legal issues.
Main focus usually on adult perspectives, and/or marital interaction.	Focus on family as well as spousal issues, especially parent-child relationships.

May put practical problems on one side while helping client to deal with emotional or psychological problems.	Seeks to settle concrete, practical issues and thereby promote positive changes in attitudes and adjustment.
Counsellor's role non-directive and relatively passive.	Conciliator's role usually very active: chairing discussions, containing conflict, identifying and clarifying options, etc.
Strongly influenced by psychodynamic theory and psychotherapy.	Theoretical bases include conflict management theory; family systems theory; communication theory; crisis theory.
May use the relationship between the client and the counsellor as a means of promoting change in other relationships.	Aims to increase the autonomy of both parties in managing their own affairs without recourse to external authority.

Differences between Counselling and Conciliation in Relation to the Reception of Referrals

Many counselling agencies offer an initial reception interview to a potential client to clarify the nature of the help sought and to explain the kind of help provided by a counsellor. The initial reception of referrals for conciliation is usually more complicated and time-consuming, because only one party may be seeking help and conciliation cannot take place at all unless both agree to participate. Seeing one party before making contact with the other may suggest a coalition between the conciliator and the party seeking help, thus jeopardising the chances of conciliation getting off the ground or being effective. When referrals are made jointly by both solicitors, they have assessed that conciliation is appropriate and both parties may have already agreed to the referral being made. However, where one of the parties makes a direct approach, he or she may be looking for partisan advice and support rather than for conciliation as such. The service's co-ordinator or receptionist needs to be skilful in assessing the viability of conciliation in a friendly manner which encourages the individual seeking help while at the same time explaining why a conciliation service always needs to involve both parties.

Experience of receiving referrals where only one partner is seeking help indicates the importance of a brief, carefully planned method of engaging both the help-seeker and the other party. The help-seeker may need to be restrained from pouring out his or her problems prematurely and the nature of possible resistance from the second party needs to be anticipated, so that an appropriate method can be devised to reach through this resistance to underlying concerns and fears. It is preferable to approach the second party via their solicitor because solicitors often encourage reluctant clients to accept an appointment, but in many cases the person concerned has not consulted a solicitor. A letter offering conciliation "out of the blue" needs to be carefully worded to convey the service's neutrality and to touch on relevant issues and concerns: these can often be deduced from even the barest details given by the other party. It is important to explain that only the minimum amount of information has been obtained from the "help-seeker"; otherwise, the other party may fear that the service has already swallowed a biased account of the situation. When resistance is anticipated, it is also helpful to tell the second party that their partner or ex-partner does not expect them to accept the offer of an appointment (e.g. to discuss access to the children) but that the conciliator cannot help at all unless he or she is able to understand both parents' points of view. This often produces a swift and positive response, to the surprise of the first party. This method of engaging both parties is applicable in voluntary out-of-court conciliation. When conciliation is initiated by the court, both parties may feel constrained to attend – though not necessarily disposed to co-operate.

Intractable Disputes

It would be easy to provide examples of disputes which failed to settle through conciliation but this would only illustrate that not all disputes are amenable to conciliation and that some criteria are needed to distinguish suitable from unsuitable referrals. We need to know much more about different kinds of disputes and how to work with them effectively. It has been suggested (Kressel, Deutsch, Jaffe, Tuchman and Watson 1980, Parkinson 1983a) that couples who are emotionally "enmeshed" in conflict may be reluctant to resolve it because the resulting emotional void would be worse than the battle itself. Conciliation may offer a means of continuing the struggle and conciliators may be beguiled into believing that just a little more help will produce agreement. Some time-limits need to be set and supervisors need to help conciliators adhere to these limits or extend them appropriately with both parties' consent. Failure to reach agreement may increase feelings of inadequacy (both in the parties and in conciliators) and conciliators may feel under pressure from the couple, the court or their agency to demonstrate "success". Research has indicated that conciliators in some services do exert authority in covert or not so covert ways (Davis and Bader 1985, Dingwall in press), despite subscribing to the doctrine of "party control". Methods of working vary considerably and conciliation techniques are being evolved gradually. Conciliators must recognise that as they cannot respond to all the demands which may be made on them, referrals to a counsellor or therapist may be needed. The referral system can work in both directions and the sequence of help needs to be planned carefully with the individual/s concerned. Good liaison is needed between different agencies to ease people's transfer between them without breaching confidentiality.

Relationship with Solicitors

Conciliation, unlike counselling, is closely linked with legal processes and there is considerable emphasis in Britain on the need for conciliators to liaise with solicitors and on the value of co-operation between them. This emphasis on the interdisciplinary nature of conciliation in separation and divorce is itself a form of conciliation between different professional disciplines. One interesting aspect is the use of a common vocabulary which promotes better understanding between lawyers and conciliators, instead of causing confusion or irritation by using obscure professional jargon. Conciliation involves finding common ground between solicitors and conciliators as well as between the parties themselves, because it needs to complement, not supplant, legal advice and assistance from solicitors. "A legal resolution that ignores the client's psychological needs is as inappropriate as a psychological resolution that conflicts with the client's legal needs" (Steinberg 1980 p. 261). This interdisciplinary approach has implications for each stage of the conciliation process and for the handling of the problems that are liable to arise at each stage.

Limited contact between solicitors and conciliation services is important because solicitors' help is generally needed to formalise agreements and apply for consent orders. Busy solicitors do not always think of recommending conciliation and they may lack information about it (some solicitors still confuse it with reconciliation) or doubt its usefulness. Conciliation services which are affiliated to the National

Family Conciliation Council can draw solicitors' attention to the code of practice (Appendix A) which sets out guide-lines on issues for referral and the status of provisional agreements.

Solicitors may be wary of interference by well-meaning, idealistic amateurs, as conciliators are sometimes perceived. Rather than holding out unrealistic hopes of solving all the difficulties, conciliators offer help on specific issues. Access disputes are notoriously time-consuming for solicitors and their lack of direct contact with both parties is a handicap. Conciliation need not delay the legal process because it can be attempted while an application for legal aid is processed by the Law Society or while the parties wait for a court hearing date. Pitching the expectations of conciliation realistically low may reassure solicitors that their recognition of substantial difficulties is acknowledged. Although conciliation may not avoid court proceedings, it may narrow the areas of disagreement or at least clarify them and reduce misunderstandings.

If there are dependent children, it is relevant to ask solicitors whether there is any direct and co-operative contact between the parents. Parents in conflict with each other often communicate only via their solicitors or via the children and although solicitors may succeed in obtaining a legal settlement of custody and access issues, "negotiations conducted by solicitors leave parents with the problem of how to resume communication when their solicitors withdraw. A solicitor typically sees, and can certainly only act for one of two parties and is therefore not well placed to promote the direct dialogue and joint decision-making" which are essential if agreements over access are to be maintained or varied informally when necessary (Parker and Parkinson 1985 p. 271). By seeing both parents together on neutral ground, conciliators can facilitate direct communication between them and consider with them both how this communication can be maintained after conciliation ends.

Solicitors may be understandably resistant to the idea of handing over their clients to another professional, in case this gives the impression that they are flummoxed by or insufficiently interested in their clients' problems. Conciliators should emphasise that although they offer an alternative means of settling disputes, they are not substitutes for solicitors: they are an additional resource in cases where there is overt dispute, ambivalence about decisions, problems involving children or problems of communication. Many parents are very concerned to do what is best for their children – although they may disagree about what this involves – and the impartial, family-oriented perspective of conciliators can usefully complement the solicitor's primarily legal perspective. Solicitors can assure their clients that in recommending conciliation, they are not withdrawing from the case: on the contrary, they are concerned to help the client weigh up different methods of dealing with particular problems and a joint approach by solicitors and conciliators offers the client a greater range of specialist help and information than either a solicitor or a conciliator can provide alone.

Solicitors can find themselves in a professional dilemma if they feel that a client is behaving irrationally or irresponsibly, especially where children are concerned. If they speak too strongly on children's behalf, the client may lose confidence in the solicitor's advocacy of their case and may transfer to another, more adversarially inclined solicitor. A referral for conciliation can ease solicitors off the professional hook of responsibility towards children whom they do not represent but for whom they feel considerable concern. In practice, solicitors rarely meet with the children and do not see this as part of their task (Murch 1980) and they may feel that the conciliator's impartial concern for the family as a whole is a particular advantage and strength.

These considerations may encourage solicitors to refer their clients to a conciliation service, preferably at an early stage. A low referral rate from solicitors is not necessarily due to active opposition or disenchantment with a particular service: it may be due to lack of information about conciliation generally. Solicitors may also suspect that in some cases the parties are simply looking for any means of keeping the battle going and that any further discussion will merely refuel the flames. Alternatively (but in my own experience, very rarely), a solicitor may neither agree to the conciliation service contacting a client nor be willing to discuss the possibility of conciliation with the client. If the solicitor seems disinclined to take positive action in a situation which may be amenable to conciliation, he or she may be asked to pass on a letter addressed to the client c/o the solicitor, together with a copy for the solicitor. This request is not easily refused and it can enable the conciliation service to put the offer of conciliation directly to the client in the service's own words, instead of relying on a discouraging mention by the solicitor. The letter should be carefully worded to relate to the client's probable concerns and anxieties, of which the solicitor may not be fully aware. If there is conflict over the children, solicitors cannot readily disregard the suggestion of conciliation, since children's welfare is paramount in law and litigation over children is undesirable.

The Nature and Extent of Conciliators' Responsibility towards Children

Reference has already been made to the assumption that conciliation benefits children and to conciliators' concern that agreements should meet children's needs as well as parents' needs. But what right do conciliators have to preach about "children's needs" and how can they claim to know what is in a child's best interests, if they do not get to know the child and if the child's parents disagree? Any attempt to push conciliators into the role of a superior expert or authority figure who automatically knows better than natural parents what their children need introduces a paternalistic, child-saving philosophy which runs counter to the main principles of conciliation. There is bound to be a conflict of values if conciliators become – or are seen as – double agents working to a double agenda, whose explicit concern is to help divorcing couples reach mutually agreed decisions, but whose implicit concern is to check up on the welfare of their children. Conciliators incur criticism if they appear to be either adult-centred or child-centred, yet there is pressure on them to protect both adults' rights and children's rights.

Davis (1983a, 1985) has accused court welfare officers and social workers of importing child-welfare ideology into conciliation because this ideology is ingrained in their traditional work with families. He suspects that conciliators with social work training may feel more comfortable and secure in the role of child-protector than in the unfamiliar role of impartial negotiator, without statutory duties or powers. Roberts (1983) takes a similar view that the conciliator should be no more than an impartial broker who facilitates negotiation between disputants and assists them to reach consensual decisions on matters of joint concern. Both these commentators consider that parents' autonomy should be absolute, and as conciliators have no formal power or right to vet parents' decisions, it may seem that they are committed solely to settling disputes between adults, regardless of the quality of the settlement from the children's point of view. For family conciliators, however, the quality of the settlement is important and they are concerned that it should take account of children's feelings and needs as well as helping both parents.

Most conciliators work from the assumption that children's best interests are promoted by agreement between their parents (Howard and Shepherd 1982) and in many independent services conciliators rely on parents' statements about their children without involving the children directly. However, there is evidence from research (Wallerstein and Kelly 1980, Mitchell 1985) of considerable discrepancy between parents' perceptions of their children's feelings and the accounts given by children themselves. Mitchell (1985) found that some children strongly disagreed with the custodial parent's view of their "wishes". One girl said to the researcher: "My Mum didn't understand how I felt. She was too busy being angry" (p. 191). One-third of the parents in Mitchell's study were unable to describe their children's feelings about the break-up of their marriage and many projected their own feelings on to their children, assuming that the children shared the same feelings about the other parent. Working solely with parents could result in arrangements being made which purport to be in children's best interests but which actually serve parents' interests at the expense of their children. Many conciliators are reluctant to accept that their responsibility is exclusively towards the two parties to the dispute, as though children were no more than sacks of corn to be haggled over or split in half. Yet the role of child advocate is incompatible with the commitment to helping people work out their own decisions. Complete neutrality is bland and permissive: at some point there has to be a dividing line between supporting parental autonomy and, to take an extreme but possible situation, colluding with child abuse.

The code of practice for conciliators (Appendix A) sets out guidelines in relation to child abuse, stating that in extreme cases conciliators have an overriding duty to report a case involving child abuse to an appropriate agency, if neither parent is willing to do so. The preface to the code states that "in the short term, the objective of conciliation is to help parties reach a workable settlement which takes account of the needs of the children and adults involved. The longer term objective is to help both parents a) maintain their relationship with their children, and b) achieve a co-operative plan for their children's future welfare." The implied bias in favour of access taking place does not square with total neutrality, since it creates a potential alliance between the conciliator and the parent seeking access. Where, on the other hand, parents agree that there should be no access, conciliators may feel that they should question whether this agreement is satisfactory from the children's point of view. Unlike social workers and divorce court welfare officers, conciliators have no responsibility to investigate and assess what is in a child's best interests, but does this mean that they should concur with whatever parents propose? A case comes to mind in which the parents were in agreement over custody and access.

One parent called the child by a girl's name and dressed her in girl's clothes and the other called her by a boy's name and dressed her in boy's clothes. Should a conciliator accept without comment any arrangements on which parents agree, however bizarre or even damaging they may be for a child? Conciliators are faced with considerable dilemmas if both parents appear to be disregarding a child's physical or psychological health, and the code of practice advises (Appendix A, par. 5) that conciliators may need to terminate conciliation if continuing discussion proves unproductive. In such circumstances, they should explain to both parents why they feel unable to continue and inform their solicitors that conciliation has ceased. The report to solicitors should not however give information or assessments to justify the conciliator's concern, since conciliators are not in a position to investigate and assess these situations. Collusion between separating and divorcing parents in making grossly unsatisfactory arrangements for their children seems very uncommon, but there is a remote possibility of psychiatric illness or subnormality affecting both parents' ability to reach responsible decisions concerning their children.

It may be questioned why conciliators need feel any responsibility for children since arrangements for the children are considered by the judge at the section 41 (children's) appointment. Research referred to in chapter 1 (Davis, MacLeod and Murch 1983a, Dodds 1983) showed however that this scrutiny may be perfunctory and many cases referred to independent conciliation services involve couples who are separating but not divorcing, couples who are already divorced and unmarried couples. The arrangements these parents make for their children will not normally be reviewed by the court unless one parent contests the other's decisions. It is of course debatable whether there should be any attempt by the state to scrutinise the arrangements which divorcing parents make for their children (Haynes 1984) but Eekelaar (1984) argues cogently that objections about unwarranted intrusion into family life take no account of the rights of the child. If it is accepted that conciliators have some ethical responsibility towards children although no statutory responsibilities for their welfare, they should explain to parents at the outset that their concern is to help them work out arrangements which meet their children's needs as well as their own. This does not mean that parents' decisions have to be submitted to the conciliator for approval, and only in extreme circumstances would a conciliator take any action without their consent. This would normally be discussed with both parents first, to see if any other way of handling the situation could be arrived at.

In practice, any question of breaching confidentiality is likely to occur very rarely and conciliators who are experienced in handling stressful situations can usually gain consent from at least one party and probably both that they will separately or jointly seek appropriate help. In one case, a divorced father who had not had any contact with the conciliator for several months suddenly telephoned her and confided that he thought he was going to kill his ex-wife's boyfriend later that night. He agreed to come to see the conciliator straight away and it was apparent that he was seriously ill. He could not eat any food without vomiting and felt he had lost all control. He had contacted the conciliator because he thought she would listen to him and take notice of what he was saying, whereas the doctor he had seen in a group practice had simply advised him to get on with his work. He agreed readily to the conciliator obtaining an emergency medical appointment for him and after a long interview with a psychiatrist, he was admitted to hospital forthwith as a voluntary patient. On his discharge ten days later, he said that the respite and isolation from the outside world had enabled him to regain sufficient control to cope with the stress he still felt, though he continued to maintain that he would have committed murder if the conciliator had not made a swift response that particular afternoon. Conciliators need to be alert to these high-risk situations and yet be able to resist pushing "panic buttons" unnecessarily, in response to manipulation or hysteria.

Another form of pressure which conciliators frequently encounter is pressure from a parent to interview the children in order to "find out what they want". Interviewing children to elicit wishes or choices from them may increase their anxiety, especially if a child is asked to make painful decisions which should be made by adults, not children. It may also expose the child to further pressure from one or both parents to say whatever that parent wants them to say, and if parents are to be informed afterwards of what the child has actually said, this may put the child in an intolerable position. On the other hand, promising confidentiality to children may place the professional in the untenable position of holding information without being able to act on it. Many judges choose not to see children on their own, recognising that children may repeat what they feel they ought to say and that they may be too afraid or confused to put their feelings into words. As two court welfare officers have observed, "generally speaking, the greater the conflict between the parents, the less reliance can be placed on children's views" (Howard and Shepherd 1982 pp. 91-

2). The experience of family court counsellors in the Family Court of Australia has similarly led many of them to conclude that the concept of "the wishes of the child" is simplistic, unreliable, and possibly damaging to the child. Marshall and colleagues, in a very useful paper on this subject (Marshall Grant and Nasser 1979) suggest that the concept of "the needs, perceptions and attachments of children" is more valid and relevant than "the wishes of the child". This is not to deny that individual children may have powerfully felt wishes or preferences which need to be taken into account, but children's feelings cannot be fully understood in isolation from the context in which they occur.

Conciliators, especially if they are accustomed to counselling adults, may share parents' fears that involving children in discussions about family arrangements draws children into marital arguments and may heighten their anxieties. Haynes (1981) recommends that children should be brought in only after agreements have been reached, to review the proposed arrangements with both parents. He has however quoted a case (1984) in which the son reminded his parents that he played in the football team on Saturday afternoons, which they had both forgotten, and a laboriously arranged access schedule had to be re-negotiated. Huntington (1982) contests Haynes' view that children should be excluded from discussions. She argues, and many court welfare officers in England and Wales agree with her (Howard and Shepherd 1982, Guise 1983, Taylor 1984), that there are helpful ways of including children in conciliation without burdening them with the weight of decisions which rightfully belong to their parents. James and Wilson (in press) take the view that children have a right to be included in conciliation meetings and that "the importance of their involvement cannot be over-emphasised" (draft, p. 32).

An adversarial legal system assumes that there are two protagonists in a dispute, one of whom may be right, and the other wrong. In matrimonial disputes, the dispute is normally assumed to be between the spouses and if the issue/s involve children, decisions are made for and about the children, but rarely with them. However, conflict in families may not be confined to parents; very often, it is transmitted to the children, who may come to play a direct part in it. Children may form an alliance with one parent against the other and in some families a child may become a substitute parent, providing protection and companionship for an abandoned adult (Saposnek 1983). These situations create great stress for children and may affect their development in the longer term (Wallerstein and Kelly 1980). If decisions are made without understanding the child's role in the divided family, the child's reactions may make parental arrangements or court orders unworkable in practice, and professionals may find themselves beating their heads against a brick wall. It is important for children to understand what role the absent parent is going to play in future, what role a new step-parent is going to play and that the adults in their lives care about them. Recent studies (Walczak 1984, Mitchell 1985) have shown the extent to which many children are left in the dark while major upheavals go on around them. They may rebel against arrangements which are imposed on them without explanation or discussion, and thus make life impossible for all concerned, including themselves. Some of them take the law into their own hands by running from one parent to the other, and if "custody" is exercised with or without "control" but without any "care" (is it a coincidence that the legal terms suggest penal incarceration?), this may be followed by further crises, in which the child may need medical treatment, help with emotional or behavioural problems, fail at school or ultimately desert both parents (Wadsworth 1979, Wadsworth and Maclean in press).

Many conciliators are uncertain whether they should concentrate on helping children indirectly, by helping their parents to co-operate, or whether they should seek to help children directly, by encouraging parents to bring their children to conciliation meetings. There cannot be a hard and fast rule, because much depends on the nature and stage of decisions and on the level of crisis. Some decisions, such as decisions whether, when and how to seek a divorce, are essentially marital decisions in which children have no proper part. However, if decisions are being made about custody and access there may be strong indications for involving children appropriately, if conciliators are able to do this in a way which helps parents and children together. They need to be as positive and supportive as possible, so that parents are not made to feel inadequate nor feel that the conciliator is the ally of a manipulative and rebellious child. Where children are actively involved in parental conflict, conciliators need to look not only for common ground between estranged parents but also for the common ground between parents and children and between the children themselves. Siblings sometimes take the side of the same-sex parent, thus reproducing the marital conflict between themselves. There is little value in settling disputes between parents if arrangements are promptly overturned by the children. Arrangements may be fully accepted only if some discussion takes place with parents and children together. In the following cases, children were directly involved in the conciliation process, with apparently beneficial results for them and for both parents.

Case Example: a Pre-adolescent Child

The referral to the conciliation service was initiated by Mrs West, who telephoned at her solicitor's suggestion to say that her twelve-year-old son, Neil, had left home a month ago after an argument with her, and had gone to live at his father's home, about three miles away. She and Mr West had been divorced for two years, and she had legal custody of Neil and his sister, Susie, aged seven. Mrs West felt that Mr West was taking advantage of her trouble with Neil to hang on to him, and that Neil would have returned to her of his own accord if he were not afraid of his father's reaction. Mrs West was considering applying to the police or the court to have her custody of Neil enforced, but her solicitor had advised her to try conciliation first. Mr West was reached by telephone the same day and he agreed to attend a joint appointment with Mrs West the following day. Neither of them wanted Neil to be present at this first meeting. It was clear that they were bracing themselves for a confrontation, having bottled up feelings about each other for a considerable time.

The first meeting was indeed an acrimonious one, but it also produced some positive movement, including an assurance from Mr West that he was not putting pressure on Neil to stay with him. Both parents frequently referred to Neil's "wishes" as a means of attacking each other and at one point Mr West warned Mrs West that if Neil were forcibly returned to her, he would only run away again. Mrs West was not convinced, and she and Mr West decided that she should have a talk with Neil with the conciliator present, followed by another meeting with both of them and Neil, to help the parents make decisions for Neil's future which all of them felt able to accept. At the meeting with his mother, Neil seemed particularly mature and reflective for his age. He explained that his decision to go to live with his father had not been a sudden one and that he wanted more freedom and independence than he was allowed by his mother and Bill (Mrs West's co-habitee). He felt that they treated him and Susie as though they were the same age and that Susie was allowed to get away with pestering him and spoiling his things. At his father's home, he had more privacy and he felt that he was settling down well in the new school and did not want to be moved back to his old school.

The discussion with Neil and his mother raised a number of issues which were then discussed with him and both his parents together. It was emphasised that the final decision about Neil's custody belonged to his parents, after different possibilities and points of view had been carefully considered. One of the main issues from Neil's point of view was the fact that he had outgrown his bike; he pointed out that he needed a bike so that he could go to see his mother, sister and stepfather, after school and at weekends. His parents could see that he was strongly attached to them both and that although he felt settled with his father, this did not mean that he had rejected his mother. The atmosphere between Mr and Mrs West became less hostile as it became clearer that this was not a competition to win Neil, but a question of sharing concern and responsibility for him and adjusting to the fact that he was almost a teenager, whose needs were inevitably changing as he grew up. The issue of the new bike initially provoked some argument about maintenance payments but this led to an agreement to share the cost of the bike, on the understanding that Mrs West would discuss the proposed arrangements with her solicitor, and unless he advised her strongly to the contrary, she would arrange for the child benefit payable for Neil to be transferred to Mr West's name. Both solicitors supported these proposals, which were outlined in a summary sent to them both by the conciliator. The court subsequently made a consent order transferring Neil's care and control to his father; no court hearing was necessary because Neil's mother concurred with the application.

Case Example: a Distressed Three-Year-Old

Mrs Nott telephoned the conciliation service on her solicitor's advice, concerning her husband's access to their three-year-old daughter, Melanie. She said on the telephone that she had insisted on her husband leaving home some weeks previously, because the arguments between them had become violent and he had hit her several times in front of Melanie. Melanie was now very afraid of her father and clung to her mother if he came to the door. Mr Nott was demanding access to Melanie and Mrs Nott was on the verge of applying for a non-molestation injunction because he kept phoning her late at night to plead for a reconciliation.

Mr Nott was at first unwilling to accept the offer of conciliation, on the grounds that it was a ploy on his wife's part to delay his getting an access order from the court. He was assured that he was free to apply to the court and it was suggested that it would be worthwhile to talk about his access to Melanie without delay, even if he began court proceedings at the same time. The offer of an appointment three days later was then accepted. At this joint appointment, Mrs Nott stated that she felt that it was important for Melanie to remain in contact with her father but Melanie now refused pointblank to be separated from her and she did not want to accompany Melanie on access visits with Mr Nott. Both parents acknowledged that Melanie screamed if her father went to the house, and Mr Nott said he felt unable to drag her away from her mother in such a distraught state. It was agreed that Mrs Nott would bring Melanie to see the conciliator and become familiar with the toys etc. in the conciliation room and that before the second visit a few days later, Melanie would be told that her father would be joining them for a while and that both her mother and the conciliator would be there with her all the time. Whereas the family home was associated with fighting between Mr and Mrs Nott, the conciliation room offered security, and after a couple of visits in which her mother remained in the room throughout, Melanie was sufficiently at ease for her mother to go out for a while to do some shopping. On the next visit, Melanie and her father went out together and thereafter he was able to collect her from the family home.

The pace of these gradual changes was geared to the pace at which Melanie seemed able to cope with them and both her parents accepted that the only way to overcome her fears was for her to experience the two of them co-operating with each other in a calm and relaxed way. They managed to do this in relation to Melanie, partly because they had other discussions with the conciliator without Melanie being present, in which they focused on the other unresolved issues between them. Previously, all the stress of the failing marriage was transmitted to Melanie and it was not surprising that it was more than she could bear. Parental issues were thus separated from marital issues and a formal agreement on access became workable in practice by restoring Melanie's trust that it was safe for her to love her father and for her parents to see each other.

Comment

In both these cases, conciliation with the parents might have produced nominal agreements but their effectiveness in practice hinged on the child's direct experience of parental co-operation and on the child receiving emotional permission from each parent to relate to the other. Children's concerns often differ from their parents' concerns and they may raise an issue or fear which provides the key to a bigger problem, as in the case of Neil's bike, which enabled him to manage his contacts with both halves of his family.

Many voluntary conciliation services in England and Wales work to a large extent with parents without including children in family meetings. Scotland, with its record of innovatory work with children's panels in the juvenile justice system (Martin and Murray 1984), seems more inclined to involve children directly in conciliation. The co-ordinator of the Scottish Family Conciliation Service (Lothian) has identified a number of reasons for involving children (Ross 1985b) which have also been noted by divorce court welfare officers south of the border. Guise (1983) suggested that in the most entrenched situations in which parents are using the children as hostages or pawns in their battles, the children's presence can help parents recognise the pressure it puts on children to take decisions for the family. Warring couples may then begin to see each other as parents with mutual concerns instead of solely as antagonists. In one case mentioned to me by the co-ordinator of the Cleveland Family Conciliation Service, a provisional agreement on access was drafted with both parents for them and for their solicitors and then a simpler version was drafted for their children. Each child had a copy of the arrangements, which referred to them individually, and both the parents and the children showed in subsequent contacts that they valued this document as a tangible record of what they had worked out together. Not all disputes settle through conciliation with this degree of satisfaction and co-operation and conciliators will continue to wrestle with conflicting needs and demands. A family systems approach used with appropriate skills can help parents and children together, without conciliators taking on the role of judge or child advocate which implies that parents are unfit to take decisions. Balancing adults' needs with children's needs in ways which maximise parents' confidence and resources is a difficult task, especially where there is a long history of difficulties. This emphasises further the need for careful selection and training of conciliators to help them develop specific skills in working with divided families.

9 MEASURING THE RESULTS OF CONCILIATION: SOME FINDINGS AND OBSERVATIONS

The philosophy of conciliation generates a great deal of enthusiasm and in a world that is constantly exposed to the horror and havoc wrought by conflict in all spheres of life, the concept of peaceful settlement has understandably powerful appeal. However, moral support does not always mean financial support and a government intent on cutting public expenditure may be interested in a new enterprise only if it promises savings. It may not be sufficient to argue that conciliation benefits both parties and their children: some evidence of financial savings is called for to justify funding even experimental schemes. Sir John Arnold, President of the Family Division of the High Court, has repeatedly emphasised that public funding of conciliation is justified on both economic and social grounds.

> With matrimonial disputes accounting for some 72% of all civil legal aid litigation outlay . . . , there is urgent need to embrace and develop every means of resolving such disputes by agreement. To the advantage of freeing limited legal aid resources for more rational expenditure may be added a large potential avoidance of resentment and unhappiness and their consequences of ill-health and of delinquency (Arnold 1981, p. 196).

Conciliation developments have been supported by judges with long experience in the divorce courts and support has also come from members of all the main political parties. In June 1981 an Early Day Motion set down in the House of Commons by Leo Abse, leader of the all-party divorce reform group, was signed by over 100 MPs. The Motion called on the government to establish a committee of inquiry to review, among other matters, "locally-oriented and funded conciliation schemes and ... to make recommendations as to the best manner of securing, on a permanent basis, the general availability of suitable schemes" (*Hansard* 24 June 1981). Later in the same year, the Law Commission also recommended that "the availability and scope of conciliation and similar services should be systematically investigated; everything possible should be done to encourage recourse to conciliation rather than litigation" (Report No. 112, par. 46). In response to the pressure for divorce law reform and for conciliation services, the Lord Chancellor set up two committees of inquiry with overlapping terms of reference: the Inter-departmental Committee on Conciliation, a committee of civil servants which was set up in March 1982, and the Matrimonial Causes Procedure Committee, appointed in July 1982 under the chairmanship of the Hon. Mrs Justice Booth[1]. The Inter-departmental Committee was asked "to review current arrangements for conciliation, . . . to report on the nature, scope and effects . . . of existing facilities and services, [and] to consider whether those or further facilities should be promoted or developed, and if so, how this could best be done within existing resource planning" (Report 1983 par. 1.1). From the outset, the government showed interest in saving money through the use of conciliation and reluctance to accept a commitment to any additional public expenditure, however desirable this might be for other reasons. The Inter-departmental Committee questioned whether there was any justification for the public funding of conciliation services, emphasising that other options should be considered before recommending that the government should intervene. The Committee took it to be "axiomatic that it is generally better for parties to civil litigation, or indeed any dispute, to settle their differences rather than fight them out to the bitter end", but observed that "if there is a justification for creating special machinery for matrimonial cases it must surely be primarily for the sake of the children" (par. 1.13). The Committee did not explain why, if conciliation is preferable to litigation, it should not be available to all potential litigants, whether they have children or not, since a caring society should be concerned to settle disputes without adding to the distress of the individuals involved.

The first problem which arises in any evaluation of conciliation is thus the political question of whose values should determine the criteria on which the evaluation is made. Davis (1983a) argued that since most disputes are eventually settled one way or another, conciliation should be assessed not by counting settlements and assuming savings but by comparing the timing and quality of these settlements with those obtained through a formal process of adjudication. The main yardstick should be "the parties' satisfaction with the arrangements" (p. 7). But should the quality of the settlement be judged by the parties alone and should their satisfaction with the outcome be the sole yardstick? It may be unrealistic to assess any method of settling disputes on the basis of consumer satisfaction, since the pain and trauma of divorce are such that people are unlikely to feel "satisfied" with any process. Unless they have already been through formal court proceedings, they cannot compare their experience of conciliation with the experience of a bitterly fought adversarial process followed by adjudication. Moreover, the time-scale in which a settlement is achieved through the courts is geared to adult and especially to professional time-scales and many divorcing individuals need to adjust emotionally to their separation over a period of time. This need may be at odds with their children's need for custody and access arrangements to be worked out at an early stage, with as little delay as possible.

There are therefore a number of different and potentially conflicting criteria for evaluating conciliation, depending on whose values take priority: a) from the court's point of view, its success in settling contested cases quickly and clearing court lists; b) from each party's point of view, the helpfulness of the process to each of them personally and the nature of its final outcome; c) from the children's point of view, the lowering of tension and conflict around access visits and their parents' willingness to communicate directly with each other, instead of using their children as messengers or spies; d) from the government's point of view, the evidence of a drop in the number of welfare inquiries and matrimonial supervision orders and of reduced legal aid expenditure; e) from the point of view of solicitors concerned to protect their professional interests, the opportunity to offload time-consuming but financially unrewarding access cases while preserving intact the bulk of their matrimonial work. It is difficult to see how any process could cater for all these interests simultaneously and financial support for conciliation from public funds depends largely on whose interests it is primarily seen to be serving and what costs are incurred. It also has to be borne in mind that a prolonged but ultimately unsuccessful conciliation effort might not benefit anyone, least of all children in need of a decision. The evaluation of conciliation seems therefore to depend on value judgements and on the interplay of numerous variables, highlighting the uneasy tension between private and public interests – which is in itself an arena for conciliation.

Attempts to measure the psychological benefits of conciliation for adults and for children lack scientific precision because of the highly subjective judgements required. Research studies have therefore tended to rely on objectively verifiable data such as the number of cases undertaken, the number of agreements recorded, the time and cost involved and, in some studies, the durability of agreements. Relitigation rates are sometimes used as a measure of "success" but this too is an unreliable yardstick since the absence of subsequent litigation does not prove that agreements are being adhered to.

Referral Rates

If courts channel all contested cases through a preliminary conciliation procedure before listing them for a court hearing the principle of voluntary participation is lost. Independent schemes, on the other hand, may fail to reach both parties and depending on their location they may remain a quiet backwater of the mainstream legal process, catering for couples who choose to use them and who can afford any travelling expenses involved. In a survey of recently divorced people carried out at Bristol University (Davis, MacLeod and Murch 1982b), two-thirds of the parents who had experienced conflict with their spouse in the course of their divorce proceedings said that they would have welcomed the help of a conciliator to help them come to agreement, whereas one-third said that they would not have done so. However, it must be borne in mind that these parents were speaking with the benefit of hindsight and that they may have wanted to make a good impression on the interviewer. Even if they expressed support for conciliation in principle, they might have rejected it in practice when they were in the midst of a dispute. The discrepancy (which may be as high as 50 per cent in some areas) between the number of self-referrals received by independent conciliation services and the number of conciliation cases that actually get off the ground suggests that even where conciliation is felt to be appropriate, one party may be unwilling or out of reach.

The Inter-departmental Committee commented (1983) on the generally low take-up of independent conciliation schemes, reporting that their average number of cases was only about 33 per year, apart from BCFCS and Bromley. Most of these schemes were then very new and running on a shoe-string and in view of their low and insecure funding it is not surprising that their take-up rate did not increase to any marked extent during 1982-84. There are so many variables in independent conciliation services, in their level of funding and staffing, the type of referrals accepted, the geographical area covered and the way conciliation is offered and organised that it is misleading to compare their referral rates and reported results. With this caveat in mind, it is possible however to note three levels of operation in independent schemes: 1) those undertaking fewer than 50 cases per year; 2) those undertaking 50-100 cases; and 3) two services (Bristol and

Bromley) undertaking well over 200 cases per year. In 1983-84, many independent services (including Cambridge, Chelmsford, East Berkshire, Kent, Leeds, Norfolk, North Devon, Sunderland) undertook fewer than 50 conciliation cases. Some (Berkshire, Cardiff, Cleveland, Coventry, Richmond, Surrey, Swindon) dealt with 50-100 cases and some were encouraged by an increase in take-up. Bromley anticipated a substantially increased referral rate of 460 cases in 1985 (Gibbons 1985), a response which contrasts with experience in the United States of a generally low take-up of voluntary conciliation schemes. This led two American researchers (Merry and Silbey 1984) to suggest that by the time a conflict is serious enough to warrant an outsider's intervention, one or both parties may refuse conciliation because they want vindication, protection of their rights, an advocate to help in the battle or a third party who will uncover the "truth" and declare the other party wrong. The take-up of voluntary conciliation services depends on recommendations from users of these services and on good support from solicitors, Citizens' Advice Bureaux workers and other agencies. They can then complement court-initiated conciliation by offering informal help at an early stage.

Are Those Who Use Independent Conciliation Services Representative of the Divorcing Population as a Whole?

Court-related conciliation procedures can catch all contested cases in their net, regardless of social class and ethnic differences, whereas independent services are likely to cater for unrepresentative sections of the divorcing population. Much depends on the image they project and on referrers' perceptions of what they are offering and to whom. Research monitoring of ten independent services undertaken by Yates (1985) on behalf of the National Family Conciliation Council found that solicitor referrals accounted for nearly half the referrals which led to conciliation, the others being self-referred or referred by other agencies. Davis (1980) in his first study of BCFCS examined solicitors' criteria for referring cases for conciliation and found a wide variation. Some solicitors thought it suitable primarily for middle-class and articulate clients, whereas others saw it as a service for lower income groups. Davis' analysis of the husband's occupation in 73 BCFCS cases suggested that the service was used more often by professional than semi-skilled and unskilled workers, compared with socio-economic differentials in the divorcing population as a whole.

In the self-referred group, fathers (37%) seemed to be slightly more likely than mothers (30%) to seek conciliation (Yates 1984), in contrast to referrals to marriage guidance (Heisler 1984), which are initiated predominantly by women. Fathers who sought conciliation were often closely involved in looking after their children and strongly motivated to fight for custody or access (Davis 1980). It is not known whether fathers in higher socio-economic groups are more likely to fight for custody and access through the courts than those in lower income groups. If so, this might explain the higher demand for conciliation from middle-class couples. An alternative hypothesis is that independent conciliation services, like marital counselling agencies, attract a proportion of middle-class couples but fail to attract working-class couples and the unemployed to a comparable extent.

Another so far unanswered question is whether independent conciliation services are acceptable to couples in ethnic minority groups. The Inter-departmental Committee referred to the concern expressed by the Commission on Racial Equality that services should be designed to cater for these groups and should recognise their different cultural traditions. There is evidence of an increasing breakdown rate among Asian marriages, despite the strong cultural and religious traditions which support marital and family ties[2]. Experience (unpublished) of the experimental Asian marriage counselling scheme in Bradford suggests that Asian couples may accept a counsellor who speaks their own language and understands their cultural traditions. Conciliation services in areas with mixed ethnic populations need to take account of these considerations in selecting and training their conciliators. To date, there seems to be only one independent service (in Yorkshire) which has recruited a black conciliator and only a few schemes have established links with leaders of their local Asian community.

Settlement Rates

Assessing the "success rate" of conciliation services in terms of full and partial agreements raises complicated technical questions as to when, how and by whom these agreements are recorded (whether subjectively by conciliators or with objective verification and follow-up), and whether the agreements reached are partly attributable to other influences or factors as well as to the conciliation process. Davis (see References) has undertaken a great deal of research into the settlement rates achieved both in in-court and out-of-court conciliation schemes. In relation to BCFCS he reported (1982b) that in 139 cases undertaken by BCFCS in 1979-80, in which he monitored the service's records and checked the outcome with the parties' solicitors, 40 per cent of the cases reached full agreement on all contested issues (including 13 per cent who agreed on a reconciliation), with a further 18 per cent partially agreed, 19 per cent having an uncertain outcome and 19 per cent not agreed.

> Measurement of outcome was often not clearcut. In some cases there was a shift from previously entrenched positions, but without firm agreement being reached in the course of conciliation. Sometimes an agreement would be reached only for this subsequently to break down. The work of BCFCS may therefore be most usefully viewed as one factor in a very complex scene (p. 356).

Two years later, BCFCS reported full settlement in 27 per cent of cases, reconciliation in 11 per cent, partial settlement in 26.6 per cent and an inconclusive outcome in 20 per cent, with the remaining couples either not agreeing or failing to attend (BCFCS 1984). It should be borne in mind, however, that these figures were based on the conciliators' records without follow-up studies to ascertain the outcome in the longer term. Davis (1983b) also studied conciliation at Bromley, where he found in a sample of 118 cases that 38 per cent were settled, 25 per cent showed "some progress", 13 per cent had an uncertain outcome, 23 per cent failed to settle and in 2 per cent the outcome was not recorded. A follow-up consumer study by Davis and Roberts at Bromley may be published in 1986.

The Conciliation in Divorce research project carried out by Davis at Bristol University from 1981 to 1984 included a detailed study of court records and observation of in-court conciliation appointments at Bristol and Newport County Courts (Davis 1982c) and a follow-up consumer study to investigate people's experience of this system (Davis and Bader 1985). The appointments achieved a high rate of settlement, with 70 per cent of cases settling where there was a dispute over access, 56 per cent settling where there were related issues over the divorce itself and custody or access and 42 per cent where both custody and access arrangements were contested. Davis and Bader (1985) have however questioned the quality of these settlements and have drawn attention to the dissatisfaction expressed by parents, especially by non-custodial parents who tended to feel that they had had a raw deal. The researchers suggested that "agreements" resulted in some cases from arm-twisting by the registrar, the court welfare officer or by the parties' own solicitors. When children were present, in 27 per cent of these cases, their views tended to determine the outcome but children were not necessarily helped to deal with their divided loyalties. The Davis and Bader study was based on two county courts and in view of the great variation of approach in different courts and by different welfare officers their findings should not be assumed to be representative of in-court conciliation generally.

The Costs of Conciliation

The Inter-departmental Committee's main preoccupation was the financial cost of conciliation and its impact on legal aid costs. The Committee used financial estimates of doubtful validity to support the conclusion that out-of-court schemes did not save money, betraying an inherent bias against them by stating that public funding of "out-of-court experimental projects would do no more than put off the day of decision against participation or responsibility by government in voluntary out-of-court schemes" (par. 5.7). The report was widely criticised for faults of methodology (Westcott 1983, Yates 1983, BCFCS Trustees 1984, Davis 1984). BCFCS was criticised (par. 4.19 footnote) for not providing information and subsequent private inquiry suggested that the Committee was unaware that about 1,000 pages of quantifiable data had been provided by BCFCS to the Committee's Study Group. The Study Group's decision to exclude cases in which no court proceedings could be traced meant that cases which led to a reconciliation or to access being agreed informally, without any application to the court, were effectively counted as failures, although the Committee's terms of reference (par. 1.1) were "to review . . . the provision of facilities and services to assist the parties to actual *or potential* matrimonial proceedings" (italics supplied). The Committee decided not to consider possible savings to the legal aid fund attributable to independent conciliation services because they "cannot be quantified" (par. 4.19). Davis (1981) found that although the relationship between conciliation and legal aid is very complicated, the evidence suggested that conciliation is associated with lower legal aid costs.

Conciliation which does not produce a settlement may increase the overall costs of a case and if cost is the decisive factor, conciliation services have to demonstrate net savings, over and above their total running costs. The costs per case in independent services vary enormously and again, valid comparisons are difficult because of the varying extent to which schemes are subsidised by parent organisations, such as the Probation Service (Bromley, North-East Essex, Surrey), the National Marriage Guidance Council (Harrogate, Northumberland and Tyneside), the Family Welfare Association (Northampton), Dr. Barnardo's (Tunbridge Wells), National Children's Home (Bury) and the Chichester Diocesan Association for Family Social Work (Brighton). If parent organisations carry some hidden costs and conciliators give their time free, the cost per case of voluntary conciliation may be recorded as nil, whereas in an independent service such as BCFCS where expenditure cannot be transferred to other budgets, the cost per case may rise to £140 or more. The Interdepartmental Committee tried to cost conciliation by using Nottingham County Court as a control but acknowledged (par. 3.20) that comparisons between Bristol and Nottingham were not valid because of special features in each area. An interesting variable which may prove to be significant in costing conciliation schemes is the proportion of conciliator time spent in face-to-face discussion with both parties together. This appears to vary greatly between different services, from an estimated 95 per cent in Bromley to a lower proportion at BCFCS where a wider range of issues is dealt with and more time is spent by conciliators on telephone and written contact with both parties and their solicitors, writing up case records and other office work. Bromley uses two conciliators per case which could increase costs but total time per case may be less. Recent figures from Bromley (unpublished) showed that the use of two conciliators was associated with a much higher rate of recorded agreements, compared with cases in which only one conciliator was involved.

The Longer-Term Benefits of Conciliation

Although it is far from easy to evaluate the benefits of conciliation in the longer term, we need to know whether both parties' participation in working out arrangements increases the likelihood of these arrangements being adhered to. Relatively little is known about the extent to which court orders are complied with but circumstantial evidence suggests that many defined access orders are ignored and that some custody orders are reversed by parents without the court being informed. Inevitably, family circumstances change over time, especially where one or both parents remarry. The real test of different methods of settling disputes may lie not so much in the type of settlement reached during the divorce but in parents' ability to negotiate and renegotiate arrangements informally. Although 55 per cent of the parents interviewed by Davis and Bader (1985) said that they had felt angry, upset or disappointed after their conciliation appointment at the court, half of those who reached some agreement on custody or access said at a follow-up interview that the agreement had survived and a further 16 per cent said that they had modified the arrangements subsequently, by mutual consent. Comparable figures in relation to independent conciliation services were not available in 1985. It would be very useful to know whether couples who engage in conciliation at an early stage of separation or divorce show a greater ability to sort out subsequent problems on their own, compared with those who are referred for conciliation during or after contested court proceedings.

Apart from the fact that conciliation may take place at different stages in the legal and emotional divorce, it is inevitably difficult for divorcing couples to assess their personal gains and losses in an objective way. Feelings of grief or bitterness over the breakdown of the marriage may colour their experience of conciliation so that they dwell on the negative feelings it has failed to assuage and underrate its benefits. The level of conflict which they bring to conciliation may vary greatly and some account needs to be taken of pre-existing characteristics and variables. This calls among other things for some means of measuring different levels of conflict, such as the scale developed in the Denver Custody Mediation Project (Pearson and Thoennes 1984a) which uses a number of measures to distinguish intrinsically co-operative couples from those who are inherently dispute-prone. These measures included subjective ratings of conflict as well as factual evidence about the frequency and length of access visits and the payment of maintenance orders. They were designed mainly from adult perspectives and no research published in Britain by 1985 had sought children's opinions as to whether conciliation benefited them. Children's opinions should be taken into account, however, since their lives are drastically affected by custody and access decisions and by the level and duration of parental conflict. If they are directly involved in conciliation, they may have useful comments to offer and even if they do not take part directly they may have a great deal of insight into their family's difficulties. Researchers (Wallerstein and Kelly 1980, Lund 1984, Mitchell 1985) have shown that it is possible to seek children's perceptions and opinions by a variety of age-related techniques without subjecting them to painful and inappropriate questioning. Some children told the researcher that nobody had ever bothered to ask their opinion before (Mitchell 1985). From their point of view, the level of family tension around access visits and the amount of time (including staying access) which they spend with the absent parent is likely to be far more important than whether custody and access are registered as "agreed" on court documents.

Research is also needed into the different methods used by conciliators. Dingwall (in press) found that in one independent service conciliators did apply various sorts of pressure to achieve or obstruct certain outcomes. As the label of "conciliation" is being applied in Britain to different forms of intervention by conciliators, further analysis of tape-recorded interviews is needed to identify the actual methods used and to correlate these with differences in recorded outcomes and in consumer reactions.

The Inter-departmental Committee on Conciliation produced a disappointing and poorly researched report (1983) which did however make the positive recommendation that a Conciliation Project Unit should be established, preferably outside central government, to monitor and evaluate different in-court schemes over a three-year period. In December 1983 members of the All Party Parliamentary Group for Children met with the Lord Chancellor to request him to include independent conciliation services in the Project Unit's terms of reference. The Lord Chancellor received this request sympathetically and in February 1984, when he announced the establishment of a Conciliation Project Unit to be funded by central government for a three-year period, he said: "There is as yet insufficient evidence about voluntary out-of-court conciliation services on which to make decisions on funding and organisation of these services. Further investigation into their costs and effectiveness is called for and it has been decided therefore that the unit will monitor one or two out-of-court schemes" (*Hansard* HL 24 February 1984). A year later, it was announced that the Conciliation Project Unit would be based at the University of Newcastle. Its brief is "to identify the factors of conciliation which seem to contribute most to success, and to make recommendations about the best model for a national conciliation service, how it might be organised and structured, whether it should be in-court or out-of-court or a combination of the two"[3]. Factors to be studied include the effects of conciliation on the parties as well as the relative cost of different models of conciliation. A number of schemes will be selected for intensive study involving the follow-through of some 90 families over an 18-month period. The directors of the research unit are the professor of law, the professor of economics and a social scientist at Newcastle University. The multidisciplinary nature of the research task presents a formidable challenge, since the presence of so many complex, interacting variables makes any definite conclusions about conciliation extremely hard to prove. The unit's final report is due by the end of August 1988 and whatever its recommendations, they should not be allowed to gather dust on government shelves as the Finer Report has done.

Experience of Conciliation in Other English-Speaking Countries

The Inter-departmental Committee was criticised for ignoring research findings from other countries whose experience of conciliation is more extensive than the British experience. Care should be taken however not to draw generalised conclusions from countries with different laws and legal systems and different social, economic and cultural conditions. Attitudes towards marriage, divorce and family life vary considerably and these public attitudes influence people's reactions to marriage breakdown and their expectations of parental roles and responsibilities following separation or divorce. Provided these differences are borne in mind, much can be learnt from the experience of conciliation in Australia, New Zealand, Canada and the United States. All these countries have responded to changes in public attitudes to divorce by introducing new legislation, setting up family courts and promoting opportunities for conciliation in preference to adversarially conducted court proceedings (Parkinson 1982b, Burgoyne, Ormrod and Richards forthcoming).

Australia

The Australian Family Law Act 1975 was a major piece of legislation which reformed divorce law and established the Family Court of Australia[4] with the objective of providing "a more humane and dignified manner of dealing with the problems of marital breakdown without delay and without overburdening the parties with expense" (Evatt 1978). The Act made irretrievable breakdown of marriage the sole ground for divorce and abolished all fault-based evidence as proof of breakdown. Twelve months' separation (living apart under the same roof is accepted) is the sole means by which irretrievable breakdown is established. The court has specially appointed judges and registrars and a court counselling service staffed by a principal director and about a hundred counsellors, all of whom have four-year qualifications in psychology or social work (Gibson 1985). When the court counselling service was set up, the counsellors unanimously selected the priority of working with families in conflict over children as "the area of greatest need" (Marshall 1978). Individuals in need of personal or marital counselling are generally referred to other agencies so that court counsellors can concentrate on brief "conciliation counselling" (in the form of joint discussions with both parents together) in contested custody and access cases. Under different sections of the 1975 Act, counsellors accept self-referred cases without court proceedings being instituted and they also undertake court-ordered conciliation conferences under section 62 (1). These conferences are confidential: evidence of anything said or of any admission made is not admissible in any court (section 62 (5)). Their other main duty is the preparation of reports to the court on matters relating to the welfare of children (section 62 (4)). The counsellor who prepares a report is a different counsellor from the one who has taken part in a confidential conciliation conference (although practice at the Parramatta registry is said to diverge from this rule).

In 1979 the Chief Judge of the Family Court of Australia outlined new directions and priorities for the court counselling service: "The Attorney-General has accepted the view that the Court resources in the pre-trial conciliation area should be expanded in anticipation of cutting down on the number of contested cases and the need for further judicial appointments" (Evatt 1979 p. 10). As a result, court counsellors spend almost half their time (46 per cent on average) on pre-court work and in Canberra this proportion was reported in 1984 to be as high as 76 per cent (Jordan 1984). Considerable energy and resources have been devoted to public education programmes and to developing good links with solicitors, who play an important part in initiating voluntary referrals.

Court counsellors use brief, dispute-focused methods in working with parents in conflict over their children. "Probably the most common structure for a conciliation conference . . . is for an intensive 'one-off' session with both parents," which may last up to two hours (Bordow, Marshall and Turner 1983 p. 10).

> The counsellor does not necessarily remain neutral . . . and . . . although amicable settlement is often a goal, . . . the families involved cannot be said to be perfectly free to decide whether or

> not to adopt the proposed terms, for they are coerced to some extent by the length, stress and cost of legal proceedings and by pressure to settle from judges, counsellors and their legal practitioners (ibid. p. 5).

Conciliation conferences are usually preceded by an information-giving session for a group of parents at which a court counsellor explains court procedures, legal terminology and the needs of children in divorce. The concept of mandatory conciliation aroused controversy in Australia but it was felt to be justified on the grounds that conciliation promotes co-operation between parents in the best interests of their children and the welfare of children is the court's paramount concern (Stewart and Harrison 1982). A report from the Family Court's research psychologist (Bordow, Marshall and Turner 1983) showed that only a tiny proportion (8 per cent) of couples who were ordered to attend a conference expected it to have any positive outcome. The majority (71 per cent) thought that settlement would be possible only if the other party "gave in" or "saw sense". However, shortly before the conference was due to take place, only a third thought it was doomed to fail and in the event 75 per cent of cases were settled. None of these couples had recommenced court proceedings when a follow-up study was carried out a year later, whereas of the 25 per cent who failed to settle at the conference, over half (57 per cent) were still involved in litigation a year later or had started fresh proceedings. Court counsellors reported improved communication and co-operation in the "successful" group and the researchers noted that couples who had been separated for shorter periods of time were more likely to reach agreement than those who had been apart for longer periods.

As well as encouraging agreement over children, the Family Law Act was designed to promote agreement and avoid litigation in property and financial matters. Regulation 96 of the Family Law Regulations provides that "where the court or a registrar is of the opinion that it may be advantageous or advisable to do so, it or he may order the parties to confer and make a bona fide endeavour to reach agreement on matters in issue between them." Regulation 96 conferences on finance and property issues produce a high rate of settlement and although the registrar's intervention may be more in the nature of arbitration than conciliation, the legal profession in Australia seems to regard the system favourably (Broun 1983). Broun was dismissive of the conciliation work of court counsellors in relation to custody and access disputes: it is not known how far his views as a barrister were based on comments from clients who were pursuing litigation, without taking account of those who reached agreement. Long waiting-lists for court appointments in the larger registries have also drawn criticism and Parramatta has suffered some violent incidents involving attacks on judges and on court buildings.

The Chief Judge of the Family Court (Evatt 1979) has suggested that a more distinct demarcation between adjudication and conciliation would help to clarify people's expectations of the court and of the role of court counsellors. "One important goal of counselling should be to build up in the mind of the public and of the legal profession an image of counselling as an independent process, as an alternative means available to assist in the resolution of family problems" (p. 2). In 1984 the Family Law Council, a federal government advisory body, issued a discussion paper by the Chief Judge recommending that the court counselling service should be distanced from the authority of the court. Decentralised services have been set up in some areas to test the effect of basing court counsellors in the community instead of in the precincts of the court. There is much to be learnt from the Australian experience and a very useful series of papers is emanating from court counsellors working in the Family Court, as well as from the Institute of Family Studies in Melbourne[5].

New Zealand

The Family Court of New Zealand was established in 1980 and divorce law was reformed at the same time. Irretrievable breakdown of marriage is the sole ground for divorce and two years' separation is the only means of establishing irretrievable breakdown. Unlike the United Kingdom, where disputes over children, money and property are treated as ancillary to the decree proceedings, the New Zealand system concentrates on settling these problems when they first arise, typically at the time of separation. The divorce itself can then be a legal formality after arrangements for children and other matters have been dealt with. Either partner to a marriage can apply to the Family Court for a separation order, custody, access or maintenance order but before court proceedings take place the applicant is usually referred to the counselling co-ordinator who is attached to each registry. The counselling co-ordinator explains the various services that are available within the court itself and in the community and tries to match individuals with the kind of help or course of action they find acceptable. Some crisis counselling and short-term conciliation are undertaken by the counselling co-ordinators and if appropriate people are then referred for further counselling or conciliation. Many problems are resolved informally at this early stage without court proceedings taking place but when a contested application is made to the court, the court can order a mediation conference which is attended by both parties, their solicitors and, if appropriate, by counsel for the child.

The mediation conference is chaired by a Family Court judge who is not acting in a judicial capacity and who would not normally preside at a subsequent court hearing of the same case (Priestley 1984). These judges have been specially chosen for their particular aptitude and interest in family work and it will be interesting to learn whether they help couples to reach agreement without directing or controlling their decisions. There has not yet been enough monitoring of the New Zealand system in the longer term to assess the extent to which agreements are adhered to and whether arrangements benefit children as well as both parents. In the short term, mediation conferences achieve a high rate of settlement, with 60 per cent of couples reaching full agreement and a further 10 per cent reaching partial agreement (ibid.). The content of mediation conferences is treated as legally privileged and cannot be used subsequently in evidence to the court in the course of litigation. Their whole objective is to help couples, especially parents, work out agreed arrangements and avoid bitter and prolonged court proceedings.

The population of New Zealand is very small (around 3 million) and cultural and social conditions such as housing provision may be particularly favourable to the evolution of the Family Court as a benign, problem-solving institution which sets out to meet the needs of the community rather than to act as an instrument of state control. A similar model would not necessarily work equally well in other cultural and legal settings where members of the judiciary acting as mediators might be more authoritarian. One of the main criticisms of the Family Court of Japan, which was set up in 1949, is that the so-called Conciliation Committees are powerful arbitrators who not only take charge of "conciliation" but also determine the legal outcome if no agreement is reached (Isono 1975). Isono reported that the composition and powers of Japanese Conciliation Committees discourage young couples from seeking assistance from them and that fewer cases were being settled because of growing disenchantment with the procedure. Comparison between the Japanese and New Zealand systems suggests that very different principles and methods of conciliation can be applied under the same label, with correspondingly different results.

Canada

A member of the Canadian Department of Justice (Macdonald 1980) has reported that "the thrust of family law has been away from the adversary system ... and towards conciliation and a concern for human values and relationships" (p. 123). Court-related counselling and conciliation services have been established in Alberta, British Columbia and Ontario, the first of these being the Conciliation Service of Edmonton Family Court, set up in 1972. This pioneer scheme was funded for the first three years by the federal government and since 1975 by the provincial government. In 1980 it became a branch of the Provincial Department of Social Services and Community Health. Voluntary referrals initiated by lawyers rather than by the Family Court increased to 60 per cent of all referrals in 1975-77 and it was found that "though reconciliation is not the primary purpose of conciliation counselling, it can be a result"[6]. Contested custody cases are often adjourned for court-ordered conciliation, which is seen as a demanding and time-consuming process calling for a high level of professional skill[7]. A follow-up study conducted in 1975 of cases closed a year previously showed "a high degree of permanence in the decisions reached by the parties at the conclusion of counselling"[8].

The unified Family Court in Hamilton (Ontario) began operating in 1977 with comprehensive jurisdiction in family law matters and a broad range of ancillary services. It represented an important development in federal-provincial co-operation, being the first unified family court established outside a superior court. The Hamilton project was welcomed by the Hamilton Bar and was generally considered very successful (Macdonald 1980). The Canadian government subsequently established three other federal-provincial projects to test different forms of court structure: one like Hamilton at county court level (Saskatoon) and the other two (in Newfoundland and New Brunswick) at the superior court level.

Research studies of conciliation were undertaken at Kingston, Ontario in 1978-79 (Frontenac Family Referral Conciliation Service 1979). The Frontenac Family Referral and Conciliation Service is a court-based conciliation service set up in 1975, offering voluntary pre-court conciliation as well as court-connected conciliation. A wide range of issues is dealt with, including disputes over maintenance, custody and access disputes and disputes connected with domestic violence and alcohol abuse. Research monitoring showed that 75 per cent of spouses to whom a letter of invitation was sent accepted the offer of conciliation and full or partial agreement was achieved in 82 per cent of cases, including reconciliation in 14 per cent. It was also found that agreement was more likely to be reached at the pre-court or court intake stage (75 per cent) than during or after court proceedings (48 per cent). The average number of interviews per case was three and the average time spent was four hours. On average, the time-span for settlement was three weeks for agreements reached through conciliation compared with an average of 12-13 weeks for resolution by court process. The research also showed that it took no longer to attempt conciliation without a settlement being reached and then use the court than it did to settle the case through the court process alone.

Extensive research into conciliation has also been carried out by Irving and colleagues in Toronto (Irving, Benjamin, Bohm and Macdonald 1981, Irving and Benjamin 1984), where a Conciliation Counselling Service was established in 1976 in the Provincial Court (Family Division) of Toronto. The 1984 study was based on a sample of 193 couples who met four criteria: 1) the referral for conciliation had been made by their lawyers or by a judge with the concurrence of both lawyers; 2) both parties were willing to accept conciliation; 3) both parties could speak and read English with reasonable fluency; 4) both parties were willing to participate in the research study. Only 4 per cent of the potential client group were excluded because they did not want to take part in the study, whereas 27 per cent were excluded because they could not speak English. Seventy per cent of the couples who took part in conciliation reached an agreement, including 12 per cent who reconciled. Detailed negotiations of financial and property matters were left almost exclusively to their lawyers but conciliation often helped them to reach agreement in principle on these matters as well. One husband commented: "Up to conciliation, my wife and I had been unable to sit down and talk things out without arguing in front of the baby. The counsellor helped us to act more maturely" (Irving, Benjamin, Bohm and Macdonald 1981 p. 29).

A follow-up study carried out a year later found that of the 70 per cent of couples who had reached some form of agreement in conciliation, 22 per cent had reconciled within six months. It is not known how far the conciliation process contributed to this remarkably high reconciliation rate nor the extent to which these reconciliations lasted over time. Of the other couples who had reached agreement in conciliation, a substantial proportion (40 per cent) had changed the terms of their agreement usually with regard to access arrangements, but most of them (74 per cent) had agreed these changes informally and only 9.8 per cent had resorted to litigation. The majority (62 per cent) said that they had not felt pressured to reach an agreement and those who did said that they would have liked more time in conciliation and follow-up contact with the service. Couples had five interviews on average, extending over six or more hours in which they were usually seen separately as well as together, with children included on at least one occasion in nearly a quarter (23 per cent) of cases. Just over half (53 per cent) reported that their family situation had improved in the year following conciliation. One wife said: "I have more time to myself and I am not as angry with my husband. Also, my daughter now sees her father, [something] I had refused before" (ibid. pp. 28-9). Sixty-nine per cent of clients said they were "satisfied" or "very satisfied" with the terms of their custody and access arrangements. Nearly all of them (92 per cent) felt that they had a clear understanding of the terms of their agreement and 76 per cent believed that this was also true of their spouse. The researchers also sought lawyers' opinions of the conciliation service and 69 per cent of those who had referred clients to the service during 1978/79 agreed to participate in the survey. Most lawyers referred cases for conciliation because of an access dispute (89 per cent) or custody dispute (85 per cent) and 60 per cent considered that conciliation facilitated agreement or that issues were clarified (52 per cent). Most of them felt that conciliation did not conflict with their role as legal advisers and that conciliators' expertise complemented their own; 82 per cent thought that conciliation helped their clients to use legal advice and assistance more appropriately and that it had a substantial effect in reducing distress and emotional turmoil.

Whereas the conciliation service in Toronto concentrates on child-related issues, the Family Conciliation Service in Montreal deals with all issues connected with separation and divorce (Camozzi 1984). The service has its own lawyer who checks agreements involving financial and property matters and whose task it is to gain the support and trust of the legal profession. Conciliators with the Montreal service are trained in marital and family therapy and use Haynes' methods (Haynes 1981). The first session lasts two hours on average and the number of sessions per case is normally two or three. The service is funded jointly by the Ministry of Justice and the Ministry of Social Affairs and after a policy decision taken in 1982 to encourage early referrals, the referral rate jumped from 100 cases in 1981 to about 600 in 1983, of which 74 per cent were voluntary pre-court referrals

(Camozzi 1984, Gibbons 1984).

Federal legislation was introduced in Canada in 1985 which, if adopted, will liberalise Canadian divorce law and encourage more widespread use of conciliation and mediation services to resolve disputes connected with divorce.

United States

Divorce conciliation in the United States developed mainly in two sectors: court-connected, publicly funded conciliation services and privately financed divorce mediation agencies. Court-connected conciliation is usually limited to custody and access disputes whereas private mediation encompasses financial and property issues (Folberg 1983). Research (Bahr 1981, Pearson and Thoennes 1984a) suggests that there are substantial differences between users of public and private services and that it is unwise to generalise from one to the other. A comprehensive study of court-based conciliation and adjudication was under way in 1985, funded by the Children's Bureau of the United States Department of Health and Human Services. Data were also being collected in Denver, Colorado on divorcing individuals who do not contest custody or access as well as on those who do so.

Roughly one in ten divorces in the United States involves a full-scale legal battle over custody and/or access (Foster and Freed 1980) – the same proportion as in England and Wales (Eekelaar and Clive 1977). From 1979 onwards, the Custody Mediation Project in Denver, Colorado undertook a systematic investigation of conciliation both in the short and longer term, comparing the results with litigation outcomes. One study (Pearson and Thoennes 1984b) sought to identify all contested custody and access cases coming to the attention of court personnel in two metropolitan judicial districts. Two-thirds of the parents were offered a free conciliation service and it was explained that any agreement reached could be incorporated in a court order made with their consent. In every third case in the sample, the parents were assigned to a control group without conciliation being offered. This resulted in three groups, as about half the couples who were offered conciliation declined it. This refusal rate is fairly common in voluntary conciliation and dispute resolution agencies in the United States (Cook, Roehl and Sheppard 1980) and may be due to various factors, including people's unfamiliarity with the concept of conciliation, their reluctance to meet and negotiate with a perceived opponent and the manner in which the offer of conciliation is made. The Denver project used an impersonal standard letter putting the daunting prospect of "sitting down with your spouse and one or two neutral outsiders for 6-8 sessions of 1 hour each". Participants were also requested "to suspend your legal activities dealing with the divorce or the post-divorce legal action during the negotiation period". These conditions, combined with the exclusion from conciliation of property and financial issues and the request to take part in a long-term research programme, may have deterred many people from accepting the offer.

The first follow-up interview showed that about 60 per cent of the conciliation group reached a settlement during conciliation and another 20 per cent settled subsequently, before a court hearing took place. In other words, 20 per cent of the conciliated cases still required a judicial decision, compared with nearly 50 per cent of the non-conciliated cases. "Successful" conciliation clients reported more satisfaction and compliance with the terms of their settlement than those who fought their case through the court; they reported having more access to their children and were more likely to have a joint custody order. These positive outcomes were associated with lower legal fees and a shorter passage through the court process. At the second follow-up nearly two years later, "successful" conciliation clients continued to report a range of positive outcomes, including regular access, low relitigation rates, improved relationships with their former spouse and confidence in their ability to work out problems without returning to court. The researchers tested a number of hypotheses, including the hypothesis that their results were spurious because the couples who reached agreement were intrinsically co-operative. They selected individuals in all three groups who had described their ability to co-operate with their former partner as "just about impossible", and found that even at this end of the conflict scale conciliation clients became more co-operative in the long run than those who did not try conciliation. Overall, their findings did not indicate that the benefits attributable to "successful" conciliation were readily explained by pre-existing characteristics.

The Denver researchers were accused by Levy (1984) of bias and oversimplification and have replied to these criticisms (Pearson and Thoennes 1984c). In their comparative study of three court-connected conciliation services, Pearson and Thoennes (1984a) noted the significant distinction between "settlement" and "resolution": some couples felt that the settlement they reached neither solved their problems nor reduced their hostility towards one another. Conversely, many of those who failed to reach agreement said that they approved of conciliation and would recommend it to others! Features of conciliation which were most often mentioned by respondents as helpful were the opportunity to air grievances and hear each other's point of view (70-80%), the conciliator's role in keeping discussions focused and under some control (70-80%) and the orientation towards children (60-70%). Negative reactions included feelings of pressure and lack of time (average time per case varied from 2.3 to 4.3 hours in different services); ambivalence about the presence of children and/or lawyers at conciliation meetings; and complaints of not feeling heard and understood. One woman who complained that the process was too hurried added that she had never expected to work out an agreement with her former husband and had no idea that this was the purpose of the meeting. She had wanted weekly counselling sessions. The research showed how important it is for conciliators to explain their role and the confidentiality of discussions in relation to court proceedings, before people are invited to explain their disagreements and problems.

Comment

Research findings from other countries provide us with a great deal of useful information, but much still remains unknown. Despite the growing popularity and use of conciliation, there have been few empirically based assessments and there is still a tendency to assume that the process must be beneficial or at least neutral, either improving situations or leaving them unchanged. However, bringing hurt and angry people into direct and ill-managed confrontations can make matters worse, and researchers in the United States (Pearson and Thoennes 1984a, Waldron, Roth, Fair, Mann and McDermott 1984) have reported that conciliation inflamed conflict in some cases. Waldron and colleagues concluded that two main factors determine whether couples are likely to benefit from conciliation. "The first determinant is a level of personality development that allows the subject to view the world not as black and white but as a gamut of greys ... The capacity for empathy, the ability to see two sides of an issue, and the capacity to separate the parenting relationship from the marital relationship are essential" (p. 18). The second important factor is that parents have let go of their marriage sufficiently to be able to work together on issues concerning their children. Waldron and colleagues found that all the children in their study whose parents reached agreement through conciliation were reported subsequently to be reacting positively to the arrangements. The two cases in which the agreement broke down immediately were cases in which the children were allowed to decide whether to spend time with one parent. This suggests that conflict is not resolved through parents shifting their responsibility for decisions on to the children. Although all the parents in this study were initially very hostile and felt they had been forced into conciliation by the family court without knowing how it might help, the researchers found a 46 per cent "success rate" on follow-up. The majority of the parents interviewed said that their relationship had improved and that they could communicate more easily than before. There is therefore substantial evidence that conciliation can enable even very hostile couples to reach workable agreements, and that the level of conflict at the outset is not a reliable predictor of the outcome. Generally speaking, a positive outcome seems to depend on the interplay of various factors, including both parties' motivation and emotional resources, the skills and methods used by the conciliators, and the co-operation of other professionals and third parties with the conciliation process.

Notes

1. The *Report of the Committee on Matrimonial Causes Procedure* (Booth Committee) is considered in chapter 10.
2. *The Times* reported on 2 May 1984 a trend of increasing marriage breakdown among Asian families, despite the emphasis in their culture on the preservation of marriage.
3. J. Walker, "Conciliation Project Unit" in *Marriage Lines, Quarterly Newsletter of the Marriage Research Centre*, no. 5 (Spring 1985), p. 3.
4. Jurisdiction under the Family Law Act 1975 is exercised by the Family Court of Australia in all States and Territories except Western Australia, where the Family Court of Western Australia exercises jurisdiction under both the Family Law Act 1975 and Western Australian legislation.
5. Some of these papers are referred to in this chapter and in the previous chapter.
6. Edmonton Family Court Marriage Conciliation Service, *Five-Year Summary of Operations 1972-77* (Report January 1978), p. 16.
7. Ibid. p. 18.
8. Ibid. p. 13.

10 RECENT DEVELOPMENTS IN THE UNITED KINGDOM AND IRELAND

In the last decade, there has been a remarkable surge of interest in conciliation as a method of settling disputes and pioneer schemes have not been confined to disputes arising from marriage breakdown and divorce. Community-based mediation schemes have been set up in some areas, offering help in connection with landlord/tenant disputes, disputes between neighbours and different ethnic groups and other kinds of dispute. These projects have been strongly influenced by developments in the United States, where the success of the Community Boards Program led to federally funded neighbourhood justice centres and crime prevention schemes. The first experimental community mediation project began in an area of San Francisco in 1977, using local residents who were trained as mediators to help other members of the community settle various kinds of dispute, rather than go to court (Shonholtz 1984). The privately funded Institute of Mediation and Conflict Resolution in New York dealt with more than 12,000 disputes during 1983 and has trained over 5,000 people as mediators in all kinds of interpersonal conflict, including family and neighbour disputes, minor criminal matters and police/community relations (Gibbons 1984).

The Newham Conflict and Change Project set up in 1983 with funds from the Cadbury Trust was the first community mediation scheme to be established in Britain. The project uses local volunteers as mediators who advise and counsel each party separately, usually without engaging them in face-to-face meetings (Marshall 1984). The project co-ordinator has observed that

> from the outside, and even to the people involved, it often seems that the conflict is more intense than the issues justify. Emotions run higher and higher, positions harden, and the fight seems unstoppable. It may culminate in a legal battle or in physical violence ... If people in conflict could sort out real differences from imaginary ones, they may be able to come to a shared understanding of their situation. In any case, they should be able to direct their energy in more constructive ways and to help improve the quality of life for everyone (quoted in Marshall 1984 p. 11).

The Edgware Mediation Service which opened in October 1984 also uses volunteers (all of whom were initially Quakers, although there is no religious qualification for selection) who receive extensive training in mediation. Neighbour and domestic disputes and consumer complaints are expected to be the issues most frequently referred by the general public and a wide range of agencies. Another conciliation initiative was taken in Worcester during 1985 by the Charity Commissioners, who intervened as mediators in a three-year dispute between rival Muslim factions over the future of a mosque. This dispute had led to violent clashes in which policemen were injured.

The philosophy of conciliation also underlies reparation schemes which have been introduced in the criminal justice field, in which the offender voluntarily agrees to compensate the victim financially or by giving some service, directly or indirectly. Reparation and community mediation schemes have features in common, as Marshall (1984) pointed out: both offer an alternative to formal systems of justice and seek to involve people personally in settling disputes and, in a deeper psychological sense, making peace with one another. In December 1984 a new organisation called the Forum for Initiatives in Reparation and Mediation was set up to link existing schemes in Britain and to foster further developments. An inaugural conference entitled "Alternatives to Confrontation" was held in London in April 1985 to bring together representatives of the different kinds of conciliation being practised in Britain: industrial conciliation, conciliation in separation and divorce, community mediation projects and victim-offender reparation schemes. Although these developments share common principles, there are also major differences between them. The Lord Chancellor's Advisory Committee on Legal Aid has pointed out (*Annual Report 1983-84*) that matrimonial and family disputes have characteristics which distinguish them from citizen v. citizen disputes, notably the need to consider children's interests and the fact that many divorced parents remain tied to each other through their children. Moreover, industrial and family conciliation does not necessarily avoid confrontation as the title of the 1985 conference implied: both these forms of conciliation are concerned with helping people to reach agreed and mutually acceptable decisions for the future, rather than seeking to redress past wrongs.

Conciliation may be appropriate at many different levels and in various settings. During 1985 senior government ministers and Downing Street officials were said to be looking for an alternative to the star chamber as a means of settling expenditure disputes between the Treasury and other government departments. The present system of confrontation between individual ministers and the Treasury followed by an adversarial battle and adjudication in the star chamber is seen as a costly and inefficient method of deciding arguments over departmental spending. In the industrial field, the need for a conciliation service operating independently of central government is demonstrated by the large number of voluntary referrals to ACAS. In 1983, ACAS completed 1,621 cases of collective conciliation, 45 per cent of which were referred jointly to ACAS by trade unions and employers[1]. Over 80 per cent of these disputes were settled without industrial action being taken (Calvert 1984). Additionally, 42,960 individual conciliation cases were completed in 1983, of which 42 per cent were settled and 25 per cent withdrawn, leaving 33 per cent for determination by an industrial tribunal. As Sir Pat Lowry, chairman of ACAS, commented at the end of ACAS's tenth anniversary year, this is "not a bad record" (Lowry 1984) and at £12 million a year ACAS has been rated "cheap at the price" (Calvert 1984).

ACAS might be described as a well-known, mature adult in the conciliation field whereas family conciliation services are still at a comparatively adolescent stage of development and suffer from problems typical of adolescence: they lack an established identity, financial independence and secure future and some of them need to detach themselves from possessive parent bodies! Despite these constraints, they are continuing to develop in many parts of the United Kingdom. New services were opened in 1985 in many places, including Birmingham, Bournemouth, Brighton, Harrogate, Northampton and Sheffield, with short-term funding from a variety of sources including charitable trusts, the Manpower Services Commission, grants from local authorities and fees paid under extensions of the Green Form scheme. Family conciliation services are also developing in Scotland, Northern Ireland and the Irish Republic. A conference on conciliation was held in the Channel Islands in April 1983 and an international conference held in London in October 1984 was attended by 140 participants from eight different countries[2].

Scotland

Developments in Scotland have been spearheaded by the Scottish Family Conciliation Service (Lothian) based in Edinburgh, which is seen as a pilot project for Scotland. The service was funded mainly by the Scottish Office for a three-year period 1983-86 under the Social

Work (Scotland) Act 1968 and is being monitored and evaluated by the Central Research Unit at the Scottish Office. In the first two years it was found that referrals from solicitors were much more likely to lead to conciliation taking place than those from other sources and that the number of solicitor referrals increased as the service became better known to and accepted by the legal profession in Lothian (Ross 1985a). The service's expenditure totalled about £35,000 in 1984-85 and its resources of specialist experience and knowledge represent a national resource which is readily shared with other Scottish schemes and with statutory and voluntary services concerned with marriage and family life in Scotland. The co-ordinator of the service was one of the organisers of the first Scottish Conference on Divorce Conciliation, held at Pitlochry in November 1984[3].

In 1985 the Scottish Family Conciliation Service (Strathclyde) obtained the offer of a grant under the Local Government Grant (Scotland) (Needs) Act 1969 for 75 per cent of the funds needed over a four-year period to provide a central office and four community-based conciliation centres, staffed by a team of about twelve conciliators working on a sessional basis. Support for the Strathclyde service came from the Sheriff Principal of North Strathclyde, the President of the Glasgow Bar Association and many other organisations and individuals. A conciliation service in Central Region was opened in June 1984, based at the Citizens' Advice Bureau in Stirling and at two other centres in the region. This service was set up with very limited funding and the part-time co-ordinator and conciliators agreed to work as unpaid volunteers. The conciliators were recruited from a wide range of mainly non-professional backgrounds and worked generally in male-female pairs. Other initiatives in Scotland to provide conciliation services were taken in Aberdeen and in Tayside and Fife, and Steering Committees were formed in these areas to explore the practical possibilities, including sources of funding.

In March 1985 Lord James Douglas-Hamilton moved an amendment to the Divorce (Scotland) Act 1976 to make statutory provision for conciliation in divorce proceedings and to place a duty on lawyers to consider conciliation at an early stage in cases involving dispute (*Hansard* 21 March 1985). After a lengthy debate in which the value of conciliation was acknowledged, the motion was withdrawn because it was considered premature and not necessarily the best way of providing opportunities for conciliation. The Solicitor-General for Scotland suggested that referrals by solicitors for conciliation might be better dealt with by means of a Court of Session practice note than by primary legislation at this stage and that future decisions concerning conciliation services would largely depend on the research evaluation taking place in Scotland and England.

Northern Ireland

Divorce legislation in Northern Ireland is closely modelled on English divorce law although historically there has often been a considerable time-lag before a reform in English divorce law was adopted in Northern Ireland. The 1857 Act which introduced civil divorce in England did not apply in Ireland, where the only provision for divorce was by private Act of Parliament, as late as 1939. In that year, divorce legislation was introduced which brought Northern Ireland broadly in line with the provisions of the 1937 Act in England and Wales. However, the English Divorce Reform Act 1969 did not apply to Northern Ireland and again there was a gulf between the two jurisdictions until 1978, when reform in Northern Ireland once more brought the two systems into broad alignment, apart from some minor differences where Scottish rather than English practice is followed.

Partly as a result of different cultural and religious traditions and other social factors the divorce rate in Northern Ireland has remained well below the English rate. There has been a sharp upward trend, however, particularly in the wake of the Matrimonial Causes (Northern Ireland) Order 1978: the number of petitions filed more than doubled from 700 in 1979 to 1,776 in 1984. Where there are children, the court must inform the Health and Social Services Board so that the case can be referred "to a suitably qualified person i) to consider the possibility of conciliating the parties to the marriage and ii) for a report on the children and the suitability of any arrangements which have been made, or are proposed by either party to be made for their welfare"[4]. Conciliation is not defined in the Order and there appears to be some confusion between conciliation and reconciliation. A survey undertaken by the Social Work Advisory Group in Northern Ireland (McCoy and Nelson 1983) showed that almost three-quarters of the divorcing couples referred to social workers from the Southern and Eastern Health Boards had been separated for more than two years before the social worker contacted them, by which time arrangements for the children were generally settled, one way or another. The figures suggested that in most Districts the children lose contact with the absent parent in about half of all divorces. The Social Work Advisory

Group concluded from the survey that the provision for conciliation was clearly not being used and the report questioned whether it was being offered at an appropriate time. The time when conciliation may be most needed is during the crisis of separation when arrangements are being worked out and both parents may still be in contact with the children. There is therefore considerable interest in pre-court conciliation services which would be available to couples before legal proceedings are started. The Northern Ireland Legal Aid Advisory Committee held a conference on conciliation in October 1981 and in 1985 a small working group consisting of a representative of the Social Work Advisory Group, the Marriage Guidance Regional Officer and a lecturer in social work at Queen's University began to look at the practical questions involved in providing an independent conciliation service in Northern Ireland which would accept voluntary referrals at all stages of separation and divorce.

The Irish Republic

Divorce was still not available in the Irish Republic in 1985 because Article 41 of the Constitution prohibits enactment of any law permitting dissolution of marriage. However, the ban on divorce has not prevented a serious and growing problem of marital breakdown and separation. The number of applications for the Deserted Wife's Allowance and for church annulments of marriage suggest that there are thousands of separated couples in Ireland and many illegitimate children whose parents are not free to marry (Duncan 1982). The report of the all-party Dail committee on marriage breakdown (Oireachtas Committee on Marital Breakdown 1985) published in April 1985 after almost two years of discussions revealed deep opposition to divorce within the two main parties and failed to provide the consensus on which divorce legislation could be introduced. Without agreement on the need for divorce, the committee's majority support for a referendum to remove the constitutional prohibition on divorce was of limited value and it may still be some years before civil divorce is permitted in Ireland. The situation in Ireland is reminiscent of that in Italy in the early 1970s, where the Italian referendum of 1974 followed a deeply emotional campaign for and against divorce.

Family law in general is a subject of intense debate in Ireland, where the problems connected with marital separation, custody of children, financial provision for wives and children, adoption and domestic violence are creating a demand for conciliation services, despite the absence of divorce. A series of conferences and seminars on conciliation was held in the Republic from 1982 onwards. The opening address at a seminar organised by the Department of Justice in June 1984 was given by Nuala Fennell, Minister of State for Family Law Reform, who pointed out that "however desirable a conciliation service may appear to be, it will have to compete as to priority with other demands on the public purse and this may mean accepting a slower rate of progress in relation to any proposals that might be considered desirable" (Fennell 1984 p. 5). Different views were put forward at this seminar of the kind of conciliation service appropriate to the Republic, with one speaker advocating the establishment of an independent, out-of-court conciliation service while a District Court Justice (Johnson 1984) believed that a very effective conciliation service could be built on the existing Court Welfare Service "at modest expense". More detailed questions concerning the needs of children whose parents separate and the methods and skills applicable in conciliation were discussed at a two-day seminar on conciliation held at Trinity College, Dublin in September 1984. In February 1985 the Minister of State for Family Law Reform announced the appointment of a steering committee with the following terms of reference:

1. To draw up plans for a pilot family conciliation service.
2. To provide a pilot scheme on an experimental basis for up to three years.
3. To arrange for independent monitoring and assessment of the scheme's effectiveness and for a report on its effectiveness to be made to the Minister of Justice at the end of the experimental period.

The steering committee was informed that £150,000 (Irish) would be made available over a three-year period to finance an out-of-court service available free of charge to married couples. The committee included representatives of the Legal Aid Board, the Irish Association of Social Workers, the Probation Service, the AIM group for family law reform and other agencies, with a Dublin solicitor as chairman. The committee drew on conciliation experience in Britain, Australia, Canada, New Zealand and the USA and hoped to have a pilot project in operation by the end of 1985.

England and Wales

In England and Wales 1985 was also an important year for the development of conciliation in divorce proceedings. The *Report of the Committee on Matrimonial Causes Procedure* (Booth Report July 1985) recommended that formal provision should be made for conciliation in divorce and other matrimonial proceedings and that the court should initiate a referral for conciliation "where it is thought appropriate" (par. 3.6). The Committee considered that

> it is of the essence of conciliation that responsibility remains at all times with the parties themselves to identify and seek agreement on the issues arising from the breakdown of their relationship. The conciliator's role is to assist the parties in this process. He should be neutral not only in the sense that he does not take sides between the parties, but also in the sense that he does not have a preconceived solution to any particular problem (par. 3.10).

The Committee was "greatly impressed by the view that in many cases conciliation is likely to be most effective before court proceedings have been started" but thought it equally important "in helping parties to resolve issues which arise, or emerge, only when proceedings have started" (par. 3.12). Despite the emphasis on early intervention, the Committee stated that "under our proposals the obvious place for conciliation is at the initial hearing" (par. 3.12). The initial hearing is the linch-pin of the Committee's proposals. Both parties would be required to attend this hearing within about ten weeks of the filing of proceedings, "with their legal advisers if so desired", in every case involving a child to whom section 41 of the 1973 Act applies and also in cases where the respondent states an intention of opposing the decree. The Committee estimated that these hearings would last only 15 minutes on average (par. 5.2) and they are expected to accomplish a great deal in this short time. The registrar would be able to exercise substantially increased powers at the hearing, including the power to grant a decree (abolishing judicial pronouncement of decrees in open court), power to express satisfaction with the arrangements for the children (replacing the section 41 appointment with a judge in chambers), power to make interim or final orders on financial and property matters and power to refer the parties to a welfare officer "for the purpose of discussing the nature of conciliation and its relevance to the nature of the dispute in which they are engaged" (par. 4.59).

The Committee's central recommendation that the court should refer contested cases to welfare officers for conciliation is closely in line with the 1971 Practice Direction on Conciliation (see chapter 4). Conciliation would thus become "a recognised part of the legal procedure" and its objective would be "to marshal such reasonableness and objectivity as exist and to direct the parties towards solving the essentially practical problems which arise" (par. 3.11). Referral for conciliation would consist of a two-stage process – an explanation of the nature and purpose of conciliation followed by actual conciliation where both parties agree to it. This two-stage procedure was intended to avoid the objections raised against mandatory conciliation: the decision to take part in conciliation would rest with the parties because "their willing participation and co-operation are essential" (par. 4.59). However, the initial discussion with the welfare officer "may quickly develop into a conciliation appointment" and the Committee saw no objection to this in principle "provided that all the necessary facilities and the time are available and that there is no doubt that each is acting freely, with full knowledge of what is involved and under no pressure from any source" (par. 4.56). The Committee recognised the problems of hasty, on-the-spot conciliation and proposed adjournments where appropriate to enable discussions to continue out of court – but only for a limited period, since the court would be concerned to facilitate "a speedy trial" (par. 3.8). This emphasis on the court's control of the time-scale for conciliation does not accord with the principle that "the primary decision-making responsibility should rest with the spouses themselves ... they should be given all necessary help in deciding for themselves what should happen to their children, their property and their marriage" (par. 3.2). If this principle is followed, it should be for the parties, not the court, to decide with the conciliator and with their legal advisers how long the conciliation process should last. Setting a time-limit at the outset may however encourage a concentrated effort at conciliation, and a time-limit may also be necessary from the children's point of view, since they may suffer from delayed decisions and prolonged uncertainty.

As far as confidentiality is concerned, the Booth Committee had no hesitation in recommending that conciliation must be legally privileged, on the ground that "conciliation requires that there should be a full and free exchange between the parties and that this is unlikely to occur if there is a possibility of matters disclosed in conciliation being referred to in subsequent proceedings" (par. 4.60). The Committee felt that this privilege should be absolute. No reference is made in the Report to the potential clash of principle between the public interest in avoiding litigation and the predominant public interest in the welfare of children, where for example parents make an admission of neglect or abuse but refuse to seek help from a statutory agency or to waive their privilege. Such situations are likely to be rare in the context of conciliation, but a few such cases have already occurred and the conciliator's position in relation to reporting to other agencies and/or giving evidence to the court must be clearly defined. The Booth Committee made a necessary but possibly oversimplified distinction between the role of conciliator and that of the welfare officer who prepares a report for the court, recommending that the same welfare officer should not conciliate in a case and later report on it (par. 4.63). This separation of roles is essential, but it raises major logistical problems for the probation service, especially in rural areas where there may be only one welfare officer available for both functions. Although the Committee was satisfied that conciliation takes less welfare officer time than the preparation of a traditional report, an initial hearing in every divorce involving children might produce a greater demand for conciliation than the probation service could meet, unless additional resources were made available. This seems very unlikely, since a Statement of National Objectives and Priorities for the Probation Service issued by the Home Office in April 1984 placed civil work at the bottom of the list, stating that "the proportion of resources allocated to civil work should be contained at a level consistent with local circumstances and the foregoing priorities" (p. 4).

The Booth Committee's proposals have substantial financial implications both for the Home Office and the Lord Chancellor's Department which neither Department may want to take on board. The administrative costs of the initial hearing would be considerable and the Committee recognised that solicitors "may have to do significantly more work" in preparation for it, since a claim for financial relief would have to be supported by a detailed statement of the claimant's financial needs and resources. Accordingly, the Committee recommended an increase in the initial limit for legal advice and assistance under the Green Form scheme and "a modified form of Assistance By Way of Representation"[5] to cover the costs of legal representation at the initial hearing. The Committee admitted that "to have three separate forms of legal aid in matrimonial proceedings is unsatisfactory and . . . may cause confusion; but we do not see how this can be avoided without radical revision of the entire legal aid system"(Appendix 1 par. 5).

These implications and the mixed reactions of the legal profession led to speculation that the Booth Committee's "important and wide-ranging[6]" proposals might be shelved indefinitely, along with the Finer Report. There are however a number of practical possibilities which could be considered. For example, arrangements could be made between a Chief Probation Officer and an accredited independent service to enable court-referred conciliation work to be sub-contracted to the independent service and paid for by the Probation Service on a sessional or hourly basis. This arrangement could apply both to in-court and out-of-court referrals and would be much cheaper than employing more full-time welfare officers. It would also have the advantage of using trained and experienced part-time conciliators who would not have a statutory relationship with the court. The National Family Conciliation Council and the Association of Chief Officers of Probation Civil Work Committee formed a Joint Working Party on Conciliation in February 1984, and in response to the Booth Report this Working Party has prepared guide-lines on the use of independent conciliators for court-referred conciliation. The sub-contracting of conciliation referrals from a statutory service to an independent one would put into effect the 1971 Practice Direction, some 15 years later! Independent conciliation services would be fully responsible for the management of the delegated work and conciliators employed by an independent service would be accountable to their own professional supervisors and not to the Divorce Court Welfare Service, so that welfare inquiries would not be influenced by prior knowledge of a case gained through supervising a conciliator. In some areas (e.g. Reading, South-East London, Surrey), independent conciliators already staff conciliation appointments at the divorce court and the magistrates' domestic courts. Other areas use a combined team of conciliators drawn from statutory and voluntary services. These combined teams may pave the way for a new Family Court Conciliation Service attached to the still-awaited family court. Opinion is divided, however, between the concept of a comprehensive service undertaking pre-court conciliation, court-related conciliation and welfare inquiries as separate tasks with firm boundaries on confidentiality or, alternatively, two completely separate services, one statutory and the other voluntary and independent.

If the combined model is preferred, the Family Court Conciliation Service of the future could have a subsidiary "welfare arm" attached to it instead of being primarily an investigative welfare service with a secondary conciliation function. This would be logical, since only a minority of divorces raise questions of child neglect or abuse, whereas many parents might welcome a crisis-oriented service to help them reach agreement over arrangements for their children and possibly other matters as well. However, perceptions of "the welfare" are not easily changed, and the stage at which parents become able to reach some form of agreement is bound to vary. Some may respond to conciliation at an early stage, whereas others may accept it only via the court, or not at all. Despite all the emphasis in the Booth Report on the parties taking their own decisions and reaching agreements, the Committee considered that if they are not able to do so at the initial hearing or in subsequent conciliation, "responsibility shifts to the court to determine contested issues according to the evidence" (par. 4.62). This abrupt switch from the "essentially inquisitorial" initial hearing (par. 3.9) to adversarially conducted proceedings followed by adjudication may not take sufficient account of the evidence (Eekelaar and Clive 1977, James and Wilson 1984) that the intervention of a welfare officer often results in agreed arrangements being presented to the court for ratification. We do not know whether such agreements are attributable to the welfare officer's use of directive authority, or to particular methods and skills, or to a combination of the two, and we need to learn more about the different degrees of authority which are needed to contain varying levels of conflict. A survey undertaken by the Association of Chief Officers of Probation showed that two-thirds of the 54 Probation regions in England and Wales were providing some form of court-related conciliation in 1985, but welfare officers have reported receiving very little training in civil work (James and Wilson 1983). Those who have sought further training in a family systems approach report that even deeply divided, hostile or non-communicating couples may become able to take some joint decisions as parents. Conciliation is not something that can be swallowed like a quick dose of salts at only one stage of the legal process. More thought needs to be given to ways of making it available at all stages of separation and divorce and to the role of the welfare officer where a report is called for. Shepherd and Howard (1985b) in an excellent article on divorce court welfare practice argue that it is in a transitional stage between the traditional, investigative model and the conciliatory, conflict-resolution model. Their work with families has convinced them that family meetings arranged with parents and children together, on neutral ground, are more helpful to all concerned than separate home visits, because parents are enabled to communicate directly with each other instead of via solicitors or the children. If the discussions are managed carefully, they may provide a more reliable basis for understanding and assessing families' problems than a traditional welfare inquiry. Parents who refuse the offer of conciliation on a voluntary basis or who take part without reaching any conclusion may nonetheless reach agreement with each other, in the context of a welfare inquiry. Much depends however on whether welfare officers are encouraged to learn new methods and skills or whether they use "old" paternalistic methods under a cloak of conciliation. In preparing a report for the court, they have a different role from conciliators working on a privileged basis because their inquiry is backed by the authority of the court, and families will inevitably perceive them as holding authority. It does not follow from this that their role should be merely investigative and that settlement-seeking methods are inappropriate.

Conciliation methods may also be applicable in matrimonial supervision and child care cases, within a framework of statutory responsibility. When there is dispute between the local authority and the parents of a child in care over access to the child, the local authority may be seen as one party to the dispute and the natural parents as the other party. There may be an area of common ground between them in their mutual concern for the child's wellbeing despite their different views of what constitutes the "best interests" of the child. If foster-parents are involved as well, it is possible to extend the conciliation model and include all parties in "participative decision-making". Round-the-table discussions can be chaired by a neutral conciliator without statutory authority or by a statutory worker with ultimate control over decisions, depending on the circumstances of the case. The House of Commons Social Services Committee in their *Second Report on Children in Care* (1984) commented that conflict would be diminished by better communication between social workers, natural parents and foster-parents and that the children themselves should be directly involved in discussions about their future. Unresolved conflict between adults is almost bound to be detrimental to children and, as the Committee pointed out, "if more consideration were given to the respective responsibilities of state, parents and child, the issues might be seen in more positive and less divisive terms" (par. 15). Conciliation which involves different organisations as well as one or more families can be described more accurately as "network conciliation" rather than simply "family conciliation".

The Booth Committee took a firm view that the state (represented by the court) and divorcing couples have a common interest in settling disputes through conciliation rather than through litigation, but the question of what part the state should play in divorce proceedings remains unclear. As it is acknowledged that in the majority of cases parents are well able to make satisfactory arrangements for their children (par. 4.127), it is questionable whether the divorce court should make custody orders in uncontested cases, except where the circumstances require the definition of custodial powers and responsibilities. The Committee's proposals were designed to increase divorcing couples' participation in and control of the legal process, but the structure and brief duration of the initial hearing could result in professionals steering bemused people into rapid decisions which might receive no more than fleeting scrutiny from a hard-pressed registrar. The Committee's support for joint custody is half-hearted, compared with the conviction in the earlier Consultation Paper (1983) that the concept of joint custody can have "immense emotional significance" and that "if joint custody was the normal order, it would encourage the parties to settle their differences and would assist conciliation on such questions as access" (par. 7.7). In the final Report, the Committee turned away from any presumption in favour of joint custody on the grounds that "it must remain a question for the court, in the exercise of its unfettered discretion, to decide in each case what order would best serve the child's interests" (par. 4.132). Does the Committee expect the court to select the appropriate custody option in the course of the initial hearing? No guidance is given to registrars as to whether they should assess the desirability of sole or joint custody with both parents during a 15-minute hearing, as well as dealing with the decree and financial matters. Should an uncontested application by one parent for sole custody be referred automatically for possible conciliation, on the grounds that the children's interests might be better served by a joint custody order? It is also disappointing that although the Committee considered that the activities of conciliation and welfare inquiries are "so different as to be incompatible" (par. 4.63), the person performing the task of conciliation is constantly referred to in the Report as "the welfare officer": the term "conciliator" is now common and its use by the Committee would have helped to distinguish the two roles.

Despite these criticisms, the adoption of the Booth Committee's proposals would make the legal process of divorce much less divisive and adversarial. The recommendations that couples should be able to file a joint application for divorce, that applications based on "unreasonable behaviour" should omit particulars of behaviour and that petitioners should no longer have to name the person with whom a spouse is alleged to have committed adultery are all constructive proposals, though they may be seen by some as an attempt to reform the substantive law of divorce through the "back door" of procedural reform. There is also some inconsistency in the recommendation that the court should issue a final decree of divorce automatically, four weeks after the grant of a provisional decree. The evidence that conciliation can lead to reconciliation even after a petition has been filed should make the court less hasty to finalise the divorce until at least one and preferably both spouses apply for a final decree. There is arguably too much emphasis in the Report on speeding up divorce proceedings from the time of the initial hearing, and too little on the urgency of providing help at an earlier stage, before the initial hearing takes place. Apart from the delays which may occur in preparing an application for divorce, the interval of ten weeks between the filing of the application and the initial hearing is a critical period in which conciliation may help both partners to consider the realities of divorce and to make practical plans for the future, before presenting the proposed arrangements to the court. The Committee's recommendation that section 6 (1) of the 1973 Act (requiring solicitors to file a certificate concerning possible reconciliation) should be repealed seems to close the door on reconciliation, since the proposed information leaflet giving details of counselling and conciliation services would not necessarily produce a substantial increase in self-referrals to these services.

The comparative lack of attention given by the Booth Committee to procedures at the pre-court and court intake stages may reflect the fact that the Committee included two judges, three registrars and a magistrate and only one solicitor in private practice, from an area in which there was no independent, pre-court conciliation service in operation[7]. If the Committee had included a second solicitor and perhaps a child psychologist, there might have been greater emphasis on procedures leading up to the initial hearing. Solicitors are uniquely placed to refer divorcing couples for conciliation before the court is involved at all and although the design of the Green Form may have been outside the Booth Committee's terms of reference, the Committee could perhaps have suggested a revision of the form to include a reference to the possibility of conciliation, where issues are unresolved or contested. Whether this would in fact encourage more referrals by solicitors to pre-court conciliation services would depend on various factors, including their availability and empirical evidence of their value. The Booth Committee recommended that parents should file a joint statement of arrangements for the children but this expectation of amicable discussion is unrealistic in many cases. "Even in the least contentious of divorces good communication is usually just what has proved a major stumbling block in the relationship and the help of a conciliator at this very early stage is therefore likely to be vital" (Parker and Parkinson 1985 p. 274). Early referrals for conciliation from solicitors, in conjunction with continuing legal advice to each party, would seem to be more logical than waiting two and a half months for a short court hearing at which proceedings may then be adjourned to allow conciliation to take place. If the court can be empowered through procedural rules to direct the parties to attend an appointment "to discuss the nature of conciliation", this power could surely be exercised in contested cases before the initial hearing takes place. Referrals by the court to an accredited conciliation service would give couples more time to consider the possibility of conciliation and understand its function, without the pressures of a court hearing. In some cases, couples who would not have attended an appointment on their own initiative may find, contrary to their expectations, that conciliation enables them to sort out their difficulties, with continuing advice from their solicitors. In other cases, issues might at least be clarified prior to the initial hearing, thus lightening the court's task.

The Lord Chancellor's Legal Aid Advisory Committee has argued (*Annual Report 1983-84*) that there are grounds for supporting voluntary conciliation services from public funds. In the first place, "it can reasonably be argued that divorcing spouses should not be allowed to conduct their emotional battles at public expense" (par. 121). Secondly, the cost of divorce should be measured in terms of the subsequent cost of other services which divorced couples and their children may need in the future. And thirdly, "there is a direct public financial interest in ensuring that, where divorce is unavoidable, it is achieved as harmoniously as possible and the arrangements made are likely to stick" (ibid.). Public funding for conciliation services need not mean that they become state-controlled services. The National Marriage Guidance Council depends on funding from the Home Office but it is an independent organisation, not an agent of central government.

The Booth Committee was faced with the difficult problem of proposing reforms in one part of a complex system without reforming other parts of the system at the same time. The tide of professional opinion is flowing strongly towards the introduction of family courts and the expansion of conciliation services[8], but as Cretney (1985) asked, can we sensibly discuss the structure of the family court without considering long overdue changes to the substantive law, or introduce new procedures without knowing what legislative framework is proposed? The Law Commission has undertaken a review of the ground for divorce which might lead to the removal of all fault-based evidence, although the Booth Committee reported that there is a minority view, strongly held, which supports the retention of the fault concept in relation to divorce. Meanwhile, the Department of Health and Social Security has embarked on a review of all legislation concerning children and a Consultation Paper on the "resource implications" of the family court is expected from the Lord Chancellor's Department and the Home Office early in 1986. It remains to be seen whether all this deliberation will produce any action. The Law Commission's proposals for reform of the law relating to illegitimacy[9] have been waiting since 1982 for implementation "when resources are available": no legislation has yet been introduced. One can understand the scepticism of a senior barrister who remarked that "efforts to find the 'best' way to resolve matrimonial disputes have not necessarily achieved better results in other countries where different ... systems prevail ... nor should one expect too much of the changes of law, whether of substance or procedure, that are promised to us on all sides"(Jackson 1983 p. vii).

Despite the inertia and procrastination which hamper efforts to reform family law and the structure of the courts, stones which are thrown into the family law pond do not necessarily sink without trace. The ripples have spread out from many local centres over the last ten years, not only in a widening circle of small practical experiments but more fundamentally in an interdisciplinary approach to the problems of marriage breakdown and divorce. As the Lord Chancellor's Legal Aid Advisory Committee observed[10], conciliation should not be the sole preserve of specialist services catering for a minority of contested cases. To be effective, it must be accepted as a general approach to problems arising from marital breakdown and its benefits should be measured not only in the number of agreed settlements in cases referred for a formal process of conciliation but also in the conciliatory approach of solicitors to bipartisan negotiations. A Canadian professor of family law has observed that "no single discipline has the omniscience that we all seek in the constructive settlement of family disputes"[11]. The expectation that either solicitors or conciliators can solve all kinds of problems in isolation, without drawing on each other's knowledge and expertise, shows a kind of tunnel vision. We should not think in terms of "dyads" which imply that one professional has to be a substitute for another one and that disputes between divorcing couples involve only two people. The Booth Committee gave insufficient attention to the professional partnership that is needed between solicitors and conciliators, especially where issues of children, finance and property are inter-related. While advancing a cautious opinion that there may be potential for conciliation on financial matters (par. 4.65) and emphasising that the parties should seek legal advice before concluding financial agreements, the Committee appeared not to recognise the difficulties that may arise in practice if consent orders are made hastily, without the parties receiving adequate legal advice. The pressure on solicitors to settle matters as far as possible in advance of the initial hearing could therefore encourage the use of pre-court conciliation services, especially if conciliation is found to promote co-operation over property and financial matters and increase compliance with financial settlements. Solicitors who support the value of conciliation but recognise its inevitable difficulties and limitations can provide a necessary counterweight of checks and balances, to safeguard the position of the less powerful party in particular. For this to work well, legal training would need to include some teaching on conciliation. A national code of practice for conciliators in statutory as well as independent services would also help to establish standards and basic rules of practice. In the United States, the American Bar Association and the Association of Family and Conciliation Courts have recently approved and distributed codes of practice which define conciliators' duties and responsibilities. The formulation of these rules, which deal with ethical as well as legal considerations, has been described as a watershed in the rapidly expanding area of dispute resolution (Bishop 1984).

In Britain, the arguments for and against conciliation still tend to rely on hearsay and hunch rather than on empirical evidence. Many countries have moved towards a combination of formal and informal procedures, usually under the umbrella of a unified family court, and experience shows that no single procedure or method can provide adequate solutions to the urgency and complexity of matrimonial and family disputes. We need a flexible combination of different methods and procedures, including bipartisan negotiation, conciliation, inquisitorial court procedures designed to facilitate settlement and, in some cases, adjudication. Above all, we need a constructive approach instead of a destructive one. Good communication is often the key to solving problems and good communication is needed between solicitors and conciliators as well as between the couples they seek to help. "All design, all policy, all that is worthwhile in human inventiveness is based as much on dialogue – even dialectic – as on agreement. Engineering design, like policy, is by its very nature a compromise between divergent requirements ... between mobility and safety, between economy and social need, between tradition and progress" (Hailsham 1981 p. 48). We do not live in a utopian society in which all differences melt into consensus and one suspects that such a society would be devoid of vitality. In the world today, where conflict and grievous loss are extremely common, we need to work out how they can be minimised. In some cases, an attempt to reduce conflict and loss may lead to mutual gain, in the sense that new and rewarding relationships may grow out of the ruins of a broken marriage, both for parents and children. If the dialogue begins early enough, some couples may decide that the marriage itself can be renewed on a different basis, but if a permanent separation is unavoidable, they may be helped to part with better understanding and with a greater capacity for co-operation on matters of joint concern.

Notes

1. ACAS, *Annual Report 1983*.
2. A report on this conference was published in *Marriage Guidance*, the National Marriage Guidance Council's quarterly journal (Spring 1985).
3. A report on the first Scottish Conference on Divorce Conciliation was published jointly by the Scottish Council for Single Parents and the Scottish Family Conciliation Service (Lothian), November 1984.
4. Article 43 of the Matrimonial Causes (Northern Ireland) Order 1978.
5. Assistance By Way of Representation was introduced under the *Legal Advice and Assistance Regulations 1980* as an administratively cheap and convenient substitute for civil legal aid in the magistrates' courts.
6. Press release on the Booth Report issued by the Lord Chancellor's Department on 1 August 1984.
7. The members of the Booth Committee included a High Court judge, a circuit judge, three registrars, a magistrate, a solicitor, a barrister, an Assistant Chief Probation Officer and the Lay Observer.
8. The Family Courts Campaign organised by the Association of County Councils sent an open letter in November 1985 to the Prime Minister and other party leaders from a range of organisations asking them to make a firm commitment to the setting up of Family Courts in England and Wales.
9. The Law Commission's *Report No. 118* (1982) made proposals for reform of the law relating to illegitimacy.
10. The Lord Chancellor's Legal Aid Advisory Committee's *32nd Annual Report 1981-82*, Appendix D.

11. J.D. Payne, Unpublished paper on "Family Conflicts Resolution: Cumulative Alternatives – Mediation, Arbitration and Judicial Disposition", University of Ottawa, 1982.

APPENDIX A: CODE OF PRACTICE FOR FAMILY CONCILIATION SERVICES

Issued by the National Family Conciliation Council's Executive Committee after consultation with the Law Society's Family Law Committee and the Solicitors' Family Law Association.

1 The Aims of Family Conciliation Services

The primary aim of conciliation is to help couples involved in the process of separation and divorce to reach agreements, or reduce the area or intensity of conflict between them, especially in disputes concerning their children.

In the short term the objective of conciliation is to help the parties reach a workable settlement which takes account of the needs of the children and adults involved.

The longer term objective is to help both parents:
a) maintain their relationship with their children, and
b) achieve a co-operative plan for their children's welfare.

2 The Function of Conciliation Services

Conciliation is a process which requires the co-operation of both parties, and which respects their autonomy and legal rights. The conciliator helps the parties to explore possibilities of reaching agreement, without coercion. Where children are involved, the conciliator helps the parties to work out arrangements which balance their individual interests with those of their children. The conciliator has an ethical responsibility to help parents focus on their children's position and needs, as well as on their own needs, without imposing the conciliator's own values on them or directing them towards an outcome preferred by the conciliator.

Appropriate matters for conciliation are:

(i) Disputes about divorce/separation: where one party wants a divorce/separation and the other does not, or is unsure; or where there is disagreement about the timing or basis of a divorce petition.

(ii) Custody: disputes about custody, care and control of children, including the question of joint custody; also disputes about specific issues such as choice of school, religious upbringing or change of name.

(iii) Access to children: disputes may be referred when separation is imminent as well as after separation, at any stage of divorce proceedings or after divorce.

(iv) Conciliation may include outline discussions on issues of finance and property where these cannot be separated from the primary issues about the divorce and/or children. The aim of such discussions should be to explore options and consider priorities in a non-adversarial manner. Both parties are then encouraged to take further legal advice and are restrained from giving premature undertakings. Where there is a dispute about property and/or finance alone, the parties should be advised to seek a settlement with the help of solicitors. Conciliation may then be an additional resource if the property or finance seems to be heavily charged with emotional or symbolic values for one or both parties.

3 Relationship with Solicitors

(i) The parties should be warned against entering into any agreement without first obtaining legal advice on its terms. They should be encouraged to seek legal advice in all cases and unrepresented clients should be advised that their situation may have legal implications on which legal assistance may be advisable. The availability of the "Green Form" scheme and legal aid should be explained to them.

(ii) At the time of referral, the parties should be asked to agree to the conciliation service communicating with their solicitors and the need for limited contact between the service and their solicitors should be explained to them. Nothing should be said by a conciliator to one solicitor which is not also said to the other solicitor and to both parties.

(iii) On accepting a referral from solicitors, the conciliation service should as soon as possible send a written acknowledgement to each solicitor, giving the date of their client's first appointment, and then periodic indications of how long the conciliation process is expected to last.

(iv) Where the circumstances require it, and especially where negotiations are prolonged, the conciliator should at a suitable stage send each solicitor an interim summary in terms agreed with both parties.

(v) At the end of conciliation, the conciliator should prepare for each party and their solicitors a summary of the outcome of conciliation, marked "Without Prejudice". This should record proposed arrangements in terms agreed with both parties, stating that these proposals are subject to legal advice. Where matters remain unresolved, the summary should give a concise statement of each party's position in terms approved by that party. The summary should not contain any statement of the conciliator's opinion. Conciliators must never give an evaluation or subjective appraisal of either party to either solicitor, either in writing or orally.

4 Confidentiality

Conciliators have a duty to explain to both parties that all communications made between them in the course of conciliation, as well as those made between them and the conciliator, and between the conciliator and their solicitors, are made in confidence. This confidentiality cannot be absolute, for the reasons explained below, and its limits need to be explained with particular care:

A. The Extent of the Confidentiality Provided by the Conciliation Service

(i) No information may be given by the conciliator or by a member of the conciliation service's staff to anyone, including a court welfare officer or the Court itself, unless both parties give their joint and explicit consent (having sought legal advice) to this information being provided or unless the Court orders the conciliator to provide evidence to the Court.

(ii) However, it must also be explained to both parties at the beginning of their first appointment that although communications made during conciliation are confidential, a conciliator cannot give a guarantee of absolute confidentiality in all circumstances, because a situation might arise in which a person's life or safety is endangered. If, during conciliation, it appears to a conciliator that there is substantial danger, particularly to a child, the conciliator should advise the party or parties concerned to seek help from an appropriate agency. If neither party is willing to do this, the conciliator should discuss the matter with his or her supervisor and may then, where it is considered necessary:

(a) Report the matter to both solicitors, and/or-

(b) If the parties are still unwilling to approach an appropriate agency, report the matter to the local Social Services Department or

to the Divorce Court Welfare Service, if they are already involved.

The latter course should be taken only where at least one of the parties admits that a child has been abused, and normally only after discussion with both parties.

B. The Confidentiality of Conciliation in Relation to the Court

(i) The Court encourages parental agreement as far as possible and is likely to refrain from detailed inquiry into arrangements that are acceptable to both parties. Conciliators should explain, however, that all arrangements made during conciliation are capable of variation by the Court if not felt to be appropriate or in the best interests of the children. Parties to current or potential divorce or judicial separation proceedings should be informed that under section 41 of the Matrimonial Causes Act 1973 a judge must consider the arrangements for the children and pronounce them satisfactory, or the best that can be devised in the circumstances, before the decree can be made absolute. It should be understood, therefore, that the judge may ask the parties about details of custody and access arrangements that have been worked out during conciliation.

(ii) Conciliation seeks to create an atmosphere of mutual trust and frankness between the parties. English law has long appreciated the value of "Without Prejudice" negotiations in avoiding unnecessary litigation, and if conciliation fails to resolve matters, the Court is unlikely to allow either party to make use of evidence derived from failed conciliation, in a subsequent trial of the issue. Both parties must explicitly agree to take part in conciliation on the understanding that it is "Without Prejudice": there seems little doubt that the Court would then hold it to be in the public interest to exclude evidence derived from a genuine, albeit unsuccessful, attempt to settle matters independently.

(iii) However, in matters relating to children, the Court also has a positive duty to protect the children's interests, and it may consider that in some circumstances it would be contrary to this policy to exclude certain evidence altogether, even if it derives from the conciliation process. This could apply particularly in the case of a crime against a child.

(iv) Once an agreement has been reached between the parties, the confidentiality afforded by "Without Prejudice" negotiations falls away, and the parties should therefore be warned against entering into an agreement without first obtaining legal advice about its terms.

(v) Where appropriate, the parties should be advised to consider trying out proposed arrangements on a trial basis, if one or both of them are uncertain, rather than agreeing to implement them immediately on a permanent basis. This may be particularly helpful in establishing an acceptable pattern of access.

(vi) If an agreement that has been reached through conciliation proves unworkable and litigation ensues, the Court will review all the circumstances of the case afresh, with a view above all to establishing what is in the best interests of the child/ren in question. The Court would not wish either party to be disadvantaged by a bona fide attempt to reach agreement and the way the previous agreement was arrived at in conciliation may therefore not be relevant.

5 Withdrawal from Conciliation

The parties are free at all times to withdraw from conciliation, and they are also free to disregard professional advice from a conciliator. In cases where it appears to the conciliator that they are acting or proposing to act in a manner that may be seriously detrimental to the welfare of their child/ren, the conciliator may decide to terminate the conciliation. In such circumstances, he or she should state in general terms the reason for discontinuing it in the summary sent to solicitors, and may recommend that a welfare officer should be involved.

6 The Suggested Role of Solicitors

(i) When a client consults a solicitor concerning unresolved issues or disputes with his or her former spouse, especially over matters concerning their children, the solicitor may like to bring the availability of conciliation to the client's attention. S/he should stress that these services provide an additional and complementary resource for dispute resolution, and while offering a different approach from the legal process of negotiation by solicitors or adjudication by the Court, conciliation should not be seen as a substitute for legal advice.

(ii) When referring a client to a conciliation service, it is desirable that the solicitor should contact the other party's solicitor to establish whether his/her client is willing to participate.

(iii) If a solicitor has grounds for advising the client to withdraw from conciliation, the solicitor should normally notify the conciliation service.

(iv) A solicitor will no doubt bear in mind the possible effect on the conciliation process of litigious acts made on his or her client's behalf and should where possible liaise with the other party's solicitor and the conciliator to ensure that acts such as the filing of a petition or an affidavit cause as little disruption as possible.

This code is currently under discussion and further amendments may be made before any decision is taken to make it mandatory for all services affiliated to the National Family Conciliation Council. Information about the Council and affiliated services may be obtained from the National Family Conciliation Council, 34 Milton Road, Swindon, Wilts. SN1 5JA. Tel. 0793 618486.

APPENDIX B: LIST OF CONCILIATION SERVICES AFFILIATED TO THE NATIONAL FAMILY CONCILIATION COUNCIL AND VOLUNTARY ORGANISATIONS ASSOCIATED WITH CONCILIATION

List of Services Affiliated to the National Family Conciliation Council (October 1985)

BIRMINGHAM
Birmingham Family Conciliation Service,
3 Kingston Row,
Birmingham B1 2NU.

BOURNEMOUTH
Bournemouth and District Family Conciliation Service,
2, St. Osmund's Road,
Parkestone,
Poole, Dorset.

BRISTOL
Bristol Courts Family Conciliation Service,
Albion Chambers East,
Broad Street,
Bristol BS1 1DX.

CAMBRIDGE
Cambridge Family Conciliation Service,
2 Pikes Walk, off King Street,
Cambridge CB1 1LF.

CARDIFF
Cardiff Family Conciliation Service,
33 Westgate Street,
Cardiff.

CHELMSFORD
Mid-Essex Family Conciliation Service,
Crown Court Probation Office,
New Street,
Chelmsford, Essex CM1 1EL.

COLCHESTER
North-East Essex Family Conciliation Service,
Ryegate House,
23 Peter Street,
Colchester, Essex CO1 1HL.

COVENTRY
Coventry Family Conciliation Service,
Trinity House,
33 Trinity Street,
Coventry, Warwicks. CV1 1FJ.

EDINBURGH
Scottish Family Conciliation Service (Lothian),
127 Rose Street South Lane,
Edinburgh EH2 5BB.

HARLOW
Harlow and District Family Conciliation Service,
Crown Buildings,
Crows Road,
Epping, Essex CM16 5DA.

IPSWICH
Ipswich and District Family Conciliation Service,
43 Elm Street,
Ipswich, Suffolk IPL 2AP.

KENT
Kent Family Conciliation Service,
The Phoenix Centre,
Central Avenue,
Sittingbourne, Kent ME10 4BX.

LEEDS
Leeds Family Conciliation Service,
26 Great George Street,
Leeds LS1 3DN.

LONDON (Central)
Divorce Conciliation and Advisory Service,
38 Ebury Street,
London SW1W OLU.

LONDON (South-East)
South-East London Family Conciliation Bureau,
5 Upper Park Road,
Bromley, Kent BR1 3HN.

LONDON (South-West)
Mediation in Divorce,
51 Sheen Road,
Richmond, Surrey TW1 1YG.

MIDDLESBROUGH
Cleveland Family Conciliation Service,
St. Mary's Centre,
Corporation Road,
Middlesbrough, Cleveland.

NEWCASTLE
Conciliation Service for Northumberland and Tyneside,
MEA House,
Ellison Place,
Newcastle-upon-Tyne NE1 8XS.

NORWICH
Norfolk Family Conciliation Service,
Charing Cross Centre,
17-19 St. John Maddermarket,
Norwich.

NORTH DEVON
North Devon Family Conciliation Service,
"Court", Alwington,
Bideford, North Devon.

READING
Berkshire Family Conciliation Service,
1st Floor, 10 Friar's Walk,
Friar Street,
Reading RG1 1LA.

SHEFFIELD
Sheffield Family Conciliation Service,
14-18 West Bar Green,
Sheffield S1 2DA.

SLOUGH
East Berkshire Family Conciliation Service,
Law Courts,
Slough, Berks. SL1 2HJ.

SUNDERLAND
Sunderland and South Shields Family Conciliation Service,
17 Hillside,
Sunderland SR3 1YN.

SURREY
Surrey Family Conciliation Service,
155 High Street,
Dorking, Surrey RH4 1AD.

SWINDON
Swindon Family Conciliation Service,
34 Milton Road,
Swindon, Wilts. SN1 5JA.

Provisionally Affiliated and Associated Services

BURY, LANCS.
Family Conciliation Service,
c/o National Children's Home Regional Office,
33-35 Wilson Patten Street,
Warrington, Cheshire WA1 1PG.

BURY ST. EDMUNDS
Contact: Mrs Pauline Sefton,
Suffolk County Council Western Divisional Office,
Shire Hall,
Bury St. Edmunds.

HAMPSHIRE
Hampshire Family Conciliation Service,
11 Beresford Road,
Chandler's Ford,
Eastleigh SO5 2LU.

HARROGATE
Harrogate District Family Conciliation Service,
1 Haywra Street,
Harrogate, Yorks.

HULL
Hull and North Humberside Family Conciliation Service,
Crown Chambers,
Land of Green Ginger,
Hull HU1 2PG.

LONDON
Institute of Family Therapy Conciliation Service,
43 New Cavendish Street,
London W1.

IRELAND
Pilot Family Conciliation Scheme,
c/o Drumiskabole,
Carraroe,
Co. Sligo, Eire.

LIVERPOOL
Barnardo's Family Conciliation Service,
c/o Barnardo's North-West Divisional Office,
7 Lineside Close,
Liverpool L25 2UD.

MIDDLESEX
Middlesex Family Conciliation Service,
7c High Street (1st floor),
Barnet, Herts.

NORTHAMPTON
Northampton Family Conciliation Service,
296 Wellingborough Road,
Northampton NN1 4EP.

PLYMOUTH
Plymouth and District Family Conciliation Service,
8a The Crescent,
Plymouth, Devon PL1 3AB.

SALISBURY
248 St. Edmund's Church Street,
Salisbury, Wilts. SP1 1EF.

SCARBOROUGH
Scarborough and District Family Mediation Service,
12, Falsgrave Road,
Scarborough,
North Yorkshire YO12 5AT.

SOMERSET
Somerset Family Conciliation Service,
37 Chamberlain Street,
Wells, Somerset.

SOUTH HUMBERSIDE
24 Priestgate,
Barton upon Humber,
South Humberside DN18 5ET.

SUSSEX
Sussex Family Conciliation Service,
22 Stanford Avenue,
Brighton, Sussex BN1 6DD.

TUNBRIDGE WELLS
The Chilston Conciliation Service,
St. George's Centre,
7 Chilston Road,
Tunbridge Wells, Kent.

YORK
York Family Mediation Service,
Tower House,
Fishergate,
York YO1 4AU.

Voluntary Organisations Associated with Conciliation

Families Need Fathers,
84 Ulleswater Road,
Southgate,
London N14 7BT.

Family Courts Campaign,
c/o Eaton House,
66a Eaton Square,
London SW1W 9BH.

Family Forum,
Cambridge House,
131 Camberwell Road,
London SE5 0HF.

Forum for Initiatives in Reparation and Mediation,
Secretary, Martin Farrell,
37 Royal Street,
London SE1 7LL.

Gingerbread,
35 Wellington Street,
London WC2.

Institute of Marital Studies,
The Tavistock Centre,
Belsize Lane,
London NW3 5BA.

Mothers Apart From Their Children (MATCH),
64 Delaware Mansions,
Delaware Road,
London W9.

National Association of Citizens' Advice Bureaux,
115 Pentonville Road,
London N1.

National Council for One Parent Families,
255 Kentish Town Road,
London NW5 2LX.

National Marriage Guidance Council,
Herbert Grey College,
Little Church Street,
Rugby, CV21 3AP.

Scottish Council for Single Parents,
13 Gayfield Square,
Edinburgh.

Solicitors' Family Law Association,
Secretary, P.H. Grose-Hodge,
154 Fleet Street,
London EC4A 2HX.

Stepfamily (National Step-Family Association),
Room 3,
Ross Street Community Centre,
Ross Street,
Cambridge CB1 3BS.

APPENDIX C: SOLICITORS' FAMILY LAW ASSOCIATION CODE OF PRACTICE

The Association recommends that members and any solicitor practising family law should adopt the following code of practice.

General

1.1. The solicitor should endeavour to advise, negotiate and conduct proceedings in a manner calculated to encourage and assist the parties to reconcile their differences and should inform the client of the approach he intends to adopt.

1.2. The solicitor should encourage the client to see the advantage to the family of a conciliatory rather than a litigious approach as a way of resolving the disputes. The solicitor should explain to the client that in nearly every case where there are children, the attitude of the client to the other party in any negotiations will affect the family as a whole and may affect the relationship of the children with the parents.

1.3. The solicitor should encourage the attitude that a family dispute is not a contest in which there is one winner and one loser, but rather a search for fair solutions. He should avoid using words or phrases that imply a dispute when no serious dispute necessarily exists, for example "opponent", "win", "lose", or "Smith v Smith".

1.4. Because of the involvement of personal emotions in family disputes the solicitor should where possible avoid heightening such emotions by the advice given; and by avoiding expressing opinions as to the behaviour of the other party.

1.5. The solicitor should also have regard to the impact of correspondence on the other party when writing a letter of which a copy may be sent to that party and should also consider carefully the impact of correspondence on his own client before sending copies of letters to the client.

1.6. The solicitor should aim to avoid or dispel suspicion or mistrust between parties, by encouraging at an early stage where possible, full, frank and clear disclosure of information and openness in dealings.

1.7. The solicitor should aim to achieve settlement of differences as quickly as may be reasonable whilst recognising that the parties may need time to come to terms with their new situation.

Relationship with Client

2.1. As a rule the solicitor should explain to the client at the outset the terms of his retainer and take care to ensure that the client is fully aware of the impact of costs on any chosen course of action. The solicitor should thereafter at all stages have regard to the cost of negotiations and proceedings.

2.2. Where appropriate, the solicitor must advise the client of his right to apply for legal aid. He should bear in mind and explain the impact of costs where the client or the other party is in receipt of legal aid, and the particular effect of the statutory charge.

2.3. The solicitor should create and maintain a relationship with his client of a kind which will preserve fully his independent judgment and avoid becoming so involved in the case that his own personal emotions may cloud his judgment.

2.4. Whilst recognising the need to advise firmly and guide the client the solicitor should ensure that where the decision is properly that of the client, it is taken by the client and that its consequences are fully understood, both as to its effect on any children involved and financially.

Dealings with Other Solicitors

3.1. The solicitor should in all dealings with the other solicitor show courtesy and where possible endeavour to create and maintain a friendly relationship.

3.2. The solicitor should seek wherever possible to foster in his own client a trust in the other party's solicitors so tending to reduce distrust and suspicion between the parties.

3.3. The solicitor should in financial negotiations make use of without prejudice discussions, that is to say discussions involving conditional offers and conditional admissions that are withdrawn and not disclosed to the court in the event of those negotiations failing. The solicitor should be mindful that an unrealistic offer may be counter-productive and delay settlement.

3.4. The solicitor should generally avoid offering or receiving comments or information "off the record", where this phrase is intended to mean that the client should not be informed.

Dealings with the Other Party in Person

4.1. In dealings with another party who is not legally represented the solicitor should take particular care to be courteous and restrained. Especial care should be taken to express letters and other communications clearly, avoiding technical language where it is not readily understandable to the layman or might be misunderstood.

4.2. Wherever proceedings are taken or negotiations conducted that may adversely affect the other party's interests, the other party should, in the interests of both parties, be advised to consult a solicitor.

Petitions and Proceedings

5.1. The solicitor should avoid allegations or procedures which may cause or increase ill-will between the parties without producing any benefit for the client.

5.2. Before instituting proceedings which make allegations about the other party's conduct, the solicitor should consider whether the other party or his solicitor should be consulted in advance as to the particulars to be alleged or the grounds to be relied on.

5.3. Where the purpose of taking a particular step in proceedings may be misunderstood the solicitor should consider explaining it in advance to the other party or his solicitors.

Children

6.1. The solicitor should treat his work in relation to children as the most important of his duties.

6.2. The solicitor should, in advising, negotiating and conducting proceedings, assist both his client and the other parent to regard the welfare of the client as the first paramount consideration.

6.3. The solicitor should aim to promote cooperation between parents in decisions concerning the child, both by formal arrangements (such as orders for joint custody); by practical arrangements (such as shared involvement in school events) and by consultation on important questions.

6.4. The solicitor must keep in mind that the interests of the child do not necessarily coincide with the interests of either parent, and that occasionally the child should be separately represented. In such case his duty is to bring the matter to the attention of the court.

6.5. The solicitor should take care to keep separate issues of custody and access on the one hand and money on the other. It is often helpful to deal with these two topics in separate letters.

6.6. "Kidnapping" of children both results from and creates exceptional fear, bitterness and desperation in the parents. The solicitor should therefore take what steps he can strongly to discourage kidnapping a child, that is to say, removing a child in breach of an order of a court of any country, or in such a manner to preempt or preclude a decision by the proper court (wherever that court may be) as to the child's custody or access.

The guide-lines set out in this Code cannot be absolute rules in as much as the solicitor may have to depart from them if the law or his professional obligations so require. They are a restatement of principles, objectives and recommendations which many solicitors practising family law already seek to follow and to which they seek to aspire in serving their clients.

October 1983

Published with the permission of the Solicitors' Family Law Association.

Enquiries concerning membership or other details should be addressed to the Secretary: P. H. Grose-Hodge, 154, Fleet Street, London EC4A 2HX.

REFERENCES

Abel, R.L. "The Comparative Study of Dispute Institutions in Society", *Law and Society Review*, vol. 8 (1973), pp. 217-347

—— "The Contradictions of Informal Justice", in R.L. Abel (ed.) *The Politics of Informal Justice*, Vol. 1 (Academic Press, New York, 1982)

Abella, R.S. "Canadian Perspectives on Procedural Aspects of Arrangements for Children upon Divorce", paper given at the 4th World Conference of the International Society on Family Law, Boston, June 1982

Abel-Smith, B. and Stevens, R. *In Search of Justice* (Allen Lane, Harmondsworth, 1968)

ACAS. See next entry

Advisory, Conciliation and Arbitration Service, *The ACAS Role in Conciliation, Arbitration and Mediation* (HMSO, London, 1979)

—— *Industrial Relations Handbook* (HMSO, London, 1980)

—— *Annual Report 1983*

Ambrose, P., Harper J., Pemberton R. *Surviving Divorce – Men Beyond Marriage* (Wheatsheaf Books, Brighton, 1983)

Arnold, J. Foreword to G. Parmiter, "Bristol In-Court Conciliation Procedure", *Law Society's Gazette*, (25 February 1981), p. 196

—— Address given at the Annual General Meeting of the Central Council of Probation and After-Care Committees, 24 May 1983

Bahr, S.J. "An Evaluation of Court Mediation", *Journal of Family Issues*, vol. 2, no. 1 (1981), pp. 39-60

BCFCS. See Bristol Courts Family Conciliation Service

Bellow, G. and Moulton, B. *The Lawyering Process* (Foundation Press, New York, 1981)

Benians, R. "Impact of Marital Breakdown on Children", *Journal of Maternal and Child Health* (October and November 1980), pp. 378-88, 423-7

Bentovim, A., Gorell Barnes, G., Cooklin, A. (eds.) *Family Therapy: Complementary Frameworks of Theory and Practice* (Academic Press, London, 1982)

Bernard, J. *The Future of Marriage* (Penguin Books, Harmondsworth, 1973)

Bishop, T.A. "Standards for Family and Divorce Mediation", *Dispute Resolution Forum* (December 1984), pp. 3-9

Black, D. "Custody and Access: A Literary Lesson", *Journal of Family Therapy*, vol. 4, no. 3 (1982), pp. 247-56

Bohannan, P. *Divorce and After* (Doubleday, New York, 1970)

Booth Committee (Committee on Matrimonial Causes Procedure), Consultation Paper, Lord Chancellor's Department, September 1983

—— *Report* (HMSO, London, July 1985)

Bordow, S., Marshall, A., Turner M. *An Evaluation of Court-Referred Conciliation Conferences* (Family Court of Australia, Sydney, 1983)

Borkowski, M., Murch, M., Walker, V. *Marital Violence – The Community Response* (Tavistock Publications, London, 1983)

Bottomley, A. and Olley, S. "Conciliation in the USA", *Legal Action Group Bulletin* (January 1983), pp. 9-11

Bowlby, J. *Attachment and Loss*, Vols. 1-3 (Hogarth Press, London, 1969, 1973, 1980)

Brannen, J. and Collard, J. *Marriages in Trouble* (Tavistock Publications, London, 1982)

Bristol Courts Family Conciliation Service (BCFCS), *Report 1979* (1979)

—— *A Review of its Functioning and Development, May 1979-August 1980* (1980)

—— *Report to the Inter-Departmental Committee on Conciliation* (1982)

—— *Annual Report 1983-84* (1984)

Bristol Courts Family Conciliation Service Trustees, "Conciliation – The Inter-

Departmental Report Examined", *Family Law*, vol. 14 (1984), pp. 48-52
British Association of Social Workers, *Family Courts – A Discussion Document* (BASW, Birmingham, August 1984)
Broun, M. "Conciliation – The Australian Experience", paper given to the Family Law Bar Association, Cumberland Lodge, 7 May 1983
Brown, D. "Divorce and Family Mediation: History, Review, Future Directions", *Conciliation Courts Review*, vol. 20, no. 2 (1982), pp. 1-37
Brown, E. "Divorce Counselling", in D.H. Olson (ed.) *Treating Relationships* (Graphic Publishing, Iowa, 1976)
Burgoyne, J. and Clark, D. *Making a Go of It – A Study of Stepfamilies in Sheffield* (Routledge and Kegan Paul, London, 1984)
——, Ormrod, R., Richards, M. *Divorce Matters* (Penguin Books, Harmondsworth, forthcoming)
Burrett, J. and Gibbons, F. "Catching the Fallout from Exploding Nuclear Families", *Social Work Today*, vol. 12, no. 33 (1981), pp. 12-14
Calvert, J.R. "Rethinking the 'A's in ACAS", *Personnel Management* (September 1984)
Camozzi, D. "Montreal Family Conciliation Service", paper given at a day conference at Bromley, "Mediation – A Wider View", 6 July 1984
Caplan, G. *A Community Approach to Mental Health* (Tavistock, London, 1961)
—— "Recent Developments in Crisis Intervention and in the Promotion of Support Systems", unpublished paper, 1985
Carter, E.A. and McGoldrick, M. (eds.), *The Family Life Cycle* (Gardner Press, New York, 1980)
Central Statistical Office, *Social Trends 14* (HMSO, London, 1984)
—— *Social Trends 15* (HMSO, London, 1985)
Chester, R. "Health and Marriage Breakdown – Experience of a Sample of Divorced Women", *British Journal of Preventive and Social Medicine*, vol. 25, no. 4 (1971), pp. 231-5
—— "Mass Divorce and its Implications", in C. Guy (ed.) *Relating to Marriage*, (National Marriage Guidance Council, Rugby, 1985)
Coogler, O.J. *Structured Mediation in Divorce Settlement* (Lexington Books, Lexington, Mass. 1978)
Cook, R.F., Roehl, J., Sheppard, D. "Neighbourhood Justice Centers Field Test", Final Evaluation Report (1980)
Cornwell, J. Paper given at a conference on "Conciliation and the Inter-departmental Committee's Report", London, 6 December 1983
Cretney, S.M. *Principles of Family Law*, 4th edn (Sweet and Maxwell, London, 1984)
—— "An Objective Assessment or Some Awkward Questions?", Bristol Law Society Conference, *Family Law* (January 1985), pp. 35-41
Crowe, M.J. "The Treatment of Marital and Sexual Problems", in A. Bentovim, G. Gorell Barnes, A. Cooklin (eds.) *Family Therapy: Complementary Frameworks of Treatment and Practice*, Vol. 1 (Academic Press, London, 1982)
Davidoff, L. "Statistics of Domestic Proceedings in 1983", in T.F. Marshall (ed.) *Magistrates' Domestic Courts*, Home Office Research and Planning Unit Paper 28, (Home Office, London 1984)
Davis, G. "Research to Monitor the Bristol Courts Family Conciliation Service", Department of Social Administration, University of Bristol, 1980
—— with Lees, P. "A Study of Conciliation: Its Impact on Legal Aid Costs and Place in the Resolution of Disputes Arising Out of Divorce", Department of Social Administration, University of Bristol, 1981
—— "Conciliation – A Dilemma for the Divorce Court Welfare Service", *Probation Journal*, vol. 29, no. 4 (1982a)
—— "Settlement Seeking in Divorce", *New Law Journal*, 8 April (1982b), pp. 355-6
—— with Bader, K. "In-Court Mediation on Custody and Access Issues at Bristol

County Court - The Observation Study", Department of Social Administration, University of Bristol (1982c)
—— with Bader, K. "In-Court Mediation on Custody and Access Issues - The Files Study", Department of Social Administration, University of Bristol (1982d)
—— with Bader, K. "Report on the Pre-Trial Reviews Held in Lump Sum and Property Applications", Department of Social Administration, University of Bristol (1982e)
—— "Conciliation and the Professions", *Family Law*, vol. 13, no. 1 (1983a), pp. 6-13
—— with Bader, K. "Report on the Bromley (South-East London) Conciliation Bureau", Department of Social Administration, University of Bristol (1983b)
—— "Mediation in Divorce - A Theoretical Perspective", *Journal of Social Welfare Law*, May (1983c), p. 133
—— "Comment on the Inter-Departmental Committee's Findings", *Family Law*, vol. 14, (1984), pp. 52-3
—— "The Theft of Conciliation", *Probation Journal*, vol. 32, no. 1 (March 1985)
Davis G. and Bader, K. "In-Court Mediation: The Consumer View" (1) and (2), *Family Law*, vol. 15 (1985), pp. 42-9, 82-6
—— MacLeod, A., Murch M. "Special Procedure in Divorce and the Solicitor's Role", *Family Law*, vol. 12 (1982a), p. 39
——, ——, —— "Divorce and the Resolution of Conflict", *Law Society's Gazette*, London (13 January 1982b), pp. 40-1
——, ——, —— "Undefended Divorce: Should Section 41 of the Matrimonial Causes Act 1973 be Repealed?", *Modern Law Review*, vol. 46 (1983a), p. 121
——, ——, —— "Divorce: Who Supports the Family?", *Family Law*, vol. 13 (1983b), pp. 217-24
Day, M., Jones, A., Owen G. "Conciliation and the Court Welfare Officer's Changing Role", *Family Law*, vol. 14 (1984), pp. 201-2
Denning Committee, *Final Report of the Committee on Procedure in Matrimonial Causes* (Cmnd. 7024, HMSO, London, 1947)
Department of Health and Social Security, *Review of Child Care Law* (HMSO, London, 1985)
Departmental Committee on Social Services in the Courts of Summary Jurisdiction *Report* (Cmnd. 5122, HMSO, London, 1936)
Deutsch, M. *The Resolution of Conflict* (Yale University Press, New Haven, 1973)
Dicks, H. *Marital Tensions* (Routledge and Kegan Paul, London, 1967)
Dingwall, R. "Some Observations on Divorce Mediation in Britain and the United States", *Mediation Quarterly* (in press)
Dodds, M. "Children and Divorce", *Journal of Social Welfare Law* (July 1983), pp. 228-37
Doran, F. "Confidentiality of Case Records", *Scottish Child*, vol. 2 (1984), pp. 11-14
Duncan, W. *The Case for Divorce in the Irish Republic*, revised edn (Irish Council for Civil Liberties, Dublin, 1982)
Edgar, D. and Harrison, M. *Children's Participation in Divorce*, Institute of Family Studies, Melbourne, Australia, Discussion Paper No. 10 (1983)
Edmonton Family Court Marriage Conciliation Service, *Five-Year Survey of Operations, 1972-77* (Edmonton Family Court, Alberta, January 1978)
Eekelaar, J. *Family Security and Family Breakdown* (Penguin Books, Harmondsworth, 1971)
—— "Children in Divorce: Some Further Data", *Oxford Journal of Legal Studies* (1982), p. 63
—— "The Democratisation of Family Law", paper given at the British Society for Population Studies Conference on the Family, University of Bath, 14-16 September 1983
—— *Family Law and Social Policy*, 2nd edn (Weidenfeld and Nicolson, London, 1984)
—— and Clive, E. with Clarke, K. and Raikes, S. *Custody after Divorce* (SSRC Centre

for Socio-Legal Studies, Oxford, 1977)
—— and Maclean, M. *Financial Provision in Divorce – A Reappraisal* (SSRC Centre for Socio-Legal Studies, Oxford, 1983)
Elston, E., Fuller, J., Murch, M. "Judicial Hearings of Undefended Divorce Petitions", *Modern Law Review*, vol. 38 (1975), p. 609
Epstein, N.B., Bishop, D.S., Baldwin, L.M. "McMaster Model of Family Functioning – A View of the Normal Family" in F. Walsh (ed.) *Normal Family Processes* (Guilford Press, New York, 1982)
Evatt, E. "The Administration of Family Law", paper presented as the Sir Robert Garran Memorial Oration, Adelaide, Australia (November 1978)
—— "New Directions for Counselling", paper presented at a meeting of Directors of Court Counselling, Family Court of Australia (1979)
Family Courts Campaign, Press Release, London, 21 November 1985
Felstiner, W.L.F., Abel, R.L., Sarat, A. "The Emergence and Transformation of Disputes", *Law and Society Review*, vol. 15, no. 3 (1980-81) p. 4
Fennell, N. *Opening Address at the Conciliation in Family Law Cases Seminar* (Department of Justice, Dublin, June 1984)
Finer Report, *Report of the Committee on One-Parent Families* (Cmnd. 5629, HMSO, London, 1974)
Fisher, R. and Ury, W. *Getting to Yes* (Houghton Mifflin, Boston, 1981)
Fisher, T. "Conjoint Working in Conciliation", *National Family Conciliation Council Newsletter*, no. 4 (February 1984)
Folberg, J. "A Mediation Overview: History and Dimensions of Practice", *Mediation Quarterly*, vol. 1 (1983), pp. 3-13
—— and Taylor, A. *Mediation – A Comprehensive Guide to Resolving Conflicts without Litigation* (Jossey-Bass, San Francisco, 1984)
Forster, J. *Divorce Conciliation* (Scottish Council for Single Parents, Edinburgh, 1982)
Foster, H. and Freed, K. "Divorce in the Fifty States: An Overview", *Family Law Quarterly*, vol. 14, no. 4 (1980), pp. 229-33
Francis, P. and Shaw, R. "Divorce and the Law and Order Lobby", *Family Law*, vol. 11 (1981), pp. 69-72
Fraser, D. "Divorce Avon Style: The Work of a Specialist Welfare Team", *Social Work Today*, vol. 11, no. 30 (1980), pp. 12-15
Freeman, M.D.A. "Towards a More Humane System of Divorce", *Justice of the Peace* (21 March 1981), pp. 173-4
—— "Freedom and the Welfare State: Child Rearing, Parental Autonomy and State Intervention", *Journal of Social Welfare Law*, vol. 70 (1983)
—— "Questioning the De-Legalisation Movement in Family Law: Do We Really Want a Family Court?" in J. Eekelaar and S. Katz (eds.) *The Resolution of Family Conflict – Comparative Legal Perspectives* (Butterworths, Toronto, 1984)
Friedmann, W. *Law in a Changing Society* (Pelican Books, Harmondsworth, 1964)
Frontenac Family Referral and Conciliation Service, *Couples in Crisis* (Frontenac Family Court, Kingston, Ontario, 1979)
Gibbons, F. *A Brief Study of Mediation Schemes in Frontenac, Montreal and New York* (South East London Probation Service, January 1984)
—— "The S.E. London Family Conciliation Bureau", *National Family Conciliation Council Newsletter*, no. 10 (August 1985)
Gibson, C. "Divorce and the Recourse to Legal Aid", *Modern Law Review*, vol. 43 (1980), p. 609
—— "Maintenance in the Magistrates' Courts in the 1980s", *Family Law*, vol. 12 (1982), p. 138
Gibson, J. "Australia and the Family Law Act", Bristol Law Society Conference, *Family Law* (January 1985), pp. 17-26
Goldstein, J., Freud, A., Solnit, A. *Beyond the Best Interests of the Child* (Free Press,

New York, 1973)
Gorell Barnes, G. *Working with Families* (BASW/Macmillan, Basingstoke, 1984)
Gorell Commission, *Report of the Second Royal Commission on Divorce* (Cmnd. 6478, HMSO, London, 1912)
Grad, J. and Sainsbury P. "Evaluating the Community Psychiatric Service in Chichester", *Milbank Memorial Fund Quarterly* (1966), p. 44
Graham Hall, J. *Proposal for a Family Court*, 1st edn (1970), 2nd edn (1973) (National Council for One Parent Families, London)
—— *Towards a Unified Family Court* (National Council for One Parent Families, London, 1978)
—— and Martin, D.F. "Towards a Unified Family Court - The Cost Factor", *Civil Justice Quarterly* (1983), pp. 223-43
——, —— "The Collecting Officer in the Unified Family Court", *Justice of the Peace* (3 November 1984), pp. 695-9
Grinnell, G.B. *The Cheyenne Indians* (New Haven, 1923)
Guise, J. "Conciliation: Current Practice and Future Implications for the Probation Service", *Probation Journal*, vol. 30, no. 2 (1983), pp. 58-60
Gulliver, P.H. *Neighbours and Networks* (University of California Press, Berkeley, 1971)
—— *Disputes and Negotiations: A Cross-Cultural Perspective* (Academic Press, New York, 1979)
Guymer, A. and Bywaters, P. "Conciliation and Reconciliation in Magistrates' Domestic Courts", in T. Marshall (ed.) *Magistrates' Domestic Courts, Home Office Research and Planning Paper 28* (Home Office, London, 1984)
Hailsham, Lord, in D. v. NSPCC, [1977] 1 All ER 605
—— "Law, Ethics and Authority", *Encounter* (February-March 1981) pp. 42-9
Haley, J. *Problem Solving Therapy* (Harper and Row, New York, 1976)
Harris, M. "How Unemployment Affects People", *New Society*, 19 January 1984
Hart, N. *When Marriage Ends* (Tavistock Publications, London, 1976)
Haskey, J. "The Proportion of Marriages Ending in Divorce", *Population Trends*, vol. 27 (HMSO, London, 1982)
—— "Social Class and Socio-economic Differentials in Divorce in England and Wales", *Population Studies*, vol. 38 (1984), pp. 419-38
Hayek, F.A. von *John Stuart Mill and Harriet Taylor* (Routledge and Kegan Paul, London, 1951)
Hayes, M. "Relatives, Care Proceedings and Wardship", *Family Law*, vol. 14 (1984), pp. 234-40
Haynes, J.M. "Divorce Mediator - A New Role", *Social Work, Journal of the National Association of Social Workers*, vol. 23, no. 1 (January, 1978), pp. 5-9
—— *Divorce Mediation* (Springer Publishing Company, New York, 1981)
—— "A Conceptual Model of the Process of Family Mediation: Implications for Training", *American Journal of Family Therapy* (Winter 1982), pp. 5-16
—— Paper given at the International Conference on Conciliation, London, October 1984
Heisler, J. *The National Marriage Guidance Client 1982* (National Marriage Guidance Council, Rugby, 1984)
Hetherington, E.M., Cox, M., Cox, R. "Family Interaction and the Social, Emotional and Cognitive Development of Children Following Divorce", in V. Vaughan and T. Brazelton (eds.) *The Family: Setting Priorities* (Science and Medicine, New York, 1979)
Hodder, E. *The Step-Parents' Handbook* (Sphere Books, London, 1985)
Home Office, *Marriage Matters*, a consultative document by the Working Party on Marriage Guidance (HMSO, London, 1979)
—— *Statement of National Objectives and Priorities for the Probation Service in England and Wales* (Home Office, London, April 1984)
House of Commons Social Services Committee, *Second Report on Children in Care*,

Vol. 1 (HMSO, London, 1984)
Howard, J. and Shepherd, G. "Conciliation – New Beginnings?", *Probation Journal*, vol. 29, no. 3 (1982), pp. 87-92
Humphreys, C. *Zen Buddhism* (Unwin Paperbacks, London, re-issued 1984)
Hunt, P. *Clients' Responses to Marriage Counselling* (National Marriage Guidance Council, Rugby, 1985)
Huntington, D. *Divorce and the Developmental Needs of Children* (Association of Family and Conciliation Courts, 1982)
Inter-departmental Committee on Conciliation, *Report* (HMSO, London, 1983)
International Chamber of Commerce, *ICC Arbitration: The Solution Way to International Business Disputes*, ICC Publication 301 (ICC, Paris, 1977)
—— and Benjamin M. "A Study of Conciliation Counselling in the Family Court of Toronto", in J. Eekelaar and S. Katz (eds.) *The Resolution of Family Conflict – Comparative Legal Perspectives* (Butterworths, Toronto, 1984)
Irving, H.H. *Divorce Mediation* (Personal Library Publishers, Toronto, 1980)
——, ——, Bohm, B., Macdonald, G. *Final Research Report on Conciliation Counselling in the Family Court of Toronto* (Ministry of the Attorney General, Toronto, August 1981)
Irving, L. and Cuthbertson, N. "Battered Beyond Belief", *Social Work Today* (14 January 1985), p. 20
Isono, S. "Some Theoretical Problems in Handling Family Disputes in the Japanese Family Court", paper given at the International Sociological Association Symposium on the Sociology of Law, Japan (September 1975)
Jackson, J.J., Preface to *Rayden's Law and Practice in Divorce and Family Matters*, 14th edn, Vol. 1 (Butterworths, London, 1983)
James, A. and Wilson, K. "Divorce Court Welfare Work – Present and Future?", *Probation Journal*, vol. 30, no. 2 (1983), pp. 50-5
——, —— "The Trouble with Access: A Study of Divorcing Families", *British Journal of Social Work*, vol. 14 (1984), pp. 487-506
——, —— *Social Work with Marital Problems* (Tavistock, London, forthcoming)
Johnson, P.K. "How Effective could Conciliation be in the Irish Legal System?", paper given at Conciliation in Family Law Cases Seminar (Department of Justice, Dublin, 1984)
Johnson, R. and Laurie, R. "A New Conciliation Service: the FBLA Conciliation Board", *Law Society's Gazette* (26 June 1985), p. 1853
Jordan, B. *Freedom and the Welfare State* (Routledge and Kegan Paul, London, 1976)
Jordan, P. "Conciliation – The Australian Experience", paper presented at the Solicitors' Family Law Association Seminar, London, 15 May 1984
Justice, *Parental Rights and Duties and Custody Suits* (Stevens and Sons, London, 1975)
Justices' Clerks' Society, *Resolving Family Conflict in the 1980s – A Unified Family Court* (February 1982)
Kaslow, F.W. "Divorce and Divorce Therapy", in A. Gurman and D. Kniskern (eds.) *Handbook of Family Therapy* (Brunner/Maazel, New York, 1981)
Kelly, J.B. "Mediation and Psychotherapy: Distinguishing the Differences", *Mediation Quarterly*, vol. 1 (1983), pp. 33-44
Kiernan, K.E. "The Structure of Families Today: Continuity or Change?" in OPCS, *The Family*, Occasional Paper 31 (1983), pp. 17-36
King, M. "Justice and Welfare in Divorce", *Legal Action Group Bulletin* (March 1981)
Kressel, K. *Labor Mediation: An Exploratory Survey* (Association of Labor Mediation Agencies, New York, 1972)
—— and Deutsch, M. "Divorce Therapy: An In-depth Survey of Therapists' Views", *Family Process*, vol. 16, no. 4 (1977b), pp. 413-43
——, ——, Jaffe N., Tuchman B., Watson C. "Mediated Negotiations in Divorce and Labor Disputes: A Comparison", *Conciliation Courts Review*, vol. 15 (1977a), pp.

9-12
——, ——, ——, ——, —— "A Typology of Divorcing Couples", *Family Process*, vol. 19, no. 2 (1980), pp. 101-16
Law Commission, *Reform of the Grounds of Divorce: The Field of Choice* (Cmnd. 3123, HMSO, London, 1966)
—— No. 112, *The Financial Consequences of Divorce* (HMSO, London, 1981)
—— No. 116, *Time Restrictions on Presentations of Divorce and Nullity Petitions* (HMSO, London, 1982)
Law Commissions of England and Wales and Scotland, *Report on the Custody of Children: Jurisdiction and Enforcement within the United Kingdom* (Cmnd. 9419, HMSO, London, 1985)
Law Society, *32nd Legal Aid Annual Report 1981-82* (HMSO, London, 1983)
—— *34th Legal Aid Annual Report 1983-84* (HMSO, London, 1985)
Law Society Family Law Sub-Committee, *A Better Way Out* (January 1979)
—— *A Family Court* (March 1985)
—— "The FBLA Conciliation Board: The Law Society's View", *Law Society's Gazette* (28 August 1985), p. 2322
Lay Observer, *5th Annual Report* (1980) HC 507
Leete, R. and Anthony, S. *Divorce and Remarriage, Population Trends 16* (HMSO, London, 1979)
Legal Action Group Bulletin (November 1982)
Legislative Commission on Expenditure Review of the State of New York, *Marital Conciliation in New York State Supreme Court* (New York, 1971)
Lemmon, J.A. "Divorce Mediation: Optimal Scope and Practice Issues", *Mediation Quarterly*, vol. 1 (1983), pp. 45-60
—— "The Mediation Method throughout the Family Life Cycle", *Mediation Quarterly*, vol. 7 (1985), pp. 5-21
Levinger, G. "Sources of Marital Dissatisfaction among Applicants for Divorce", *American Journal of Orthopsychiatry*, vol. 36 (1966), p. 803
Levy, R.J. "Comment on the Pearson-Thoennes Study and on Mediation", *Family Law Quarterly*, vol. 17, no. 4 (1984), pp. 525-33
Lord Chancellor's Legal Aid Advisory Committee, *32nd Annual Report 1981-82* (HMSO, London, 1983)
—— *34th Annual Report 1983-84* (HMSO, London, 1985)
Lowry, P. "ACAS: Adviser and Peacemaker", *Industrial Society* (December 1984)
Lund, M. "Research on Divorce and Children", *Family Law*, vol. 14 (1984), pp. 198-201
McCoy, K.F and Nelson, M.A. *Social Service Departments and the Matrimonial Causes (NI) Order* (Social Work Advisory Group, Belfast, 1983)
McCrory, J. Paper given at a day conference at Bromley, 23 April 1985
Macdonald, E.I. "The Future of the Family Court in Canada", *Family Law*, vol. 10, no. 4 (1980), pp. 123-6
McGregor, O.R. *Divorce in England* (Heinemann, London, 1957)
McMurray, L. "Emotional Stress and Driving Performance: The Effect of Divorce," *Behavioural Research in Highway Safety*, 1 (1970)
MacQueen, J.F. *The Rights and Liabilities of Husband and Wife* (1849)
Madison, M. "Defining Levels of Intervention in Dispute Resolution", Family Court of Australia, unpublished paper, 1982
Maidment, S. "A Study in Child Custody", *Family Law*, vol. 6 (1976), pp. 195, 236
—— *Child Custody – What Chance for Fathers?* (National Council for One Parent Families, London, 1981)
—— *Child Custody and Divorce: The Law in Social Context* (Croom Helm, London, 1984)
Marriage Matters, a consultative document by the Home Office Working Party on Marriage Guidance (HMSO, London, 1979)

Marshall, A. "The Work of the Counselling Service of the Family Court of Australia in Conciliating Family Disputes and in Related Tasks", paper given at the Association of Conciliation Courts Conference, Vancouver (May 1978)
——, Grant, A. and Nasser, J. "Children's Wishes in Custody and Access Disputes", *Australian Social Work*, vol. 31, no. 4 (1979), pp. 15-18
Marshall, T.F. *Reparation, Conciliation and Mediation*, Home Office Research and Planning Unit, Paper 27 (Home Office, London, 1984)
Martin, F. and Murray, K. "Principles, Practice and Policy in the Juvenile Justice System", *The Scottish Child* (January 1984), pp. 6-10
Mattinson, J. and Sinclair, I. *Mate and Stalemate* (Basil Blackwell, Oxford, 1979)
Merry, S.E. "The Social Organisation of Mediation in Non-industrial Societies", in R.L. Abel (ed.) *The Politics of Informal Justice*, Vol. 2 (Academic Press, New York, 1982)
—— and Silbey, S.S. "What Do Plaintiffs Want? Re-examining the Concept of Dispute", *Justice System Journal*, vol. 9, no. 2 (1984), pp. 151-7
Millward Brown Market Research, *Woman*, 27 February 1982, pp. 23-6
Milne, A.L. "Divorce Mediation: The State of the Art", *Mediation Quarterly* no. 1 (September 1983), pp. 15-31
Minuchin, S. *Families and Family Therapy* (Harvard University Press, Cambridge, 1974)
—— and Fishman, H.C. *Family Therapy Techniques* (Harvard University Press, Cambridge, 1981)
Mitchell, A. *Someone to Turn to – Experiences of Help before Divorce* (Aberdeen University Press, Aberdeen, 1981)
—— *Children in the Middle – Living Through Divorce* (Tavistock Publications, London, 1985)
Mnookin, R. "Child Custody Adjudication: Judicial Functions in the Face of Indeterminacy", *Law and Contemporary Problems*, vol. 39 (1975), p. 226
—— "Divorce Bargaining: The Limits on Private Ordering", in J. Eekelaar and S. Katz (eds.) *The Resolution of Family Conflict – Comparative Legal Perspectives* (Butterworths, Toronto, 1984)
—— and Kornhauser L. "Bargaining in the Shadow of the Law – The Case of Divorce", *Yale Law Journal 88* (1979), p. 950
Moore, C.W. "Training Mediators for Family Dispute Resolution", *Mediation Quarterly*, vol. 2 (1983), pp. 79-89
Mortimer, J. *Clinging to the Wreckage* (Weidenfeld and Nicolson, London, 1982)
Mortlock, W. *The Inside of Divorce* (Constable, London, 1971)
Morton Commission (Royal Commission on Marriage and Divorce), *Report* (HMSO, London, 1956)
Mostyn, F.E. *Marriage and the Law* (Oyez, London, 1976)
Murch, M. *Justice and Welfare in Divorce* (Sweet and Maxwell, London, 1980)
National Association of Citizens' Advice Bureaux, *Evidence Paper E/6/82*
—— *Annual Report 1984*
National Family Conciliation Council, Criteria for Affiliation, unpublished paper, December 1982
—— Code of Practice, *Family Law*, vol. 14 (1984), pp. 107-8
—— Code of Practice, *Family Law*, vol. 15 (1985), pp. 274-6
Oberg, B. and Oberg, G. *I'm Leaving* (Norman and Hobhouse, London, 1982)
Office of Population Censuses and Surveys, *Marriages 1983* (HMSO, London, 1984)
—— *General Household Survey* (HMSO, London, 1984)
Oireachtas Committee on Marital Breakdown, *Report* (Dublin, April 1985)
Order of Christian Unity, *Reconciliation and Conciliation in the Context of Divorce* (Winchester, 1982)
Pahl, J. (ed.) *Private Violence and Public Policy* (Routledge and Kegan Paul, London, 1985)

Palazzoli, M.S. "The Emergence of a Comprehensive Systems Approach", *Journal of Family Therapy*, vol. 7, no. 2 (1985), pp. 135-46
——, Boscolo, L., Prata, G. *Paradox and Counterparadox* (Aronson, New York, 1978)
Paolucci, B., Hall, O.A., Axinn, N. *Family Decision-Making – An Ecosystem Approach* (John Wiley, New York, 1977)
Parad, H.J. (ed.) *Crisis Intervention* (Family Service Association of America, New York, 1965)
Parker, D. and Parkinson, L. "Solicitors and Family Conciliation Services – A Basis for Professional Co-operation", *Family Law*, vol. 15 (1985), pp. 270-4
Parkes, M. *Bereavement: Studies of Grief in Adult Life* (Penguin Books, Harmondsworth, 1975)
Parkinson, L. Application to the Nuffield Foundation on behalf of Bristol Courts Family Conciliation Service, unpublished paper, 1978
—— *Joint Custody*, One Parent Times No. 7 (National Council for One Parent Families, London, October 1981)
—— "Bristol Courts Family Conciliation Service", *Family Law*, vol. 12, no. 1 (1982a), pp. 13-16
—— "Conciliating Matrimonial Disputes – An International Perspective", *Law Society's Gazette* (20 October 1982b), p. 1307
—— "Conciliation – A New Approach to Family Conflict Resolution", *British Journal of Social Work*, vol. 13 (1983a), pp. 19-37
—— "Conciliation – Pros and Cons", *Family Law*, vol. 13, nos. 1 and 6 (1983b), pp. 22-5 and 183-6
—— "Conciliation – The English Experience", paper presented at the Solicitors' Family Law Association Seminar, London, 15 May 1984 (1984a)
—— "Mediation – A Wider View", *Family Law*, vol. 14 (1984b), p. 267
—— "Conciliation in Divorce", *Marriage Guidance* (Spring 1985), pp. 18-23
—— and Sullivan, G. "Bristol Courts Family Conciliation Service", *Justice of the Peace*, vol. 144, no. 39 (September 1980)
—— and Westcott J. "Bristol Courts Family Conciliation Service", *Law Society's Gazette* (21 May 1980)
Parmiter, G. "Bristol In-Court Conciliation Procedure", *Law Society's Gazette* (25 February 1981), p. 196
Patrician, M. "Child Custody Terms: Potential Contributors to Custody Dissatisfaction and Conflict", *Mediation Quarterly*, no. 3 (March 1984), pp. 41-57
Payne, J.D. "Family Conflicts Resolution: Cumulative Alternatives – Mediation, Arbitration and Judicial Disposition", unpublished paper, University of Ottawa, 1982
Pearson, J. "Mediation: Assumptions, Approaches and Outcomes", paper given at the 59th Annual Meeting of the American Orthopsychiatric Association, March 1982
—— and Thoennes, N. "A Preliminary Portrait of Client Reactions to Three Court Mediation Programs", *Mediation Quarterly*, no. 3 (1984a), pp. 21-40
——, —— "Custody Mediation in Denver: Short and Longer Term Effects", in J. Eekelaar and S. Katz (eds.) *The Resolution of Family Conflict – Comparative Legal Perspectives* (Butterworths, Toronto, 1984b)
——, —— "Mediating and Litigating Custody Disputes: A Longitudinal Evaluation", *Family Law Quarterly*, vol. 17, no. 4 (1984c), pp. 497-524 and 535-9.
Pearson, J., Ring, M., and Milne, A. "A Portrait of Divorce Mediation Services in the Public and Private Sector", *Conciliation Courts Review*, vol. 21, 1 (1983), pp. 1-24
Price, D., Bilmes, M., Day, M. "Conciliation in Access and Custody Cases – Some Alternative Thoughts", *Family Law*, vol. 15 (1985), pp. 231-3
Priestley, J.M. "Mediation Conferences – The New Zealand Family Court's Alternative to Litigation", in J. Eekelaar and S. Katz (eds.) *The Resolution of Family Conflict – Comparative Legal Perspectives* (Butterworths, Toronto, 1984)
Pugsley, J. and Wilkinson, M. "The Court Welfare Officer's Role: Taking It Seriously?",

Probation Journal, vol. 31, no. 3 (1984), pp. 89-92
Putting Asunder: Divorce Law for Contemporary Society (SPCK, London, 1966)
Reid, W. and Epstein, L. *Task-Centred Casework* (Columbia University Press, New York, 1972)

REPORTS (in chronological order)
Report of the Second Royal Commission on Divorce (Gorell Commission) (Cmnd. 6478, HMSO, London, 1912)
Report of the Departmental Committee on Social Services in the Courts of Summary Jurisdiction (Cmnd. 5122, HMSO, London, 1936)
Final Report of the Committee on Procedure in Matrimonial Causes (Denning Report) (Cmnd. 7024, HMSO, London, 1947)
Report of the Royal Commission on Marriage and Divorce (Morton Commission) (Cmnd. 9678, HMSO, London, 1956)
Putting Asunder: Divorce Law for Contemporary Society (SPCK, London, 1966)
Report of the Legislative Commission on Expenditure Review of the State of New York, Marital Conciliation in New York State Supreme Court (New York, 1971)
Report of the Committee on One-Parent Families (Finer Report) (Cmnd. 5629, HMSO, London, 1974)
Marriage Matters, a consultative document by the Home Office Working Party on Marriage Guidance (HMSO, London, 1979)
Report of the Inter-departmental Committee on Conciliation, Lord Chancellor's Department (HMSO, London, 1983)
Report of the House of Commons Social Services Committee, Second Report on Children in Care, Vol. 1 (HMSO, London, 1984)
Report of the Scottish Conference on Divorce Conciliation, November 1984 (Scottish Council for Single Parents and the Scottish Family Conciliation Service (Lothian), Edinburgh, 1984)
Report of the Oireachtas Joint Committee on Marriage Breakdown (Oireachtas Committee, Dublin, 1985)
Report of the Committee on Matrimonial Causes Procedure (Booth Committee) (HMSO, London, July 1985)
Department of Health and Social Security Review of Child Care Law, Report to Ministers of an Inter-departmental Working Party (HMSO, London, 1985)

Richards, M.P.M. "Post-Divorce Arrangements for Children – A Psychological Perspective", *Journal of Social Welfare Law* (1982), p. 133
—— and Dyson, M.P.M. *Separation, Divorce and the Development of Children: A Review* (University of Cambridge Child Care and Development Group, March 1982)
Roberts, S. *Order and Dispute* (Penguin Books, Harmondsworth, 1979)
—— "Mediation in Family Disputes", *Modern Law Review*, vol. 46, no. 5 (1983), pp. 537-57
Robinson, M. and Parkinson, L. "A Family Systems Approach to Conciliation", *Journal of Family Therapy*, vol. 7, no.4 (1985), pp. 357-77
Roman, M. and Haddad, W. *The Disposable Parent: The Case for Joint Custody* (Holt, Rinehart and Winston, New York, 1978)
Ross, J. "The Scottish Scene", *National Family Conciliation Council Newsletter*, no. 10 (August 1985a), pp. 6-7
—— "The Place of Children in the Conciliation Process", *The Scottish Child*, no. 7 (1985b), pp. 10-13
Rutter, M. "Parent-Child Separation – Psychological Effects on the Child", *Journal of Child Psychology and Psychiatry*, vol. 12, no. 4 (1971), pp. 233-66
—— "Stress, Coping and Development", *Journal of Child Psychology and Psychiatry*, vol. 22, no. 4 (1981), pp. 323-57

Samuels, A. "Refusal or Failure to Observe Access Order – The Remedy for the Aggrieved Party", *Family Law*, vol. 11 (1981), pp. 156-8

Sanctuary, G. *Marriage under Stress* (Allen and Unwin, London, 1968)

Saposnek, D.T. *Mediating Child Custody Disputes* (Jossey-Bass, San Francisco, 1983)

Schmidt, T.S. "The Scandinavian Law of Procedure in Matrimonial Causes" in J. Eekelaar and S. Katz (eds.) *The Resolution of Family Conflict – Comparative Legal Perspectives* (Butterworths, Toronto, 1984)

Seale, S. *Children in Divorce: A Study of Information Available to the Scottish Courts on Children Involved in Divorce* (Scottish Office Central Research Unit, Edinburgh, 1984)

Shepherd, G. and Howard, J. "Theft of Conciliation? The Thieves Reply", *Probation Journal* (June 1985a), pp. 59-60

——, —— "Custody, Access and Home Visits", *Family Law*, vol. 15 (1985b), pp. 136-7

Shonholtz, R. "Neighborhood Justice Systems", *Mediation Quarterly*, vol. 5 (1984), pp. 3-30

Shropshire Probation Service, *Report on the Work of the Shropshire Divorce Unit, July 1981-July 1983* (Shropshire Probation Service, 1983)

Simmel, G. *Der Streit* (1908), trans. Wolff, (Illinois, 1955)

Simon, J. "Recent Developments in the Matrimonial Law", Riddell Lecture (1970), in *Rayden on Divorce*, 11th edn Appendix VII, pp. 3227-40

Smart, C. "Marriage, Divorce and Women's Economic Dependency", in M. Freeman (ed.) *The State, the Law and the Family* (Tavistock Publications and Sweet and Maxwell, London, 1984)

Solicitors' Family Law Association Code of Practice, *Family Law*, vol. 14 (1984), pp. 156-7

Southwell, M. "Children, Divorce and the Disposal of the Matrimonial Home", *Family Law*, vol. 15 (1985), pp. 184-6

Steinberg, J.L. "Towards an Interdisciplinary Commitment", *Journal of Marital and Family Therapy* (July 1980), pp. 259-67

Stewart, D.E. and Harrison, M. *Divorce in Australia* (Institute of Family Studies, Melbourne, Working Paper 5, October 1982)

Sutton, A. "Science in Court", in M. King (ed.) *Childhood, Welfare and Justice* (Batsford, London, 1981)

Taylor, P.M. "Conciliation – Divide and Rule?", *Family Law*, vol. 14 (1984), pp. 300-2

Visher, E.B. and Visher, J.S. *Stepfamilies: A Guide to Working with Stepfamilies and Stepchildren* (Brunner Mazel, New York, 1979)

Wadsworth, M. *Roots of Delinquency* (Martin Robertson, Oxford, 1979)

—— and Maclean, M. "Parents' Divorce and Children's Life Chances", *Children and Youth Services Review* (in press)

Walczak, Y. with Burns, S. *Divorce: The Child's Point of View* (Harper and Row, London, 1984)

Waldron, J.A., Roth, C.P., Fair, P.H., Mann, E.M., McDermott J.F. "A Therapeutic Mediation Model for Child Custody Dispute Resolution", *Mediation Quarterly*, no. 3 (March 1984), pp. 5-20

Walker, J. "Conciliation Project Unit", *Marriage Research Centre Quarterly Newsletter*, no. 5 (Spring 1985), pp. 2-3

Wallerstein, J. and Kelly, J.B. *Surviving the Breakup – How Children and Parents Cope with Divorce* (Grant McIntyre, London, 1980)

Watzlawick, P., Beavin, J., Jackson, D. *Pragmatics of Human Communication* (W. W. Norton, New York, 1967)

——, Weakland, J., Fisch, R. *Change: Principles of Problem Formation and Problem Resolution* (W.W. Norton, New York, 1974)

Weiss, R.S. *Marital Separation* (Basic Books, New York, 1975)

Westcott, J. Report of the Inter-departmental Committee on Conciliation – A Review,

Law Society's Gazette (12 October 1983), p. 2509
Wilkins, N. "Conciliation: A Friendly Feeling?" *Family Law*, vol. 14 (1984), pp. 122-4
Wilkinson, M. *Children and Divorce* (Basil Blackwell, Oxford, 1981)
Yates, C. "The Inter-departmental Committee on Conciliation – A Step Backwards", *Journal of Social Welfare Law* (1983), pp. 335-41
"National Family Conciliation Council Research Project", unpublished report, University of Essex Law Department, 1984
—— "National Family Conciliation Council Research Project – The Latest Findings", *National Family Conciliation Council Newsletter*, no. 8 (February 1985), pp. 4 and 6
Zetzel, G.W.K. "In and Out of the Family Crucible: Reflections on Parent-Child Mediation", *Mediation Quarterly*, vol. 7 (1985), pp. 47-67

INDEX